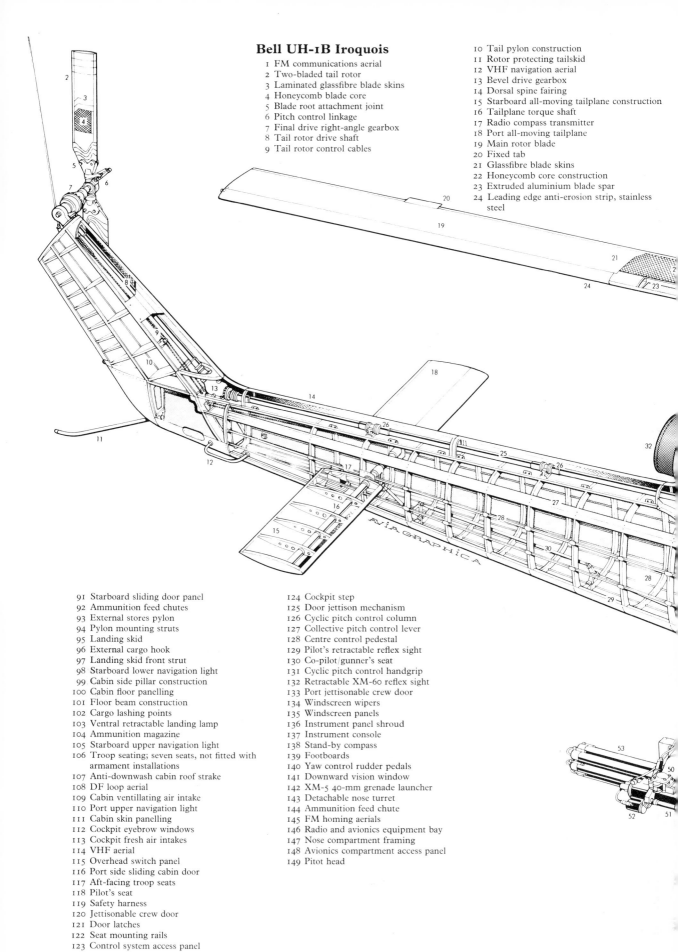

Bell UH-1B Iroquois

1 FM communications aerial
2 Two-bladed tail rotor
3 Laminated glassfibre blade skins
4 Honeycomb blade core
5 Blade root attachment joint
6 Pitch control linkage
7 Final drive right-angle gearbox
8 Tail rotor drive shaft
9 Tail rotor control cables

10 Tail pylon construction
11 Rotor protecting tailskid
12 VHF navigation aerial
13 Bevel drive gearbox
14 Dorsal spine fairing
15 Starboard all-moving tailplane construction
16 Tailplane torque shaft
17 Radio compass transmitter
18 Port all-moving tailplane
19 Main rotor blade
20 Fixed tab
21 Glassfibre blade skins
22 Honeycomb core construction
23 Extruded aluminium blade spar
24 Leading edge anti-erosion strip, stainless steel

91 Starboard sliding door panel
92 Ammunition feed chutes
93 External stores pylon
94 Pylon mounting struts
95 Landing skid
96 External cargo hook
97 Landing skid front strut
98 Starboard lower navigation light
99 Cabin side pillar construction
100 Cabin floor panelling
101 Floor beam construction
102 Cargo lashing points
103 Ventral retractable landing lamp
104 Ammunition magazine
105 Starboard upper navigation light
106 Troop seating; seven seats, not fitted with armament installations
107 Anti-downwash cabin roof strake
108 DF loop aerial
109 Cabin ventillating air intake
110 Port upper navigation light
111 Cabin skin panelling
112 Cockpit eyebrow windows
113 Cockpit fresh air intakes
114 VHF aerial
115 Overhead switch panel
116 Port side sliding cabin door
117 Aft-facing troop seats
118 Pilot's seat
119 Safety harness
120 Jettisonable crew door
121 Door latches
122 Seat mounting rails
123 Control system access panel

124 Cockpit step
125 Door jettison mechanism
126 Cyclic pitch control column
127 Collective pitch control lever
128 Centre control pedestal
129 Pilot's retractable reflex sight
130 Co-pilot/gunner's seat
131 Cyclic pitch control handgrip
132 Retractable XM-60 reflex sight
133 Port jettisonable crew door
134 Windscreen wipers
135 Windscreen panels
136 Instrument panel shroud
137 Instrument console
138 Stand-by compass
139 Footboards
140 Yaw control rudder pedals
141 Downward vision window
142 XM-5 40-mm grenade launcher
143 Detachable nose turret
144 Ammunition feed chute
145 FM homing aerials
146 Radio and avionics equipment bay
147 Nose compartment framing
148 Avionics compartment access panel
149 Pitot head

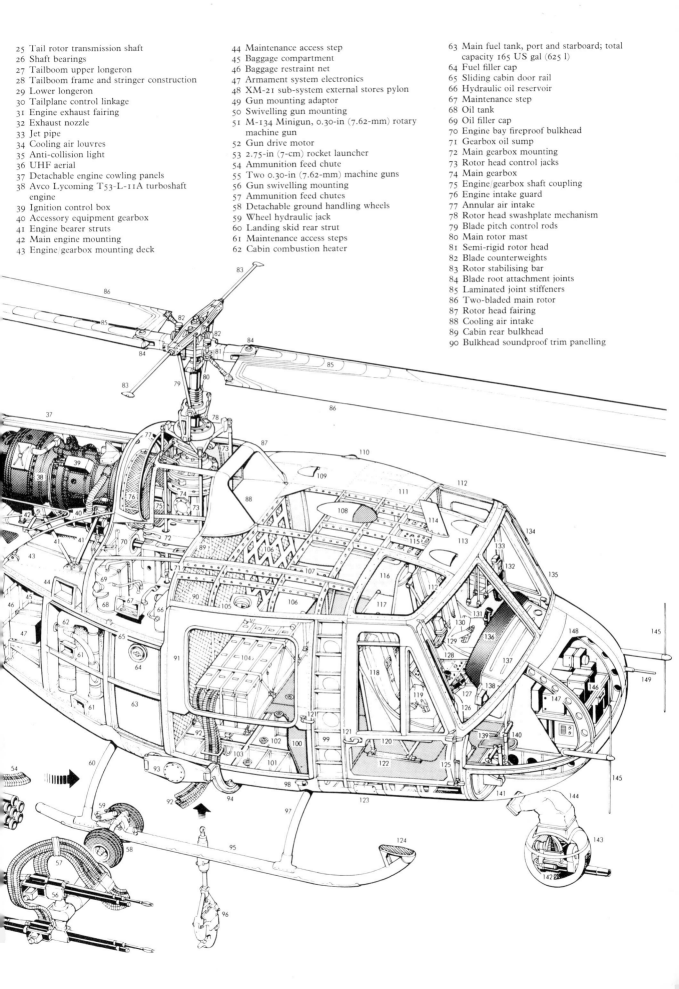

25 Tail rotor transmission shaft
26 Shaft bearings
27 Tailboom upper longeron
28 Tailboom frame and stringer construction
29 Lower longeron
30 Tailplane control linkage
31 Engine exhaust fairing
32 Exhaust nozzle
33 Jet pipe
34 Cooling air louvres
35 Anti-collision light
36 UHF aerial
37 Detachable engine cowling panels
38 Avco Lycoming T53-L-11A turboshaft engine
39 Ignition control box
40 Accessory equipment gearbox
41 Engine bearer struts
42 Main engine mounting
43 Engine/gearbox mounting deck

44 Maintenance access step
45 Baggage compartment
46 Baggage restraint net
47 Armament system electronics
48 XM-21 sub-system external stores pylon
49 Gun mounting adaptor
50 Swivelling gun mounting
51 M-134 Minigun, 0.30-in (7.62-mm) rotary machine gun
52 Gun drive motor
53 2.75-in (7-cm) rocket launcher
54 Ammunition feed chute
55 Two 0.30-in (7.62-mm) machine guns
56 Gun swivelling mounting
57 Ammunition feed chutes
58 Detachable ground handling wheels
59 Wheel hydraulic jack
60 Landing skid rear strut
61 Maintenance access steps
62 Cabin combustion heater

63 Main fuel tank, port and starboard; total capacity 165 US gal (625 l)
64 Fuel filler cap
65 Sliding cabin door rail
66 Hydraulic oil reservoir
67 Maintenance step
68 Oil tank
69 Oil filler cap
70 Engine bay fireproof bulkhead
71 Gearbox oil sump
72 Main gearbox mounting
73 Rotor head control jacks
74 Main gearbox
75 Engine/gearbox shaft coupling
76 Engine intake guard
77 Annular air intake
78 Rotor head swashplate mechanism
79 Blade pitch control rods
80 Main rotor mast
81 Semi-rigid rotor head
82 Blade counterweights
83 Rotor stabilising bar
84 Blade root attachment joints
85 Laminated joint stiffeners
86 Two-bladed main rotor
87 Rotor head fairing
88 Cooling air intake
89 Cabin rear bulkhead
90 Bulkhead soundproof trim panelling

VIETNAM CHOPPERS

VIETNAM CHOPPERS

Helicopters in Battle
1950-1975

Simon Dunstan

Published in 1988 by
Osprey Publishing Ltd
Member company of the George Philip Group
12–14 Long Acre, London WC2E 9LP
© Copyright 1988 Osprey Publishing Ltd

British Library Cataloguing in Publication Data

Dunstan, Simon
    Vietnam choppers: helicopters in battle
    1950–1975.
    1. United States. *Army Air Force*
    2. Vietnamese Conflict, 1961–1975—
    Aerial operations, American   3. Military
    helicopters
    I. Title
    959.704'348   DS558.8

    ISBN 0-85045-572-3

Editor: Martin Windrow

Filmset by Tameside Filmsetting Ltd,
Ashton-under-Lyne, Lancs.
Printed by BAS Printers Ltd,
Over Wallop, Hampshire

Dedication:
To J. S-S

Cover photographs:
Three studies of UH-1 'Hueys', taken in 1965 by the
remarkable British photographer Tim Page. *Back
cover, top left* is an unusual viewpoint, taken during a
firing run by a 'Huey B' gunship north of Vung Tao;
three 2.75-in. rockets can just be made out in flight.
The Marine 'Dust Off', *below*, was photographed at
Hoi An south of Da Nang.

Half-title page:
A CH-47A Chinook airlifts 105mm howitzer
ammunition to an artillery unit in the field during
1968. (US Army)

Title pages:
'Hueys' of the 1st Cavalry Division (Airmobile)
approach a landing zone on 7 March 1967 during
Operation 'Pershing', a search-and-destroy mission on
the Bong Son Plain. (US Army)

CONTENTS

FOREWORD

This book is the second remarkable effort by a very able author and historian toward capturing and recording the rôle of major arms of service during the Vietnam War. I was also privileged to prepare the foreword for Simon Dunstan's *Vietnam Tracks*, the story of armour in that war. This present work is an excellent portrayal of, in the author's words '. . . the most significant tactical advance of the Vietnam War . . . representing the most radical change in warfare since the *blitzkrieg*'.

His introductory chapter summarizes early helicopter employment in Korea, Indo-China, Malaya, Algeria and Borneo, actions which were studied in detail by US Army personnel who had the necessary vision to look to the future. It is of some interest to note that the story of 'Vietnam choppers' actually commenced about two years prior to the studies by the Howze Board and the formation of the 11th Air Assault Division (Test) in February 1963 which marked the birth of 'sky cavalry'. The story began on 1 November 1961, when the 57th and 8th Transportation Companies (Light Helicopter) from Ft. Lewis, Washington and Ft. Bragg, North Carolina were alerted for deployment to an unknown destination . . . That destination was Vietnam; and the author covers literally the full spectrum of operations from that first deployment of over a quarter-century ago to the final, tragic and pitiful agonies of the American effort in Vietnam.

Dunstan's book is both technical and tactical in content. The major capabilities and limitations of each type of aircraft are addressed in some detail; and for the military or civilian reader who may be interested in what was done, how, and where, methods of employment, tactics and techniques are carefully described. We learn of the organization and evolution of the helicopter units of various types within the US Army, Navy, Air Force and Marine Corps; and their capabilities and limitations in action are well covered. The author offers an excellent treatise on the logistical rôle of the helicopter; and his section on medical evacuation is superb.

Perhaps the most unique aspect is contained in the combat after-action reports which the author has woven into his story. One cannot read the accounts of 'Mad Man' Kelly, Gary Wetzel or Chief Warrant Officer Novisel without a clear recognition of the incredible professionalism, sense of duty and dedication of the thousands of helicopter crews who experienced Vietnam. The actions selected here were 'beyond the call of duty', but are representative of all the crews who did their duty in the most frustrating and complex combat environment yet faced by the American military.

Recognition must also be given to the more senior soldiers who broke the 'helicopter trail'. Here we remember those early pioneers Hamilton Howze, Robert Williams, Jay Vanderpool, Phil Seneff, Harry Kinnard, Jim Smith, Delk Oden and Bob Shoemaker. These fine soldiers were closely followed by those whom I would identify as 'operators', refining and modifying the earlier pioneer work: men such as Archie Clapp, Bill Maddox, Kit Sinclair, Jim Patterson, Charlie Canedy, Bob Molinelli, Ben Harrison and Doc Bahnsen. All these great personalities, and many more too numerous to mention, have indirectly contributed to the stuff of Simon Dunstan's volume, and their influence in the maturing of air mobility for ground combat forces frequently shows throughout his text.

Among a few personal memories which the reader may find of passing interest was one incident which occurred in 1963, and which for me encapsulates the whole Vietnam experience. The American Embassy, where I then worked, was informed that Astronaut Gordon Cooper would pass over Vietnam in the course of his earth orbital flight. Naturally, there was some concern as to the consequences if Cooper were for some reason forced to abort his mission and drop into South Vietnam. I was directed to co-ordinate search areas with the few transportation helicopter companies then present in-country. After I had briefed the commander of an H-34 company stationed at Pleiku on the mission and a suggested search area, he graciously accepted the task, but informed me that two of his 'birds' were in a 'down status' . . . during a routine Special Forces resupply mission that morning they had been hit by arrows fired by some angry Montagnards! As I gazed at the aboriginal crossbow arrows protruding from the bubble of one helicopter, effectively preventing it from rendering help to the most advanced space vehicle then known to man, I became somewhat reflective. This absurd, but true story held implications for the US experience across the whole spectrum of the Vietnam conflict.

Another incident was representative of the acuteness of helicopter personnel in recognizing and capitalizing upon enemy mistakes. In mid-1968 I was commanding the 11th Armored Cavalry Regiment ('Blackhorse'). One day an OH-6A scout commanded by Warrant Officer (now Lieutenant Colonel) Justin Ballou on a routine reconnaissance was flying 'low and slow' over an area which had sustained very heavy B-52 bomb damage, and was pockmarked with water-filled craters. Looking down, Ballou did a 'double take' before turning back again over his flight path, not believing his eyes. What he was looking at were numbers of fairly large fish swimming around in several craters close to heavy jungle growth but far from a river. We quickly inserted the aerorifle platoon of the Regimental Air Cavalry Troop, who immediately came into contact with a sizeable enemy force (we later learned that this was the headquarters of the Dong Ngai Regiment). Before the action ended, in our favour, the best part of a brigade equivalent was deployed and in battle. The betrayal of the enemy's position, and its costly consequences, were due to Ballou's imagination in recognizing a 'fish supply point'.

Another example of the quality of the helicopter crews came in early 1969. During that period the ARVN 36th Ranger Battalion, a fairly capable unit commanded by Captain Thang, was operating under the control of the 11th Cavalry, and attached to it was a small US Army advisory section. In the course of a sharp fire-fight the senior adviser, an infantry major, sustained a serious head wound. A 'Dust Off' mission was called, and within minutes a ship appeared on the scene. There was no landing zone; the time was late evening; the area was 'hot', with small arms fire aplenty; and there was no one on the ground who could talk to the 'Dust Off' pilot in English. He was forced by the nature of the terrain to employ a jungle penetrator; and to make matters worse, the major's wounds were such that extraction would have to be performed with his body in a vertical position.

As I monitored the evacuation from another aircraft, the 'Dust Off' pilot hovered over this very active area for no less than 45 minutes before the casualty was safely aboard. In the calmest possible way, he repeatedly gave instructions to the ARVN soldiers on the ground as to how to apply and rig the special equipment. This was an exercise in self-control the like of which I had not observed before, and have not since. When the 'Dust Off' called to say that everything was OK and he was en route for Long Binh hospital, I violated security regulations by asking the pilot his name and unit so that I could recommend him for an award. I will never forget his answer: 'No name provided, Colonel. I know who you are, and I thank you. I was simply doing my job, which took a little longer than usual. Good luck!' He flew off into the darkness; and the Ranger major survived.

* * *

In view of Simon Dunstan's kind permission to provide a few complementary thoughts to this excellent work: it is always as well to evaluate a weapons system against the nine 'principles of war' as they have come down to us from the days of Clausewitz. Of these, the helicopter enhances at least six: mass, economy of force, security, surprise, offensive and manoeuvre. The remaining three—objective, unity of command, and simplicity—may be applied advantageously by a chain of command which has a clear understanding both of the ground, and of that special aerial environment in which the helicopter is normally found. Adherence to these principles may well be the key to battlefield success, as much today as two hundred years ago.

The abiding lesson from the 'Vietnam chopper experience' was the importance of ground branch affiliation—personified, in the main, by the air cavalry. Those air crews knew the ground! They were sympathetic to, and enjoyed a constant tactical and even personal association with the ground combat soldier, who faced incredible difficulties against a crafty and capable adversary on challenging terrain.

In this writer's view, one of the primary characteristics of so-called counter-insurgency operations is the 'meeting engagement'. This difficult type of fighting is principally governed by the apparent inability of our combat formations to retain contact with the enemy throughout a protracted action. The phrase, 'If we can hold on to 'em, we can kill 'em', was frequently heard. Despite devastating material superiority, the ability to retain enemy contact was practically non-existent. Thus, the great majority of actions commenced with a carefully planned reconnaissance, followed by a meeting engagement, during which the primary effort involved the retention of contact, hopefully followed by the compression and eventual destruction of the enemy force.

Over 90 per cent of the contacts experienced by formations under my supervision were meeting engagements initiated by air cavalry elements on reconnaissance which had been generated by good intelligence. In that type of environment air cavalry, with the all-important ground affiliation, is a vital 'combat multiplier' of the highest order. Its absence spells disaster, if not defeat, in the long term.

While air cavalry personnel must develop understanding of the environment in which the ground combat soldier lives, fights, and sometimes dies, the same requirement should also apply to other elements of the current aviation branch of the US Army. More thought must be given, particularly, to the projected career patterns of the officers who will serve within that branch. Currently this is an initial entry speciality: junior officers begin their careers in the aviation branch with no experience of ground battle conditions, and never gain appreciation of them while serving in repeated aviation assignments. When the next war comes, the price could be paid in blood.

The simple alternative is to accept the commissioned officer into the aviation branch only after several years' service in the ground combat arm of his choice; and the segment of the aviation branch which he joins should be in affiliation with that ground combat arm. For example, attack helicopter and air cavalry units have an 'armor base'; air assault recognizes an 'infantry base', while lift units relate to the transportation corps, and so forth. After an officer is admitted into the aviation segment which is doctrinally 'hooked' to his ground combat or support 'base', his service in that type of unit should be constant. Simple tracking of assignments from the ground combat base to its aviation counterpart would surely solve the principal shortcomings of our separate aviation branch, whose activation was probably inevitable due to the complex and highly technical nature of the post-Vietnam helicopter force.

Vietnam Choppers tells a great story, effectively and well. It brought back a barrel of memories and reflections on matters which seem to me of great importance not only to the future of aviation, but also to the discharge of their responsibilities by those entrusted with our success in war. I would urge those who maintain an abiding interest in the military profession to study this volume. It will enhance understanding of what was done, right or wrong; and certain lessons will emerge which could be applied with advantage to another Vietnam-type scenario.

George S. Patton
Major General
US Army, Retired

1 HELICOPTERS AT WAR

After many years of experimentation the concept of rotary-wing flight, originally documented by Leonardo da Vinci, was finally realized during the 1930s; but it was not until the closing months of World War 2 that the helicopter was actually utilized for military purposes, with the deployment of the Sikorsky R-4 to the 1st Air Commando in the Far East for casualty evacuation and the retrieval of airmen shot down behind enemy lines. All helicopters at this time were fragile and temperamental machines with pitifully small payloads. However, by the late 1940s new designs such as the Bell Model 47 displayed markedly improved performance and reliability and were readily adopted by the armed services, particularly for rescue operations and reconnaissance missions. Although many military planners debated the rôle of the helicopter on the battlefield, it was the US Marine Corps which first experimented with the transport of troops into action by helicopter, a doctrine termed 'vertical envelopment'—the forerunner of airmobility.

Thus, the first large scale use of the helicopter occurred during the Korean War. Soon after the outbreak of hostilities in June 1950, USMC and US Air Force helicopters began flying medical evacuation missions, often from hillsides inaccessible to any other form of transport. Approximately 30,000 casualties were evacuated by helicopter during the war, and this remained its fundamental rôle throughout; a mission primarily undertaken by US Army helicopter detachments flying in support of three of the four MASH (Mobile Army Surgical Hospitals), with the fourth by USAF Air Rescue Service helicopters. The latter also performed their principal

RIGHT: 'Miss Alice II', an HO3S-1 (Sikorsky R-5) of Marine Observation Squadron Six takes off from a Korean hilltop bearing a wounded Marine who, because of the narrow configuration of the fuselage, had to be carried with his feet sticking out of the cabin. (USMC)

ABOVE: *A US Army H-13 (Bell 47) of the 2nd Helicopter Detachment, attached to the 8055 MASH, lifts off for the Korean front lines on a casualty evacuation mission. (US Army)*

ABOVE RIGHT: *HRS-1 (Sikorsky S-55) helicopters of HMR-161 land 4.5in. rocket launchers of the 1st Rocket Battery at Panjong-ni, Korea, on 25 August 1952 during Operation 'Ripple'. HMR-161 provided a rapid means of shifting personnel and equipment after the firing of rockets, whose huge backblast exposed their positions to retaliatory fire. (USMC)*

BELOW RIGHT: *A seriously injured casualty is lifted on to the side pannier of a French H-23 Raven (Hiller 360): in Tonkin, 1953. The Hiller 360 was flown by one of the most celebrated pilots of the Indo-China campaign, Médicin-Capitaine Valérie André, who in 120 combat missions rescued 165 casualties. During the Algerian War she flew a further 365, and subsequently became the first woman general in the French Army in April 1976. (Hiller Helicopters)*

function of combat rescue of downed aircrews. During the war the 3rd Air Rescue Squadron flew 9,860 rescue missions, often behind communist lines, and 996 airmen were recovered. On Friday 13 April 1951, a Sikorsky H-5 from the cruiser USS *Manchester* flew far behind enemy lines to retrieve the pilot of a Royal Navy Fleet Air Arm Sea Fury from No. 807 Squadron operating from the carrier HMS *Theseus*. The naval pilot, John Humphreys, was badly injured: his face had been smashed on the instrument panel, and his feet were trapped by the rudder pedals. The helicopter crewman attempted in vain to extricate him from the mangled cockpit; so the pilot, mindful of the unreliability of helicopter batteries, shut down the engine in order to assist, while Sea Furies and Corsairs circled overhead keeping communist troops at bay. After the successful rescue Humphreys made a full recovery, and subsequently became a successful test pilot.

Whereas the Army and the Air Force employed the helicopter principally for missions of mercy, the Marines pioneered its use as a tactical transport of men and *matériel* within the combat zone, following their pre-war experimental doctrine. On 13 September 1951, Marine Helicopter Transport Squadron 161 (HMR-161) conducted the first major resupply operation by helicopter in warfare, codenamed 'Windmill I'. The Sikorsky HRS-1 helicopters airlifted one day's supplies to the 2nd Battalion, 1st Marines during an attack on Hill 673, and returned bearing the wounded. One week later the squadron performed the first tactical lift of troops in combat when a Republic of Korea unit on the frontline was relieved by a Marine reinforced reconnaissance company. In four hours, Operation 'Summit' lifted some 224 troops and 17,772 pounds of cargo onto Hill 884, which subsequently became known as 'Mount Helicopter'. Thereafter, HMR-161 claimed several firsts including Operation 'Blackbird', the first large scale helicopter operation conducted at night, and Operation 'Bumble Bee', the first movement

by helicopter of an entire battalion into the frontline area. In the final weeks of the war the US Army deployed its first helicopter transport squadron to Korea, and it was utilized in much the same manner as by the Marines.

Despite the limited performance and numbers of the helicopters employed in Korea, they became an essential item of equipment in all military services, although their complexity and vulnerability were considered a deterrent to their routine use in airmobile operations. To the French, during the First Indo-China War, helicopters proved to be equally invaluable but, due to lack of numbers, they were employed almost exclusively for medical evacuation. The first helicopters to see service in Indo-China were a pair of Hiller 360s in April 1950, which were flown by a trio of valiant pilots including the famed aviatrix Valérie André. In order to extend their capability, the Hillers were routinely disassembled and carried by Bristol Freighter the length and breadth of Indo-China to successive operational areas. By the end of 1952 nine Westland Sikorsky S-51s and four Hiller 360s were serving in Indo-China. Up to this time four had been destroyed, but the helicopters had saved over 1,200 casualties. In 1953 six Sikorsky S-55s and four more Hillers (H-23 Raven) were provided by the United States. During the first days of the Battle of Dien Bien Phu three helicopters were destroyed on the ground at the beleaguered fortress. Thereafter it was deemed too dangerous for helicopters to evacuate casualties and they only returned to Dien Bien Phu after the camp had fallen on 7 May 1954 to retrieve the critically injured at the behest of the Viet Minh.

The first concerted use of helicopters in counter-insurgency warfare occurred during the Malayan Emergency of 1948–1960. Originally deployed in 1950, the first helicopters were used for casualty evacuation, liaison and rescue operations. They included the Westland Dragonfly, a licence-built version of the Sikorsky H-5, and from 1954 the Bristol 171 Sycamore. In March 1953 ten Sikorsky S-55s of No. 848 Naval Air Squadron arrived in Malaya, to be followed by No. 155 Squadron RAF equipped with Westland Whirlwind Mk 2s. Together, these twenty-six medium helicopters were used mostly for lifting troops into and out of remote jungle areas as well as for casualty evacuation, aerial reconnaissance, crop-spraying to contaminate enemy food cultivation, dropping psychological warfare leaflets, and the insertion and extraction of Special Air Service (SAS) troops. During its five years in Malaya No. 155 Squadron carried annually an average of 16,000 troops and 225,000 pounds of supplies. Although the helicopter provided considerable flexibility and was considered to have increased the effective utilization of ground troops by a factor of four, it required extensive maintenance because of its relative complexity, and its performance was significantly impaired by the tropical climate. Nevertheless, with the advent of more powerful helicopters the concept of airmobility in counter-insurgency warfare was further refined during the Borneo campaign of 1962–1965, when the helicopter proved its worth as a force multiplier in protecting 1,000 miles of border against incursion from Indonesia.

One of the most significant advances in the application of airmobility was during Operation 'Musketeer', the Anglo-French military action to regain control of the Suez Canal in 1956. At 0610 hours on 6 November, ten Westland Whirlwind Mk 22s of No. 845 Naval Air Squadron took off from HMS *Theseus*, followed by six Whirlwind Mk 2s and six Sycamore Mk 14s from HMS *Ocean*—a combined Army and RAF formation known as the Joint Helicopter Unit. Together, they flew Royal Marines of 45 Commando some ten miles from the carriers out at sea to Port Said in the first helicopter assault during an opposed landing. Within eighty-nine minutes, a total of 415 men and twenty-five tons of supplies were lifted into the bridgehead, while casualties were carried on each return sortie—one wounded Marine being on the operating table within twenty minutes

BELOW: *A Westland Whirlwind Mk 2 (Sikorsky S-55) of No. 155 Squadron RAF lands in a jungle clearing during an operation in Malaya. The limited number of helicopters employed during the Malayan Emergency of 1948–1960 were used for a variety of innovative tasks which became widespread during the Vietnam War. (Westland Helicopters)*

of leaving his ship. During the day, ninety-six casualties were evacuated by helicopter; one naval Whirlwind with wounded aboard ran out of fuel and ditched in the sea, but the pilot saved his casualties. In a further incident, a Royal Navy Sea Hawk crashed some thirty miles inland but the pilot was successfully rescued by helicopter.

Further important innovations were introduced by the French during the Algerian War of 1954–1962 which heralded the first major and sustained use of helicopters for airmobile operations. In the early stages of the conflict the French Army flew Sikorsky H-19s (S-55)—*l'éléphant joyeux*—as a cargo transport and to a lesser degree as a troop carrier; but with the advent of the Vertol H-21—*la banane*—in June 1956, air assault by combat troops became commonplace. In the same month the French Air Force introduced the Sikorsky H-34 (S-58) and employed it for the same purpose. Helicopters for troop support were provided by both the Army and the Air Force (and indeed the Navy), with the Army responsible for the eastern half of Algeria and the Air Force for the western half. Their methods of operation differed significantly; but, faced with the same hazards on contested landing zones, both services developed armed helicopters to deliver suppressive fire during the critical moments when transport helicopters were unloading troops on the ground.

The Air Force devised a flexible mounting to carry a 20mm cannon which could be fitted to any H-34 within minutes, while the Army fitted rocket pods and small calibre machine guns to a proportion of its H-21s. Both proved highly successful and reduced losses from ground fire dramatically. Further protection for helicopter crews from guerrilla marksmen was provided by body armour and armoured seats. With the introduction of the Sud-Est Alouette II into the Algerian conflict in 1958—the first turbine-powered helicopter to see combat service—the rôle of fire suppression was assumed by this agile machine, and most of the more cumbersome transport helicopters reverted to their troop-lifting function. Known as *le papillon à cornes* (the horned butterfly), it was armed with rockets and machine guns, and in some cases with SS-10/SS-11 anti-tank missiles to engage targets masked in gullies and caves. While the

ABOVE: *Troops of the 11th Air Assault Division (Test) land from UH-1D Iroquois helicopters in an attack against 'Redland', a hypothetical nation occupied by the 82nd Airborne Division acting as aggressors, during Exercise 'Air Assault II' which was conducted over four million acres of the Carolinas between 14 October and 12 November 1964 as the final test to prove the concept of airmobility. (US Army/Military Review)*

Alouette was used extensively for casualty evacuation and liaison, its other most important function was as an airborne command post during airmobile operations. Through these tactics of helicopter-borne shock troops, motorized infantry and armour, supported by airpower, the French had virtually defeated the guerrilla forces in the field by 1960 when the war shifted to the political arena, culminating in Algerian independence in 1962.

All these campaigns were studied in great detail in the United States. Since the Korean War, both the Marines and the Army had continued to develop helicopter tactics and doctrine. In 1955 the first experimental 'Sky Cavalry' unit was organized and tested by the Army during Exercise 'Sage Brush'. In the following year it came under the command of a dynamic officer, Colonel Jay Vanderpool. With few funds and no formal charter, he and his handful of enthusiastic subordinates—known as 'Vanderpool's Fools'—devised a variety of makeshift helicopter armaments which were demonstrated in a series of spectacular and often unpredictable field tests, following the dictum 'whatever you hit, call it the target'. Gradually official approval was gained, and the unit was expanded to become the 7292nd Aerial Combat Reconnaissance Company (Provisional) in March 1958.

Up until this time the ACR Company had used whatever

ABOVE: *A Vertol H-21 'banane' and a trio of Alouette IIs of the* Groupe d'Hélicoptères No. 2 *participate in an assault landing during an operation with the 2ᵉ Régiment Étranger de Parachutistes near Sétif, Algeria in the late 1950s. (Jim Worden)*

helicopters were to hand; but in 1960 the Rogers Board was convened to study Army requirements for all types of aircraft for observation, surveillance and transport, leading to a new generation of helicopters of greatly enhanced capabilities. This was followed in 1962 by the Howze Board, which studied the whole concept of airmobility and recommended the formation of an air assault division to test the board's findings in its wholehearted endorsement of airmobility for the Army. This was duly achieved with the creation of the 11th Air Assault Division (Test) in February 1963 and, in a series of extensive field exercises during 1964, confirmed the validity of the airmobile concept as an innovative means of improving tactical mobility on the battlefield. No field exercise, however, compares with the harsh reality of combat, and battlefields in a far-distant Asian country were beginning to impinge upon the national consciousness—Vietnam.

2 US ARMY HELICOPTERS IN VIETNAM

'The Flying Bananas'

On 1 November 1961 two units of the Strategic Army Corps, the 8th and 57th Transportation Companies (Light Helicopter), were alerted for deployment to an unknown destination. Neither knew if the alert was an actual one or just another exercise. After each company had filled its Table of Organization and Equipment (TOE) of twenty CH-21C Shawnees and two OH-13E Sioux, the helicopters were preserved by cocooning to protect their fuselages from salt water spray at the Alameda Naval Station, California. Thirty-two of the CH-21s were loaded on the flight deck of the USNS *Core*, and the ship set sail on 21 November. The remaining eight CH-21 Shawnees, belonging to the 8th, and all four OH-13 Sioux were boxed and loaded aboard a conventional cargo ship which departed the west coast a week later.

Rough seas were encountered during the trip, and it was soon discovered that salt water spray was causing corrosion in the rotor heads of the deck-loaded helicopters. The problem was resolved by the use of canvas covers and frequent servicing of exposed parts. The other ship was less fortunate: one of the CH-21s broke loose in its box, and the vessel was diverted to Hawaii for replacement of the damaged aircraft by one from the 81st Transportation Company (Light Helicopter). This caused considerable delay, and the remaining aircraft did not arrive until the 8th Transportation Company moved from Saigon to its permanent location at Qui Nhon. The OH-13 Sioux helicopters were returned to the United States without being used in action. The USNS *Core* arrived at Saigon Port on 11 December 1961. Depreservation was begun while sailing up the Saigon River, and rotor blades were installed at the dockside in Saigon, allowing the helicopters to be flown off the ship directly to Tan Son Nhut airport from where the two units were to operate.

Training of ARVN (Army of the Republic of Vietnam) units in airmobile operations began immediately and, during the first ninety days, the 57th familiarized over 25,000 ARVN troops with its helicopters, as well as conducting twenty combat assault missions. The 8th and 57th carried out their first joint training exercise on 22 December 1961 when over 1,000 paratroopers of the ARVN Airborne Brigade were transported in thirty of the thirty-two CH-21 aircraft then available in-country from an assembly area to assault positions several miles away. The first air assault operation in Vietnam was conducted by the 8th and 57th on 2 January 1962, when the two companies transported 1,036 ARVN soldiers into a small jungle landing zone approximately 300 by 150 yards in size. The operation did not result in significant contact with the enemy, but it demonstrated to ARVN commanders the real potentiality of

ABOVE RIGHT: *The 'Spraylat' protective cocoon is removed from a CH-21C Shawnee at the dockside in Saigon as the helicopters of the 33rd Transportation Company (Light Helicopter) are unloaded from the freighter 'Ocean Evelyn' on 19 September 1962. The 33rd 'Trans Company' was the fourth CH-21 unit to be deployed to Vietnam, where it was based at Bien Hoa. (US Army)*

BELOW RIGHT: *ARVN troops undergo instruction in helicopter operations soon after the arrival of the 8th and 57th Transportation Companies (Light Helicopter) in Vietnam. One of the first modifications to the helicopters was the fabrication of an additional step at the doorways to allow the short-statured Vietnamese troops to embark more easily. (US Army/Military Review)*

18

airmobile operations, and rapidly generated more requests for aviation support than could be accommodated.

Following the 8th and 57th, the 93rd Transportation Company (Light Helicopter) arrived off Vietnam aboard the USNS *Card* on 26 January 1962. When the sister ship of USNS *Core* reached a point ten miles out in the South China Sea, the aircraft were flown off the carrier deck to Da Nang Air Base. The first thirty days were spent in unit readiness and training of ARVN troops in airmobile operations. The first operational missions were undertaken to resupply and rotate personnel at several jungle outposts in I Corps Tactical Zone. Some of these outposts had been virtually isolated from their parent units for as long as a year. An appalling state of inadequate supply existed and, in some instances, a total breakdown in troop morale and discipline was evident. Aerial missions did much to restore the situation and, by mid-1962, ARVN forces were actively patrolling the region whereas units had previously seldom ventured beyond the immediate vicinity of their fortifications.

In April 1962 the first US Marine Corps squadron of HUS-1 helicopters arrived in-country and was established at the former Japanese airfield at Soc Trang in the Mekong Delta (see Chapter 8— US Marine Corps Helicopters in Vietnam). The 57th Medical Detachment (Helicopter Ambulance) arrived in late April 1962 equipped with five HU-1As, the first Hueys to serve in Vietnam[1].

[1] The original designation of HU-1A Iroquois—Helicopter, Utility, Model 1—from which the nickname 'Huey' derived was changed to UH-1A on 18 September 1962 under the unified designation system that applied to all branches of the US Armed Forces. However, by then the nickname Huey had stuck and it was rarely known by its official name of 'Iroquois'—one of the North American Indian tribes after which most types of US Army aircraft were named. Similarly, the Marine HUS-1— Helicopter, Utility, Sikorsky, Model 1—was redesignated UH-34D Sea Horse, but again, to Marines it was always known by its nickname of 'Huss'.

The unit soon demonstrated the feasibility and desirability of battlefield evacuation of casualties by helicopter (see Chapter 5— Dust Off: US Army Helicopter Ambulances in Vietnam). In the following month the Military Assistance Command, Vietnam-Military Assistance Advisory Group (MACV-MAAG) Flight Detachment was augmented by ten HU-1A helicopters, which were positioned with the III Corps Advisory Group to support adviser operations. The 45th Transportation Battalion from Fort Sill, Oklahoma, was deployed to Vietnam on 1 July 1962 and assumed command of the three CH-21 helicopter companies, and of the 18th Aviation Company which flew U-1A Otters throughout the country delivering aircraft parts and supplies to aviation units widely separated from their support elements.

During September two more helicopter companies, the 33rd and the 81st, were committed, while the 93rd Transportation Company exchanged bases at Da Nang with the Marines because of the greater capability of the Marine HUS-1 helicopters to operate in the higher elevations of the northern regions. In the following month the 611th Transportation Company (Aircraft Direct Support) arrived in Vietnam to supplement the 339th Transportation Company (DS) —which had been based at Da Nang since February—in its mission to support the field maintenance detachments operating with the helicopter companies and other aviation units.

During these early days, due to the inadequate supply and maintenance support system as well as the hostile operating environment, the 339th had accomplished its tasks by ingenuity and improvisation. For example, approximately sixty rotor blade sets per month were needed during the monsoon season to support the fleet of approximately one hundred CH-21s, while the 57th Transportation Company required over fifty engine replacements in its first year of operations. Crash- and battle-damaged aircraft in the 'boneyards'

RIGHT: *In order to increase their payload in the high temperatures of Vietnam the CH-21s were stripped of their heaters, seats, doors, cabin insulation and sound-proofing, which reduced weight by some 300 pounds. The removal of the seats also facilitated loading and unloading, and obviated the problem of weapons becoming entangled in the canvas web backs—which, on occasion, resulted in accidental discharges in flight. Here, a crew chief of the 57th 'Trans Company' crouches by the doorway with an M-2 automatic carbine, one of several types of weapons carried by crew members for self-protection, during an operation in Kien Hoa Province in the Mekong Delta on 23 July 1962. (US Army/Military Review)*

were cannibalized for every usable part and component. The maintenance personnel worked all hours, day and night, to keep the aircraft flying. On many occasions dedicated crew chiefs literally taped and wired their aircraft together to enable them to be flown back to base rather than have them face possible destruction in hostile areas. Despite the seemingly insurmountable difficulties due to the critical shortage of engines and the deterioration of rotor blades and avionics equipment from high humidity, the helicopters consistently exceeded Department of the Army programmed flying hours and availability rates. By the end of the year, the Army had thirteen aviation units flying 199 aircraft of eight different types at ten locations in Vietnam.

The Genesis of the Gunship

Despite the best efforts of the US Army aviators, airmobile operations were severely handicapped by the unfamiliarity of ARVN commanders—and indeed, of many American advisers—with the capabilities and limitations of helicopters. This was compounded by the woeful lack of training of most ARVN troops. Helicopter company personnel had to devote an inordinate amount of time to teaching the Vietnamese such basic skills as loading and off-loading, as well as ensuring that weapons were on 'safe' when boarding: many CH-21s had holes in the fuselage from accidental discharges in flight. ARVN troops displayed a marked reluctance to jump from a hovering helicopter, and they tended to congregate in the immediate landing zone instead of rapidly securing the area for following helicopters. Such failings needlessly prolonged the exposure of aircraft and their crews to hostile fire.

The dangers were exacerbated by the inadequacy of ARVN artillery and air support. Because of its inaccuracy, mortar and shell fire had to be proscribed within a one kilometre radius of the landing zone, which effectively deprived helicopters and ground troops of fire support at a time when they needed it most. Vietnamese Air Force (VNAF) fighter-bomber escort aircraft were equally ineffectual. Their napalm and bomb strikes often cratered the actual landing zone and the resulting fire and smoke constituted serious hazards to the helicopters. Moreover, the incompatibility of US Army UHF helicopter radios and Vietnamese fighter aircraft VHF radios, let alone the language barrier, repeatedly compromised missions when rapid communications in fast-moving tactical situations were required. During late 1962 air support flown by Vietnamese pilots was described by US helicopter personnel as 'inadequate, inaccurate, unco-ordinated and useless'. Attempts by US Air Force instructors to overcome these deficiencies met with such limited success that many 'Jungle Jim'/'Farm Gate' pilots (the codenames of the training programmes) flew illicit missions in support of helicopter operations in T-28s accompanied by Vietnamese student fliers who were derisively named 'sandbags'.

In order to alleviate these problems and provide some form of self-protection, helicopter crewmen carried rifles or M-3 'grease guns' and mounted light machine guns in the doorways. These measures

LEFT: *CH-21C Shawnees of the 57th Transportation Company (Light Helicopter) approach a landing zone at Bau Cham, fifty miles north-west of Saigon, to off-load troops of the 1st Battalion, 9th Regiment, ARVN 21st Division, on 24 March 1963. Set alight and cratered by VNAF airstrikes, such landing zones were potentially hazardous to helicopter operations. (US Army)*

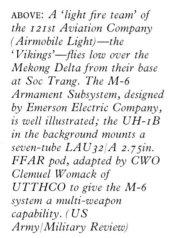

ABOVE: *A 'light fire team' of the 121st Aviation Company (Airmobile Light)—the 'Vikings'—flies low over the Mekong Delta from their base at Soc Trang. The M-6 Armament Subsystem, designed by Emerson Electric Company, is well illustrated; the UH-1B in the background mounts a seven-tube LAU32/A 2.75in. FFAR pod, adapted by CWO Clemuel Womack of UTTHCO to give the M-6 system a multi-weapon capability. (US Army/Military Review)*

ABOVE RIGHT: *A complete helicopter landing force returns from an operation near Rach Gia, Kien Giang Province in 1963. The first nine aircraft are CH-21C Shawnees of the 93rd Transporation Company (Light Helicopter), followed by six UH-1B Hueys of the 114th Aviation Company (Airmobile Light) in V formation, with six armed Hueys of the Utility Tactical Transport Helicopter Company bringing up the rear. (US Army)*

proved generally ineffective; and to meet the requirement the Army formed its first armed helicopter company to act as escort to the troop-carrying CH-21s. The unit, designated the Utility Tactical Transport Helicopter Company (UTTHCO), was activated on 25 July 1962 in Okinawa using fifteen HU-1A helicopters drawn from the 53rd Aviation Detachment which employed them as part of the Aviation Support Activity on the island. Experiments were conducted with various weapons both hand-held and aircraft-mounted; in a manoeuvring helicopter shoulder-fired weapons were ineffective, and in an effort to stabilize them they were suspended by elastic cord from the cabin ceiling—a procedure which became widespread in Vietnam. After a further period of experimentation and preparation in Thailand, UTTHCO, under the command of Major Robert Runckle, arrived in Vietnam on 9 October 1962, and flew its first escort mission seven days later during Operation 'Morning Star'.

During this period various heavier armament systems, in the form of rocket launchers attached to the Hueys, were devised and tested. Under the guidance of innovative UTTHCO personnel such as Chief Warrant Officers Carter, Heck and Womack, seven- and eight-tube 2.75 in. Folding Fin Aerial Rockets (FFAR) were skid-mounted beside the .30 calibre M-37C or 7.62mm M-60C machine guns to give a multiple weapon capability. On 20 November eleven UH-1Bs arrived at the unit's base at Tan Son Nhut airport. The UH-1B embodied the more powerful T53-L-5 engine rated at 825shp at 6,600rpm, as against the 700shp at 5,800rpm of the L-1 engine fitted to the UH-1A. Numerous other improvements increased performance; but, most importantly, the UH-1B incorporated a purpose-designed weapon system rather than the jury-rigged contraptions used hitherto. Behind and below each cargo door was a 'Universal Mount' capable of taking the M-22 (SS-11 anti-tank missile system for which it was originally designed), the XM-6 Emerson helicopter fire suppression kit, 'quad-machine gun', or a rocket launcher such as the XM-3 (which is described later, together with the M-22).

The XM-6 'quad guns' or 'flex guns', as they were called, were a vast improvement over the fixed, forward-firing machine guns of the UH-1A. Originally designated XM-153, the equipment was renumbered to XM-6 when the M-73C machine guns proved unsatisfactory. When retrospectively fitted to the UH-1A it was designated XM-6E2 and on the UH-1B as XM-6E3. The system was type classified as M-6 Armament Subsystem in May 1963. Each side mount supported two M-60C machine guns with a total rate of fire of

ABOVE LEFT: *The increased mobility of ARVN forces from 1962, thanks to the introduction of CH-21 helicopters and M-113 APCs, posed a serious threat to the Viet Cong insurgents and constrained their freedom of movement during daylight hours. They quickly evolved counter-tactics. Here, a US Army officer indicates a VC training aid to shoot down UH-1 helicopters drawn on the wall of an abandoned building. (US Army)*

2,200 rounds per minute to a maximum effective range of 750 yards. Ammunition was carried in twelve 500-round boxes located in four rows of three on the rear cabin floor. At a weight of 830 pounds when fully loaded, 6,700 rounds were available with 700 in the flexible metal chuting that fed the guns by means of electric drive motors on the mount casings. The co-pilot/gunner controlled the 'flex guns' by depressing a 'deadman' switch on the roof-mounted flexible pantographic sight whereby the guns could be aimed independently of the helicopter line of flight through an elevation of fifteen degrees and depression of sixty degrees, with twelve degrees deflection inboard and seventy degrees outboard. When the 'deadman' switch was released, for instance if the co-pilot was incapacitated, the guns returned to the stowed position and the pilot had the capability to fire them in the fixed-forward mode. The system was rugged and dependable and, combined with the 'bungee'-slung M-60 machine guns of the two door gunners, gave the UH-1B over twice the firepower of its forerunner.

Under the auspices of the Army Concept Team in Vietnam (ACTIV), the effectiveness of the armed helicopter company in its escort rôle was evaluated from 16 October 1962 to 15 March 1963. Testing was only undertaken during actual operations, mainly in support of the 33rd, 57th and 93rd Transportation Companies; but until late February rules of engagement precluded offensive action by the armed helicopters unless fired on directly. Thereafter the 'rules' were modified to allow helicopters to initiate fire against clearly identified insurgents. Many of the tactical doctrines for armed helicopter employment evolved during the test period, including techniques for escort of transport helicopters, and fire suppression of landing zones prior to and during the landing of ground troops (see Chapter 4—'US Army Helicopter Gunships in Vietnam'). The UTTHCO flew 1,779 combat hours during the test period, mostly in the III and IV Corps Tactical Zones of southern Vietnam. Whereas the rate of Viet Cong hits against unescorted helicopters doubled in number, against escorted craft it decreased by twenty-five per cent. Eleven armed Hueys were hit by ground fire but only one was shot down and seriously damaged. This experience demonstrated that the vulnerability of armed helicopters was within acceptable risk limits.

Viet Cong Counter-Measures

LEFT: *A CH-21C Shawnee lifts off after dropping a load of twelve ARVN troops in a rice paddy in the Mekong Delta. Usually eight to ten helicopters comprised the first 'lift' at the outset of an operation; more troops were then inserted during subsequent lifts. Helicopters rarely landed in such terrain for fear of becoming stuck in the glutinous mud, and troops disembarked by jumping from the hovering aircraft. (US Army/Aviation Digest)*

The Viet Cong did not remain idle in face of the threat posed by the increasing effectiveness of helicopters in airmobile operations, and soon developed counter-tactics. Probable landing zones were covered by fire, or booby-trapped by means including spears planted in the ground to puncture the bellies of helicopters or arrows strung in bows that were automatically released by their rotor downdraft. Specific instructions were issued to the Viet Cong to combat the various helicopters, as a document captured in 1963 indicates: 'The type used to carry troops is very large and looks like a worm [CH-21]. It has two rotors and usually flies at an altitude of 200 to 300 metres. To hit its head, lead by either one length or two thirds of a length when it flies horizontally. The type used by commanders or casualties

looks like a ladle [UH-1]. Lead this type one length when in flight. It is good to fire at the engine section when it is hovering or landing.' In one instance these strictures proved unproductive when a CH-21 pilot dropped onto a landing zone only to see a Viet Cong squad debouch from the trees and open fire at point blank range. Convinced of the necessity to 'lead' the helicopter, they poured their fire into the ground twenty yards in front of him, and he took off without a single hit.

Not all encounters were quite so painless as this, for the transport helicopters remained highly vulnerable in a contested landing zone without an adequate rotary- or fixed-wing escort. The Battle of Ap Bac in early 1963 resulted in a Viet Cong victory that breathed new life into the insurgency. On 2 January elements of the ARVN 7th Division, including a company of M-113 APCs, were ordered to assault the hamlet of Ap Tan Thoi in Dinh Tuong Province, on the edge of the Plain of Reeds about thirty-five miles southwest of Saigon. Intelligence reports suggested that an enemy headquarters was situated there, protected by a reinforced company. In fact, the fierce and formidable 514th VC Battalion held the area in strength, with the bulk of its 500-odd men near the neighbouring village of Ap Bac. The plan included air assault landings by ten CH-21 Shawnees of the 93rd Transportation Company but, due to the deployment of all VNAF fixed-wing aircraft to Operation 'Burning Arrow' at Tay Ninh, the only air support available was five armed helicopters of UTTHCO.

The first three helicopter lifts landed without incident around the hamlet. However, the operation soon became bogged down, and to force the pace of the action the senior American adviser suggested that the reserves be committed close to Ap Bac itself. Unfortunately, the place he chose for the insertion was in the heart of the Viet Cong's most heavily defended positions. As the ten Shawnees approached the landing zone, the VC opened fire with mortars, automatic weapons and at least two heavy machine guns, downing the fourth CH-21. When another CH-21 moved in to rescue the crew, it too was shot down. The armed Hueys flew repeated passes in an attempt to suppress the enemy fire but were unable to destroy many of the gun positions, which in turn shot down two more CH-21s and an armed Huey. One UTTHCO pilot recalled: 'The Viet Cong were brave men. My God, we got a fix on one machine gun position and made fifteen aerial runs at it, and every time that gunner came right back up firing.'

Eventually, fixed-wing aircraft arrived to augment the ineffectual artillery support and, after numerous attacks with bombs, rockets and napalm, the enemy fire was silenced—but only because the Viet Cong had slipped away through gaps in the ARVN lines. The challenge of the helicopter was met that day, and the insurgents proclaimed a triumph over Saigon's puppets and Washington's machines. Ap Bac was to remain a rallying cry to the Viet Cong throughout the war.

'Eagle Flights'

The increased activity of the Viet Cong and the nature of guerrilla warfare itself were such that, prior to helicopter operations, accurate and timely intelligence was essential to pinpoint their bases and staging areas so that the enemy could be engaged in force before they melted into the countryside. In order to reduce the planning time and maintain security for such air assaults, UTTHCO introduced in April 1963 the 'Eagle Flight', which had been devised by the Marine Shufly squadron in the previous year. A typical 'Eagle Flight' comprised a command and control Huey, seven transport helicopters carrying ARVN troops, five armed Hueys as escort and fire support and, often, a medical evacuation helicopter. Eagle Flights were usually held on a standby basis, or sometimes were airborne searching for suitable targets. The quick reaction missions were normally of short duration within range of supporting weapons, but also provided the basis for larger operations when several Eagle Flights were combined or reserve forces were available for immediate reinforcement. They were particularly useful against small targets of opportunity such as Viet Cong tax collection points; the interception of suspects fleeing an operational area; the blocking of escape routes during cordon operations; and the recovery of crews or bodies from downed aircraft.

Subsequently, most helicopter companies organized their own Eagle Flights as the build-up of US Army Aviation units continued. In the spring of 1963 the 45th Batallion relinquished control of aviation units in I and II Corps areas to a newly arrived unit, the 52nd Aviation Battalion. The 114th Aviation Company (Airmobile Light) arrived on 10 May equipped with UH-1Bs. The company comprised three platoons of which two were each made up of eight troop-carrying UH-1s, and the third was an armed platoon of eight gunships plus a reserve Huey in the service platoon. Totalling twenty-five helicopters in all, this was the basic unit organization, and armed platoons were progressively incorporated into the other helicopter companies in Vietnam. On 23 June 1963 the in-country units were redesignated when the 45th became the 145th Aviation Battalion while the 8th, 33rd, 57th, 81st and 93rd Transportation Companies (Light Helicopter) became respectively the 117th, 118th, 120th, 119th and 121st Aviation Companies (Airmobile Light). These redesignations coincided with the transition from the CH-21 Shawnees to UH-1 Iroquois helicopters. In May 1963 four CH-37 Mojave medium transport helicopters of A Flight, 19th Aviation Company arrived from Korea, and a pair each were assigned to both the 611th and 339th Transportation Companies (Aircraft Direct Support). The CH-37s were capable of recovering many aircraft intact without major disassembly, thereby reducing both exposure time in hostile areas and man-hours required to return damaged aircraft to flying duty. In its first two years of operations the 611th recovered 139 downed aircraft including fifty-four CH-21s and forty-three UH-1s.

ABOVE: *A CH-37B Mojave of the 611th Transportation Company (Aircraft Direct Support), operating out of Vinh Long, strains to lift a CH-21C of the 57th Transportation Company (Light Helicopter) shot down near Ben Cat during 1964, when there were nine Army Mojaves in Vietnam. (US Army/Military Review)*

The Early Years

In early 1964 the transition from CH-21s to UH-1s was completed; and the last 'Hog Two-One' (Serial No. 56-2049), which had arrived in Vietnam in December 1961 flew its final mission at the hands of Lieutenant-Colonel Robert Dillard, the original CO of 57th Transportation Company (Light Helicopter), on 27 June 1964. At the beginning of that year the US Army had 388 aircraft in Vietnam including 248 helicopters, the majority of which were Hueys. The newly formed Huey companies continued to fly troop lift missions in support of ARVN forces, but now they were escorted by Huey gunships from their own company's armed platoon. However, the Huey troop carriers—known as 'slicks' because of their uncluttered contours—flew twenty knots faster than the heavily laden gunship escorts with their drag-inducing armament systems. Consequently the 'slicks' were obliged to fly at less than top speed when escorted. Also the armed helicopters were unable to regain *en route* formation if they attacked targets of opportunity when escorting an air assault mission. This problem was not satisfactorily resolved until the introduction in 1967 of the first purpose designed gunship, the AH-1G Cobra.

Nevertheless, the early years in Vietnam had proved the rôle of the helicopter in counter-guerrilla warfare. In the First Indo-China War the Viet Minh, forerunners of the Viet Cong, had evolved a strategy to whittle away the will and combat power of the French Union

ABOVE: *UH-1B Hueys of the 'Soc Trang Tigers'—the 121st Assault Helicopter Company— land ARVN troops in a rice paddyfield during an operation in the Mekong Delta during 1964. A standard low-visibility camouflage and markings scheme for Hueys was introduced in 1965. (US Army/Military Review)*

Forces by investing isolated posts. The defenders would promptly demand reinforcement and a relief column would be mounted but, being predominantly truck-borne and confined to the inadequate road network, this invariably fell victim to mines and ambushes in a debilitating process of attrition. Arriving days later and exhausted at their destination, the 'rescuers' usually found that the enemy had slipped away or that the post had fallen. By the large scale use of helicopters, American planners sought to cut this tactical Gordian knot at the stroke of a rotor blade, flying reinforcements to any point of contact within minutes or hours at 100 knots, fresh and ready for battle; providing direct fire support by gunships; resupplying troops with ammunition and rations, and whisking their wounded from the battlefield with merciful efficiency.

Such was the theory; but in 1964 there were too few helicopters to accommodate all the expanding activities of American advisers and Special Forces and the increasing scale of ARVN operations, as well as support missions for engineer, signal and logistics units. It soon became evident what a brutal testing ground Vietnam was for men and machines, in a war without fronts where the Viet Cong more often than not chose the place and time of battle. Terrain varied from the glutinous rice paddy fields that sucked at landing skids, to the dense jungle where helicopters had to ease down through holes blasted in the canopy by explosives; and from mountain peaks where every ounce of power was vital, to the always frightening 'hot LZ', where every second spent hovering over ground bristling with jagged tree stumps and blasted by artillery was an open invitation to enemy gunners to rake the fragile machines with bullets and rocket-propelled grenades. The environment itself was equally hostile. The hot and humid atmosphere consistently sapped the power of engines and the strength of men, while on or near the ground even the soil presented a hazard. In many areas the bright red clay called laterite became a bottomless mire when wet, and as fine as talcum powder when dry. On take-off and landing, dust clouds clogged the turbines and abraded rotor blades while obscuring vision to mere feet. Even on routine missions the weather could change from clear skies to lashing rain within minutes.

ABOVE: *A platoon leader's UH-1B of the Utility Tactical Transport Helicopter Company executes a firing pass with the M-60C machine guns of its M-6 Armament Subsystem on 12 February 1964. Up until this time UTTHCO was the principal exponent of the armed helicopter concept, and provided personnel to assist other units being similarly equipped. (US Army)*

On 14 December 1964 two further helicopter units—Companies A of the 501st and 502nd Aviation Battalions—arrived in Vietnam at Bien Hoa and Vinh Long respectively. As the new year dawned there were 406 US Army aircraft in Vietnam with 250 Hueys, nine CH-37 Mojaves and the remainder fixed-wing types. The helicopters came under the command of three major organizations: the 13th Aviation Battalion 'Guardian' at Can Tho supported IV Corps area with three Huey companies—the 114th, 121st and Company A, 502nd; the 145th Aviation Battalion 'Old Warrior' (also nicknamed 'America's Foreign Legion', since it never served in the continental United States) at Tan Son Nhut supported III Corps area with four Huey companies—the 68th (formerly UTTHCO), 118th, 120th and Company A, 501st; and the 52nd Aviation Battalion 'Flying Dragons' at Pleiku supported I and II Corps areas with two Huey companies—the 117th and 119th. This made it possible to place a US Army aviation company or a US Marine Corps helicopter squadron in support of each ARVN division with additional aviation supporting each Corps Tactical Zone.

Due to intensified communist activity and, specifically, increased overt action against US personnel, 1965 saw the transition from an advisory and support capacity to the commitment of US ground troops. The first major combat unit of the US Army to be deployed was the 173rd Airborne Brigade stationed at Okinawa. On 7 May 1965 the brigade arrived to provide security for the airbase at Bien Hoa and also the airfield at Vung Tau, in conjunction with the attached 1st Battalion, Royal Australian Regiment. Such a defensive posture did not last long. On 27 June the 173rd Airborne Brigade participated in the largest troop lift operation of the war so far when 144 Army helicopters penetrated War Zone D in an area where allied forces had not operated for a year. Additional forces arrived in July with the deployment of the 1st Brigade, 101st Airborne Division, and the 2nd Brigade, 1st Infantry Division, followed by the remainder of the 'Big Red One' in October. At the same time the US Army Support Command, Vietnam, was redesignated simply US Army, Vietnam.

The early operations of the 173rd Airborne Brigade were made

possible only by the expertise of the helicopter units already in Vietnam. For the first three months the brigade was supported by the 145th Aviation Battalion, but in September a helicopter company was attached under brigade command. This had several advantages, not least of which was the aviation company's ability to move a complete battalion anywhere in the brigade's TAOR (Tactical Area of Operational Responsibility) within two hours, whereas previously, on a mission basis from a separate aviation unit, it took two or three times as long. After a six month trial period of three months in support and three months attached, it was shown that the effectiveness of an integral aviation company was markedly higher: after attachment the total sorties flown per month increased twenty-four per cent, the number of combat sorties increased by a factor of 1.65, and the average tonnage carried increased by fifty per cent, whereas the average number of hours flown monthly per pilot decreased twenty-four per cent and the average number of hours each aircraft was utilized decreased by twenty-three per cent. These early experiences also demonstrated that an airmobile operation was not simply a matter of moving troops between two points, but was a complete integration of reconnaissance, tactical air support, helicopter gunships, field artillery, troop lift helicopters and the essential rifleman. The practice of airmobility was still in its infancy.

'The First Team'—1st Cavalry Division (Airmobile)

Meanwhile, on 1 July 1965, the 11th Air Assault Division (Test) was redesignated as the 1st Cavalry Division (Airmobile) and was simultaneously ordered to Vietnam. On 27 August an advance party arrived at An Khe under the command of the divisional deputy, Brigadier-General John Wright Jr., who, wielding a machete himself, ordered the scrub to be cleared until it was as smooth as a 'Golf Course', a name which became synonymous with the divisional base area throughout its service in Vietnam. The 1st Cavalry Division (Airmobile) was the first major formation specifically equipped and trained for airmobile warfare. The division comprised 15,787 officers and men, 1,600 vehicles (approximately one-half the number of a standard infantry division) and 434 aircraft, all except six OV-1 Mohawks being helicopters. Since helicopters were the

ABOVE: *With the divisional insignia emblazoned on its nose, a UH-1D eases down into a jungle landing pad to resupply Alpha Company, 2nd Battalion, 8th Cavalry, 1st Cavalry Division (Airmobile). This is typical of the terrain encountered during the fighting in the Ia Drang Valley (US Army/Infantry)*

primary means of movement, weight was a vital consideration in all operations, and the division's total weight of 10,000 tons was less than one-third that of an infantry division.

Within ninety days of its establishment the 1st Cavalry Division (Airmobile) was ensconced at An Khe in the midst of a combat zone. In the first week of October it was assigned a TAOR of approximately 150 by 150 miles with the An Khe 'Golf Course' at its hub. Its primary mission was to protect the key communications centre at Pleiku, but within weeks it was heavily involved in what became known as the Battle of the Ia Drang Valley.

On 19 October elements of a division of the north Vietnamese Army (NVA) consisting of three regiments—the 32nd, 33rd and 66th—assaulted the Special Forces camp at Plei Me, twenty-five miles south-west of Pleiku. Within two days it became apparent that the ARVN, supported by a Special Forces team, was unable to repulse the attackers, and the 1st Cavalry was ordered to support the besieged camp. When the NVA broke contact and melted into the jungle the division was given the mission to seek out and destroy the enemy. On 1 November the 1st Squadron, 9th Cavalry, the divisional reconnaissance unit, uncovered an enemy hospital complex west of Plei Me Camp, and by the end of the day had committed most of its rifle and gunship platoons into the contact that developed.

The battle lasted thirty-five days, and the enemy's plan to cut South Vietnam in two was thwarted. By 26 November 1965 the 1st Cavalry Division (Airmobile) had completed its mission of pursuit and destruction up to the borders of Cambodia, whither the enemy retreated. To a large extent the statistics of the aviation units involved reveal how the mission was accomplished. The assigned and attached aviation units were directed by divisional subordinate headquarters, the 11th Aviation Group and the Support Command. The units of the 11th were the 227th and 229th Assault Helicopter Battalions (UH-1s), the 228th Assault Support Helicopter Battalion (CH-47), and the 11th Aviation Company, which provided general support helicopters and the six OV-1 Mohawks for aerial surveillance and target acquisition. The Support Command controlled the attached 17th Aviation Company (C-7 Caribou) and the attached 478th Aviation Company (Heavy Helicopter)—the four CH-54s of the Flying Crane Company. In addition were the rocket-firing gunships of 2nd Battalion, 20th Artillery (Aerial Rocket) under command of the division's artillery.

During the thirty-five days of the battle, the aircraft delivered 5,048 tons of cargo to the troops and transported a further 8,216 tons into Pleiku from various depots, primarily Qui Nhon and Nha Trang. In all, 54,000 sorties were flown carrying 73,700 personnel; and fifty-nine helicopters were hit by enemy fire, three while on the ground. Fourteen helicopters were forced down, but all except one were recovered; in addition one was destroyed on the ground by mortar fire. Eleven aviation personnel were killed, eight of these due to the mid-air collision of two Hueys, and a further nine were wounded. Whole infantry battalions and artillery batteries were moved by air. During the first six weeks in Vietnam the CH-54 Flying Cranes carried 5,700 tons of cargo and 840 passengers in 180 hours of flying time. To keep this fleet of helicopters flying, up to 77,000 gallons of fuel were consumed during a peak day, but

30–40,000 gallons was a more normal quantity. The concept of airmobility had been proven in battle beyond any doubt.

The 428 authorized helicopters of the 1st Cavalry Division (Airmobile) were distributed as follows:

The three brigades each had eight LOHs and two UH-1Bs.

The Air Cavalry Squadron (1st Squadron, 9th Cavalry) had thirty LOHs, thirty-eight UH-1B gunships and twenty UH-1Ds.

Division Artillery had twelve LOHs and forty-three UH-1Bs, including thirty-six rocket-firing Hueys and three UH-1Bs in the aerial rocket artillery battalion (2nd Battalion, 20th Artillery).

The Aviation Group (11th) comprised two Aviation Battalions (Assault Helicopter)—227th and 229th. Each battalion had three LOHs, and was divided into three lift companies (A to C) of twenty UH-1Ds each and an armed helicopter company of twelve UH-1B gunships (D Company).

One Aviation Battalion (Assault Support Helicopter)—228th— had forty-eight CH-47 Chinooks, divided into three companies (A–C) with sixteen in each, and three LOHs.

One General Support Company (11th Aviation Company) had sixteen Hueys and ten LOHs.

The Support Command incorporated the Medical Battalion— 15th—with twelve UH-1Ds; and two Maintenance Battalions—15th and 27th—with eight LOHs and eight UH-1Ds between them.

In addition, four CH-54 Tarhe 'Flying Cranes' were provided by the attached 'Hurricane' 478th Aviation Company, which was replaced in 1969 by the 'Skycranes' 273rd Aviation Company.

From 1967, the OH-13 light observation helicopters were replaced by OH-6A LOHs and, from 1968, the UH-1B/C gunships were replaced by AH-1G Cobra attack helicopters. All UH-1D Hueys were progressively replaced by the improved 'Hotel' model.

'The Golden Hawk'—1st Aviation Brigade

With the increasing scale of US Army Aviation activity in Vietnam and the growing number of aviation units dotted all over the country, it became essential to form a unified command organization to control these diverse and far-flung assets. Although each infantry division had its own integral aviation battalion for general duties, the majority of its aviation support was provided by non-divisional units assigned on a temporary basis under the operational control of the division's larger formations, either for a specific operation or on attachment for a period of time. In the early days the aviation companies had developed individual methods of operating in conjunction with the formations that they supported. As a result, it proved difficult to move a company from the Highlands to the Delta or vice versa because it entailed a complete change of technique in procedures and command relationships, as well as a fresh understanding of the terrain. In order to achieve standardization, the 1st Aviation Brigade was formed to command all non-divisional aviation units on 23 May 1966.

ABOVE: *Troopers of the 1st Cavalry Division (Airmobile) roll an M101 105mm howitzer down the ramp of a CH-47A Chinook near Plei Me during October 1965. During November artillery batteries were relocated sixty-seven times by the CH-47 Chinooks, and provided twenty-four-hour artillery support to every platoon-size or larger unit. One artillery battery was moved four times in one day to keep up with the fast-moving operations during the Battle of the Ia Drang Valley. (US Army/News Features)*

Fundamentally, the brigade was responsible for promulgating standard procedures of training, maintenance, safety, supply and methods of operations; but the actual control of aviation units in combat remained vested in the supported ground commander, for maximum operational flexibility. Each infantry division was assigned a combat aviation battalion headquarters which controlled all the aviation companies provided to the division for a specific mission. To enhance flexibility and familiarity, an assault helicopter company was habitually located with each infantry brigade and an air cavalry troop was attached to each division for aerial reconnaissance. Additional aviation support in the form of gunships, medium lift Chinooks and heavy lift Skycranes, as well as specialized helicopters for missions such as night operations, were assigned as and when required.

The swooping golden hawk insignia of the 1st Aviation Brigade soon became a familiar sight throughout Vietnam. During 1967 the brigade airlifted more than five million troops—the equivalent of 313 infantry divisions—in more than 2.9 million sorties, flying for 1.2 million hours—the equivalent of 137 years. By mid-1968 it was one of the largest formations in Vietnam, with a strength of 25,181 men and 4,230 aircraft in almost 100 separate aviation units under its command, as shown in the accompanying table.

1st Aviation Brigade Organization, 1 August 1968

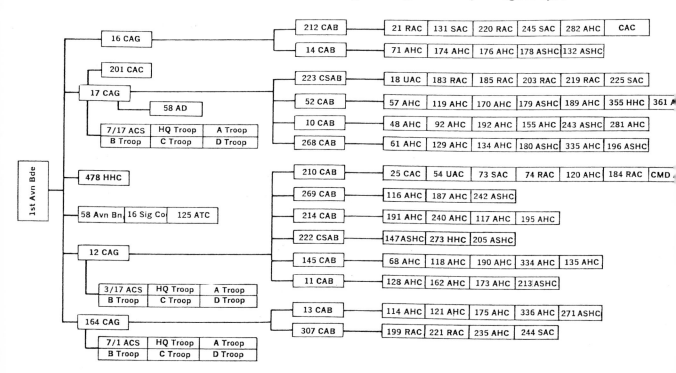

Key

CAG: Combat Aviation Group
CAB: Combat Aviation Battalion
AHC: Assault Helicopter Company
UAC: Utility Airplane Company

HHC: Heavy Helicopter Company
RAC: Reconnaissance Airplane Company
ASHC: Assault Support Helicopter Company
AD: Aviation Detachment
CSAB: Combat Support Aviation Battalion

CAC: Corps Aviation Company
SAC: Surveillance Airplane Company
ACS: Air Cavalry Squadron
ATC: Air Traffic Control Detachments

As indicated above, an infantry division incorporated an aviation battalion as part of its TOE. From 1966 onwards an air cavalry troop was added in Vietnam to enhance reconnaissance capabilities. On account of their varying rôles and differing tactical areas of responsibility in Vietnam, the divisional aviation battalions had no standard organization; but the 9th Aviation Battalion 'Condor' of the 9th Infantry Division, which fought in III and IV CTZ south of Saigon, serves as an example for the 1968/69 period. The battalion was divided into two companies. Company A, 'Jayhawks', was authorized twenty-five UH-1D/H Hueys for troop lift, resupply, command and control, and other general support duties; while Company B, 'Stingrays', was authorized two UH-1D/Hs, six AH-1G Cobras and four OH-6A LOHs for armed escort, fire support and reconnaissance. In addition, Company B, 709th Maintenance Battalion had two UH-1D/Hs; each infantry brigade, four OH-6A LOHs; and the division artillery, nine Loaches and two Hueys. As its air cavalry element, D Troop, 3rd Squadron, 5th Cavalry was authorized six UH-1D/Hs, two UH-1Cs, nine AH-1G Cobras and nine OH-6A LOHs. Thus, units of the 9th Infantry Division were authorized eighty-six helicopters, and two U6-A Beaver utility transports which operated with Company B; however, the actual number of aircraft assigned to them did fluctuate.

The Peak Years

By mid-1966 US troop strength in Vietnam had grown to 300,000 which, for the first time, allowed the High Command to adopt the offensive on a broad and sustained basis. General Westmoreland, the commander of US forces in Vietnam, remarked: 'During 1966, airmobile operations came of age. All manoeuvre battalions became skilled in the use of the helicopter for tactical transportation to achieve surprise and out-manoeuvre the enemy.' Increasingly, US troops bore the brunt of the ground fighting in I, II and III Corps Tactical Zones, and sought, in a series of large scale operations, to crush the enemy. Typical of these was Operation 'Attleboro' conducted by the 1st Infantry Division, elements of the 4th and 25th Infantry Divisions and the 173rd Airborne Brigade against the Viet Cong 9th Division in Tay Ninh Province during October and November. Over 1,100 of the enemy were killed and huge quantities of weapons and supplies were captured.

Operation 'Attleboro' was supported by the 12th Combat Aviation Group with three aviation battalions. During the three-week operation they flew 37,425 sorties in 15,658 flying hours and airlifted 46,000 troops and 6,404 tons of combat supplies. Most of the troops were transported by UH-1D Hueys, carrying a typical load of eight combat troops. CH-47 Chinooks were used mainly to move and resupply artillery units, while infantry units were resupplied for the most part by slicks. Eight aircraft were hit by enemy fire, of which three were forced down and two LOHs lost. Aircrews flew an average of 127 hours a man, of which almost a quarter were flown at night.

In another large scale offensive against the Viet Cong 9th Division, Operation 'Cedar Falls' was launched on 8 January 1967 when the 1st

Infantry Division, the 173rd Airborne Brigade and the 11th Armored
Cavalry Regiment moved into the Viet Cong sanctuary known as the
'Iron Triangle', just north-west of Saigon. In the early morning
darkness, sixty Hueys packed with troops and their ten gunship
escorts lifted off from Dau Tieng airstrip. Flying in two V
formations, each containing three flights of ten helicopters, the air
armada headed at tree-top level towards the VC-controlled village of
Ben Suc. Denied the usual preparatory bombardment in order to
achieve surprise, the troops of the 1st Battalion, 26th Infantry landed
in the midst of the village and sealed it off. The Viet Cong were too
stunned to react and, while Chinooks transported away 6,000
villagers, bulldozers of the 1st Engineer Battalion razed their
dwellings to the ground. Ben Suc ceased to exist. In a series of
massive sweeps by mechanized and armoured units numerous Viet
Cong caches and facilities were uncovered and destroyed; but the VC
9th Division had slipped away.

Undaunted, US forces unleashed another multi-division offensive,—codenamed Operation 'Junction City'—into War Zone C
during February. On the 22nd, in one of the largest mass helicopter
lifts ever, 249 helicopters of the 12th Combat Aviation Group
airlifted over 5,100 troops into ten separate landing zones in under
eight hours. This time the enemy stood and fought. The battle
continued until mid-May, by which time three regiments of the 9th
VC Division were shattered—but War Zone C had not been
neutralized.

Operation 'Cedar Falls/Junction City' marked a watershed in the
Vietnam War. After their defeat in conventional fighting against the
overwhelming firepower and airmobility of the Americans, the
enemy withdrew their main forces to sanctuaries in Cambodia and
Laos, from where they prepared for the Tet Offensive against
population centres in 1968. Thereafter, US forces adopted an enclave
and pacification strategy against guerrillas and local forces, and these
multi-division operations were rarely repeated. However, the scale of
operations remained high. During the first half of 1967, 12th Combat
Aviation Group logged over 175,000 flying hours in the support of

ABOVE: *Troops of the ARVN 1st Infantry Division disembark from Hueys of the 223rd Combat Aviation Battalion during 'Lam Son 719'. (US Army/Aviation Digest)*

every US and ARVN unit in III CTZ. Hundreds of airmobile combat assaults were executed by helicopters, which flew 113,000 of the total flying hours, in over 200,000 sorties. A further 110,000 logistical sorties were flown by helicopters transporting artillery pieces and supplies. A total of 541,000 troops were airlifted during the six-month period, with a weekly average of over 20,000. At the same time Hueys and Chinooks transported 41,000 tons of cargo, or approximately 1,600 tons per week.

Throughout the war the enemy sanctuaries in Cambodia, comprising at least fourteen major NVA bases, remained a constant threat to the heart of RVN, whose capital Saigon lay only thirty-five miles from the border region known as the 'Parrot's Beak'. For years the High Command had wished to raid these sanctuaries, but political restraints denied them this course of action. With the fall of the Cambodian leader Prince Sihanouk on 18 March 1970 the situation altered, and permission was granted for a limited incursion. In a classic example of airmobility, 1st Cavalry Division (Airmobile) thrust into Cambodia on 1 May. With the Cobra gunships and Loaches of 1st Squadron, 9th Cavalry screening the advance and attacking targets of opportunity, the tanks and armoured personnel carriers of the 11th Armored Cavalry Regiment and the 25th Infantry Division crashed across the border and headed for Snoul in a massive combined arms operation, codenamed TOAN THANG 43 ('Total Victory'). Using USAF 15,000 pound 'Commando Vault' bombs to create instant landing zones, airmobile assaults were executed and temporary fire support bases established to cover the advance. Within days many enemy caches were found and, on 5 May, a vast logistical storage area was discovered, which was immediately dubbed 'the city'. Further supply depots were uncovered as airmobile assaults and mechanized units swept through the 'Fishhook' area. Enemy resistance was sporadic and unco-ordinated and, in late June, the American forces withdrew with an immense haul of enemy supplies. The last US Army aircraft to depart Cambodia was a 'Pink Team' of 1/9th Cavalry which re-entered Vietnam at 1728 hours on 29 June.

The Cambodian campaign proved to be a most successful combined arms operation, using air cavalry, armour and mechanized infantry with USAF air support to considerable effect; and it owed much to the airmobile expertise of the 1st Cavalry Division (Airmobile). Enemy base areas had been penetrated and disrupted to such a degree that the NVA was unable to mount any major offensive for the remainder of the year. The respite allowed the process of 'Vietnamization' and the withdrawal of American troops to proceed apace.

Lam Son 719

After the Cambodian incursion of 1970, the NVA heavily reinforced their supply complexes on the Ho Chi Minh Trail in Laos as insurance against any further cross-border raids. In February 1971 these bases became the targets for a major ARVN operation codenamed LAM SON 719. In the first real test of Vietnamization, ARVN forces, without the benefit of American ground troops or advisers, were to destroy them, and so disrupt the flow of enemy troops and supplies into South Vietnam. US assistance was restricted to tactical air support and artillery coverage from fire support bases in RVN. Under the operational control of the 101st Airborne Division (Airmobile), 659 helicopters were committed to what became the ultimate test of airmobility.

Throughout the battle helicopter units faced the most extensive anti-aircraft defences of the war. Almost every LZ or PZ was heavily contested and numerous helicopters were hit, the majority by heavy machine gun fire. In one air assault into LZ 'Lolo' on 3 March, eleven UH-1 helicopters were shot down in the immediate vicinity of the LZ and a further thirty-five were damaged. On 6 March the largest helicopter combat assault of the war was launched when 120 Hueys of the 223rd Combat Aviation Battalion lifted off at Khe Sanh for LZ 'Hope' close to Tchepone, the furthest objective in Laos. Escorted by scores of gunships and tactical aircraft, the air armada flew some fifty miles and landed the 2nd Regiment, ARVN 1st Infantry Division against only light resistance in the wake of concerted B-52 airstrikes. One Huey was shot down and a further fourteen were damaged.

Following the destruction of enemy supply caches, the ARVN forces began their difficult withdrawal from Laos. The isolated firebases, established astride the axis of the attack, came under intense enemy pressure; and single-ship sorties, such as emergency resupply or medical evacuation, became extremely hazardous, requiring an escort of four gunships whenever possible. Although officially proscribed, nap-of-the-earth flying tactics became increasingly commonplace. Single helicopter missions were routinely flown at extreme low level, while combat assaults and extractions were conducted by single-ship landings with half-minute separations, and gunships made their attack runs from higher altitudes than previously normal.

However equivocal the results of the ground campaign may have been, nothing can detract from the fortitude and professionalism displayed by the helicopter crewmen during LAM SON 719. In the forty-five days of the operation, units of the 101st Aviation Group flew 204,065 sorties in 78,968 flying hours, during which sixty-eight per cent of the helicopters committed suffered combat damage and fourteen per cent were lost. Regrettable as these losses were, the doctrine of airmobility had been proven in a theatre of mid-intensity warfare, and the helicopter had accomplished everything that was demanded of it.

During 1971 the 1st Aviation Brigade decreased from 18,000 men to approximately 6,000. Throughout the year the brigade continued to provide air cavalry, gunship and lift support to ARVN forces in all four military regions. On 30 March 1972 the NVA unleashed a conventional invasion against the RVN, spearheaded by Soviet T-54 and Chinese T-59 tanks. Throughout the course of the campaign the 1st Aviation Brigade flew virtually twenty-four hours a day in support of ARVN forces, not the least of their tasks being armed helicopter gunship sorties to stem the armoured onslaught. In one instance near Quang Tri, the pilot of an OH-6A Loach flew his helicopter through a fusillade of small arms fire at a speed of ten knots just above an enemy tank while a crew member dropped a white phosphorous grenade into the open hatch, incapacitating the vehicle. However, more efficient methods of attacking AFVs were at hand: helicopters armed with anti-tank guided missiles were now deployed with devastating effect against enemy armour for the first time in warfare (see Chapter 4—US Army Helicopter Gunships in Vietnam).

BELOW: *Emblazoned with the shark's mouth markings that adorned many HueyCobras, an AH-1G of D Troop, 3rd Squadron, 4th Cavalry returns from a mission in support of the 25th Infantry Division during the Cambodian incursion of 1970. The shark's mouth encompasses the XM-28 A1 Armament Subsystem while the wing stores are XM-159 and XM-158E1 rocket pods. (US Army)*

3 AIRMOBILITY – TACTICS & TECHNIQUES

The Helicopter War

The widespread use of the helicopter was the most significant tactical advance of the Vietnam War. Initially deployed simply as a machine for the transport of men and cargo, it became the cornerstone of airmobility. Its remarkable versatility was employed for numerous tasks, from the original rôle of troop and cargo transport—although even this expanded beyond any predictions—to aerial bombardment and battlefield surveillance. Once transported into the battle area, ground forces were supported by helicopters throughout their mission for observation, command and control, direct fire support, resupply, medical evacuation, reinforcement and withdrawal, many of these missions having been initiated by the surveillance and reconnaissance capabilities of the helicopter.

Airmobile operations dominated the battlefields of Vietnam, and only the helicopter enabled US forces to overcome the problems of the appalling terrain and the lack of roads. However, the hot and humid climatic conditions constantly constrained helicopter operations due to a condition known as 'density altitude'. With increasing altitude and temperature the air became thinner and less lift was generated, so helicopters were unable to fly as far or carry as much payload as under normal conditions. Since high temperatures and high elevations were a feature of much of Vietnam, the lifting capacity of helicopters was severely reduced; but tactical considerations often demanded that they fly in breach of gross weight limitations, which caused many accidents.

Up to 1971, 4,128 helicopters were lost in Vietnam, of which 1,846 were due to hostile action and the remaining 2,282 to operational accidents. Despite these figures, the helicopter did not prove to be as vulnerable as many had predicted. During the four peak years of 1967–1970, US Army helicopters in Vietnam flew a total of 26,733,403 sorties of which 21,126,070 were in combat. 21,166 helicopters were hit by enemy fire of which 1,364 were lost. Thus only one aircraft was hit for every 1,263 sorties, and only one aircraft was shot down and lost for every 19,599 sorties.

In January 1967 there was a total of 1,515 US Army helicopters in South-East Asia. By January 1968 the inventory had increased to 2,636; in January 1969, to 3,359; and by January 1970, to 3,720. In 1967 the helicopter fleet comprised approximately sixty per cent UH-1D/H models, thirty per cent UH-1B/C Huey gunships and almost ten per cent CH-47 and CH-54 types. Throughout the four years the UH-1D/H comprised between fifty and sixty per cent of the fleet, whereas the UH-1B/C had gradually diminished to seven per cent by December 1970. The CH-47/-54 averaged close to ten per cent throughout the period. From September 1967, the AH-1G built up to ten per cent by December 1968 and increased to twelve per cent of the fleet through 1969 and 1970. From its introduction in

BELOW: *Aircraft losses in Vietnam due to accidents were more numerous than combat losses; this Huey of the 11th Aviation Company (GS), 11th Aviation Group crashed on take-off at An Khe on 5 May 1967. High density altitude and high gross weight, especially for laden gunships, were the principal factors. By 1968, twenty per cent of the aircraft inventory in Vietnam was damaged or destroyed in non-combat accidents every year. (US Army)*

ABOVE: *ARVN troops and their American adviser hurry to a UH-1B at the conclusion of an operation in the Mekong Delta in 1965. Typical of Hueys up to 1966, the UHF blade aerial on the roof of this UH-1B is painted white and bears the logo of the manufacturers, the Collins Corporation; thereafter it was painted black. (US Army/Military Review)*

September 1967, the OH-6A increased steadily to almost twenty per cent of the fleet.

The peak number of US Army helicopters in Vietnam was 3,926 in March 1970, and it then decreased until by the end of December 1970 there were 3,484 helicopters. It is estimated that between 1961 and 1972 13,000 Army aircraft were employed in Vietnam. At the height of the conflict, the US Army possessed the third largest air force in the world. To serve this massive fleet, over 3,000 pilots and 21,000 aircraft mechanics were trained each year; and an estimated 22,000 helicopter pilots served in Vietnam. From 1961 to 1973, 1,103 Army aviators lost their lives in Vietnam, of whom 1,045 were killed during flying operations.

Aviation units varied markedly among the divisions and the four military regions in Vietnam. They consisted of platoons, detachments, teams, companies, batteries, squadrons, battalions and groups. However, the basic types of aviation units around which the concept of airmobility was built were the Assault Helicopter Company (AHC), the Assault Support Helicopter Company (ASHC) and the Air Cavalry Troop.

A typical AHC comprised twenty-four to twenty-seven UH-1s in three platoons, with two lift platoons of UH-1D/H Hueys and one gunship platoon of UH-1B/Cs or AH-1G Cobras. Its authorized strength was twenty-three UH-1D/Hs, with ten in each lift platoon and three for company headquarters and service personnel, and eight UH-1B/C or AH-1G gunships. Some AHCs formed three lift platoons with seven Hueys in each. An ASHC consisted of two cargo helicopter companies, with eight CH-47 Chinooks each, and two OH-6A light observation helicopters for liaison and command and control. A typical Air Cavalry Troop had twenty-seven helicopters with nine to ten UH-1B/C gunships or AH-1G Cobras, ten to eleven OH-6A or OH-58 light observation helicopters, and seven UH-1D/H Hueys. However different their rôles, most aviation units had one thing in common—and that was a remarkable helicopter called the Huey.

ABOVE: *The standard weapon carried by Huey slicks was the M-23 Armament Subsystem, Helicopter, 7.62mm Machine Gun; Door Mounted. It comprised two 7.62mm M-60D machine guns and two mounts, one on each side of the aircraft. A 500-round ammunition box was attached to the base tube assembly; rounds were either fed to the weapon by flexible chuting, or else the belt was free, as shown here, when a B-3 size C-ration can was usually fitted to the assault bag fastening slide as a feed guide to reduce the likelihood of stoppages. (John Graber)*

The Huey—Workhorse of Airmobility

In the panoply of US involvement in Vietnam, nothing symbolized that commitment more than the Huey helicopter. To this day it represents the indelible image of that long and frustrating conflict, and the thumping of its two-bladed rotor remains the distinctive keynote. Developed by the Bell Helicopter Company to fulfil the US Army requirement for a light utility helicopter, the Model 204 entered service as the HU-1A Iroquois on 30 June 1959. Its most important feature was a free-shaft turbine engine which, for the first time, provided what earlier helicopters had lacked—power and reliability. This was a dramatic technological advance. Essentially, the turbine engine produced three horsepower for every pound of its own weight, whereas the outmoded reciprocating engine had weighed three pounds for every horsepower produced. With fewer moving parts and a compact configuration, it was reliable and simpler to maintain. The helicopter had come of age.

From 1962 onwards, thousands of these tough and dependable aircraft flew in all weathers to undertake numerous missions in support of ground troops. Their many and diverse tasks can be divided into three general categories: combat support, combat service support and administrative duties.

Combat support missions constituted the majority of the total sorties and hours flown. They included the movement of manoeuvre elements and *matériel* to execute combat assaults, movement of reserves, shifting and relocation of units and individuals in the battle area, insertion and extraction of long-range reconnaissance patrols, direct fire support, armed reconnaissance, command and control, search and rescue, night operations, forward air control, aircraft recovery and many others. The most important of these within the airmobility concept were the tactical air movement of combat troops, and armed helicopter employment.

As with its forerunner the CH-21 Shawnee, all models of the UH-1 were fitted with machine guns in the doorways for suppressive fire. The early 'fold-away' version had mounts attached to the external stores hard-points below and behind the cargo doors; this allowed the guns to be locked in place during flight but swung clear for passenger and cargo loading. It was superseded by the M-23 Armament Subsystem which became standard on all UH-1D/H Hueys. The pintle mount for the M-60D 7.62mm machine guns was attached to a base tube assembly which was fastened to two hard-points on the aircraft fuselage.

From 1962 armour protection kits were fitted to the Huey, primarily to protect the crew from small arms fire. The first kit consisted of Doron/Perforated Steel/Tipping Plate armour in the door panels and side plates on the pilots' seats. In 1965 it was replaced by the MOD-IV Hard Face Composite (HFC) armour kit which incorporated armoured seats for the pilots; this provided much enhanced protection against small arms fire from the sides, below and behind. The armoured seat was developed at the Von Karman Center of the Aerojet-General Corporation within five weeks, and the first example was delivered in April 1965. Incorporating sliding shoulder panels, it weighed 140 pounds and was able to withstand a 15g crash load. It also had a tilt-back feature to permit the application of first-

RIGHT: *A Viet Cong prisoner clambers from a UH-1B under the watchful eye of a helicopter crewman wearing standard fatigues and M-1952 body armour. This vest was preferred to the later M-69 because the collar of the latter interfered with the flight helmet—here, the Army APH-5A Flyer's Helmet. This Huey is fitted with an M-60 machine gun on an early 'fold-away' mount. (US Army/Aviation Digest)*

RIGHT: *From 1969 helicopter crewmen were issued with fire-resistant flying suits made of Nomex, together with gloves, shown here worn by a VNAF airman as he loads an XM-229 2.75in. FFAR into an XM-157B rocket pod on 19 January 1972. He also wears the later aircrew body armour of ceramic plates which gave protection over the torso area against small arms fire. The Huey is fitted with a 7.62mm GAU-2B/A (M-134) minigun, which was designated as the XM-93/-93E1 Armament Subsystem. It proved very popular with Vietnamese Huey crews but, because of its prodigious rate of fire, the VNAF reverted to the M-23 late in the war to reduce the expenditure of its diminishing stocks of 7.62mm ammunition. (USAF)*

RIGHT: *An everyday sight in
Vietnam: a sky full of Hueys
on their way to an air combat
assault or 'CA'. To the troops,
a 'Charlie-Alpha' was
commonly referred to as a
'Romeo-Foxtrot'—which in the
vernacular stood for 'Rat
F***', because a combat
assault was deemed to be just
as difficult and unrewarding.
Each aircraft had the radio
callsign 'Chalk' followed by a
number referring to its
position: thus 'Chalk 5' was
the fifth helicopter within the
flight. (US Army/Military
Review)*

BELOW LEFT: *Landing beside a
B-52 bomb crater, a UH-1D
resupplies troops of Company
A, 1st Battalion, 16th
Infantry (Mechanized), 1st
Infantry Division on 7 June
1967 during Operation
'Bluefield', a search-and-
destroy mission in War Zone C
north-east of Lai Khe. (US Army)*

RIGHT: '*Hot refuelling*'—*a UH-1D/H, with rotors turning, is replenished with JP-4 prior to an air combat assault into the Bai Long Valley in Quang Tri Province during September 1970. On an average day, a Huey consumed over 4,000 pounds of fuel. (US Army)*

BELOW RIGHT: *A UH-1H slick lands to extract members of Company C, 1st Battalion, 327th Infantry (Airmobile), 101st Airborne Division (Airmobile) after a patrol in the vicinity of Fire Support Base Birmingham on 15 April 1971. (US Army)*

LEFT: *With the aid of a smoke grenade, a member of Company D, 3rd Battalion, 60th Infantry (Riverine), 9th Infantry Division guides in a UH-1D/H during Operation 'Speedy Express' in the Mekong Delta during early 1969. The 9th Division's 2nd Brigade provided the ground forces for the Mobile Riverine Force whose area of operations was the many waterways, swamps and rivers of the Mekong Delta and parts of III CTZ. Although helicopter resources were always limited, airmobility proved valuable in this unusual type of warfare. (US Army)*

49

ABOVE: *Before and after—SP4 Gary Wetzel refuels his UH-1D of the 173rd Assault Helicopter Company prior to the mission on 8 January 1968 for which he was awarded the Medal of Honor. After the action near Can Giuoc, in which the 'Robin Hood' slick was repeatedly hit by enemy RPG and machine gun fire, the Huey was recovered; note the impact points of the RPGs to the left front. All fourteen Hueys participating in this combat assault were damaged and three were shot down. (Gary G. Wetzel)*

aid to an injured pilot or co-pilot, as well as expediting the removal of either from the control area. Armoured seats were fitted to the Hueys of the 1st Cavalry Division (Airmobile) before shipping to Vietnam.

From the outset, aircrews wore M-1952 body armour which was designed to provide protection against shell fragments but not against small arms fire. It was, however, relatively comfortable, and afforded good protection against fragmentation wounds from shattered plexiglass after penetration by projectiles. For this reason aircrews sometimes lined the chin bubbles and the cargo compartment floor with several body armour vests to protect themselves from spall fragmentation; but this expedient obstructed the pilots' downward vision, and the 'flak carpet' rarely lasted very long. To protect the frontal torso area of the pilots, aircrews were originally issued with a Doron chest protector until one made of HFC was introduced with the MOD-IV kit. This was extremely uncomfortable and interfered with the flight controls, so it was rarely worn until three inches were cut off the bottom to create what became the T65-1 Aircrew Torso Armor. This, in turn, was superseded by a ceramic plate which was standardized as Body Armor, Small Arms Protective, Aircrewman, for crew chiefs and helicopter gunners who required both back and front protection; pilots and co-pilots, who sat in armoured seats, wore frontal ceramic plates only. Known as 'chickenplates', the aircrew body armour was designed to defeat a .30 calibre/7.62mm AP round at 100 yards but often proved even more effective and, on occasions, withstood hits from .50 calibre projectiles[1]. Despite these measures, it was impossible to protect the Huey against the concentrated fire of machine guns and rocket propelled grenades in a 'hot LZ'—as this account by William Dismukes of the 173rd Assault Helicopter Company, the 'Robin Hoods', vividly reveals of an action on 8 January 1968:

'Our mission was to insert a blocking force in a large LZ on the east bank of the Can Giuoc River five miles south of Can Giuoc. The Viet Cong was trying to break contact with the 9th Division troops to the prepared positions in the treelines east of the river. The blocking force was inserted in the north-west corner of the large LZ along the river and were immediately caught in a crossfire from bunkers in the trees along the north and west sides. The majority of the infantrymen were wounded or pinned down in the open rice paddy as soon as they left the ships.

'We were flying in the number four position of the first element. I had control of the ship with the aircraft commander following through to take the ship if necessary. Looking out the right side I could see the LZ under the aircraft ahead. It looked like about thirty or forty acres of wet rice paddy bounded on all sides by heavy stands of palm and banana trees. An air strike had been placed across the river by mistake and our gunships had time for only one pass on the treelines before we started our approach. The lead ship took us in close to the west treeline. At fifty feet from touchdown we were met by heavy automatic weapons fire but continued on in. Just before touchdown a rocket propelled grenade was fired from a bunker to our

[1]For a fuller account of aircrew body armour in Vietnam, see the author's *Flak Jackets—20th Century Military Body Armour* (Osprey Publishing Ltd, 1984).

ABOVE: *Under the watchful gaze of their sergeant, three young troopers of the 173rd Airborne Brigade prepare themselves for action moments before touch-down during an air combat assault. With a crew of four, weapons, ammunition, tool box and rations, a Huey slick commonly carried eight to nine US or ten to twelve ARVN troops. (US Army/Military Review)*

RIGHT: *With a bank of loudspeakers attached to its side, a 'Thunderbird' UH-1B of the 118th Assault Helicopter Company drops propaganda leaflets during a mission in November 1965. Normally escorted by a gunship to suppress enemy fire, PSYWAR helicopters carried personnel of the Vietnamese Information Service who broadcasted the 'Chieu Hoi' or 'Open Arms' programme promising the Viet Cong amnesty if they surrendered to government forces. (US Army/Military Review)*

left front and exploded in the left chin bubble. I was knocked unconscious by the blast.

'The explosion tore out the left front of the cockpit and mortally wounded the aircraft commander. The gunner and the crewchief were thrown out of the aircraft and reached cover behind nearby dikes. The two passengers who went out the left door were killed within five feet of the aircraft and three were wounded and pinned down fifteen feet from the aircraft on the right side. The sixth man never left the cabin. The aircraft settled by itself into the water less than thirty meters from the treeline beside a low dike. The rest of the flight took off after dropping their troops. Two of the aircraft went down within 500 meters of the LZ. Their crews were extracted before the Viet Cong could get to them. Any attempt to rescue my crew would have been suicidal. The automatic weapons fire from the two treelines was so heavy the few infantrymen not wounded or killed in the LZ could not lift their heads out of the water without drawing heavy fire from the enemy gunners.

'The engine was still running when I came to so I shut it down and reached over for the aircraft commander. The Viet Cong in the trees were tearing the aircraft apart with their fire. I saw the crew chief, Specialist 4 Jarvis, coming back across the paddy to help me. He was knocked down by a hand grenade but got back up and climbed into the aircraft behind my seat. Together we started to pull the aircraft commander across the radio pedestal. The doorgunner PFC Wetzel got up from the dike on the other side and waded up to the aircraft. He was starting to open the left door when the second rocket propelled grenade hit the doorframe a foot away, tearing his left side to pieces and mutilating his left arm. He hung onto the aircraft a moment and then pulled himself up into the cockpit to push the aircraft commander out of his seat. The aircraft commander was halfway over the radios when Wetzel fell back out of the aircraft. I saw him start to crawl back towards his machine gun. I looked up and saw the Viet Cong coming out of their bunkers. They were forming an assault wave in the trees to sweep the LZ. There was almost no return fire from the LZ to stop them!

'Wetzel managed to climb back into the gunner's well behind his machine gun despite his terrible wounds. The lead men in the assault wave were on the paddy dike twenty feet away when he opened up on them. They fell and those behind them started falling. The Viet Cong covering the assault from the bunkers in the trees turned their fire on us and I could hear bullets rattling all along the left side of the aircraft. The charge faltered in the spray of water and mud thrown up by Wetzel's machine gun and those that could struggled back through the mud to the safety of the bunkers. I saw over twenty men fall in the twenty meters between the trees and the dike before he ran out of ammunition. The crewchief and I finally got the aircraft commander over the radio pedestal and out into the water on the right side. Wetzel toppled out of his seat and fell face down in the water on the other side.

'While the full attention of the enemy gunners was turned on him the other men in the LZ reached cover behind the paddy dike that ran alongside the aircraft and formed a weak defense behind it that held until dark. I crawled under the boom of the aircraft in an attempt to reach the dike but was immediately wounded and pinned down. I lay in the dark and then joined up with an artillery observer behind the dike.

'The artillery observer had just gotten in contact with his unit and the first rounds were starting to hit around the bunkers and the trees. Our gunships had been orbiting the LZ since we first went in and I contacted them through the artillery unit. They had withheld their fire until they were sure of our position. I directed them to the tree line and under their fire we were able to pull back across the paddy with our dead and wounded. We formed a perimeter on high ground 600 meters to the east and by midnight had secured enough area for medevac aircraft to come in. I have no idea how Wetzel survived, as badly wounded as he was, but he had been brought into the perimeter with the rest of the wounded and was sent out on the first aircraft. I saw him the next morning in the 93rd Evacuation Hospital. He had been in surgery all night and the doctors said they had almost lost him. They had taken out as much shrapnel as possible and had amputated his left arm below the elbow. While I was there he asked me if I thought his family would be proud of him. I told him I was sure they would be.'

They were indeed; on 20 November 1968, Gary Wetzel was awarded the Medal of Honor and became the first man in the 1st Aviation Brigade to be so honoured.

The RPG (Rocket Propelled Grenade) was a formidable weapon against helicopters, especially during assault landings when helicopters were hovering or on the ground. In 380 incidents involving RPGs up to 1971, a total of 128 helicopters were lost. Although there were fifty-four times as many helicopters hit by other weapons, only nine times as many aircraft were lost. RPGs also caused a disproportionately high number of fatal casualties. In one incident on 26 August 1970, a CH-47B Chinook was on short final for troop insertion into LZ 'Judy' with a crew of five, twenty-six passengers and a load of 105mm ammunition when it was hit by an RPG. The aircraft lost control, crashed into trees and burst into

ABOVE: *After a night of 'flashlight maintenance', a mechanic of the 101st Airborne Division (Airmobile) catches some sleep in a hammock suspended from the 'tail stinger' of a Huey. The unsung heroes of airmobility, chopper mechanics worked around the clock to keep their birds flying; without their unstinting efforts the helicopter war in Vietnam would have been impossible. (US Army)*

flames, causing the ammunition to explode. Twenty-nine of those on board were killed and eleven others were injured, including nine on the ground. Hueys represented almost seventy-three per cent of the helicopters involved in RPG incidents, with the majority of hits occurring in and around landing zones.

One of the most important tactical innovations of the Vietnam War was the use of the helicopter as an aerial command post. In 1963 the increasing number of airmobile operations created the need for a 'Command and Control' (C&C) helicopter, and a communications system was improvised by mounting three AN/PRC-10 radios on the floor of a UH-1B. Since this was limited to FM communications only, the ACTIV studied the problem and devised the 'Heliborne Command Post' (HCP). A typical command group in the HCP consisted of the ARVN commander, his senior US adviser, the air liaison officer and an artillery co-ordinator. The aviation element commander as a member of the command group occupied the co-pilot's seat. In 1965 a basic console was developed comprising two FM radios (AN/ARC-44), one VHF AM radio (AN/ARC-73) and an HF SSB radio (AN/ARC-102). Designated the AN/ASC-6, the console was designed for rapid installation and removal. In 1966 a less bulky console, the AN/ASC-10, was introduced with an intercom system for the command group on board the aircraft. From 1967 it was superseded by the AN/ASC-11 and -15 which incorporated secure voice devices.

The composition of the command group varied depending on the mission, but the range of radios allowed the commander and his staff to exercise considerable control over combat operations, with one FM channel used for communications with the ground units, one FM with the higher formation, one FM for the artillery co-ordinator and one FM for the air liaison officer to maintain contact with forward observers on the ground, as well as a UHF radio for communications with forward air controllers directing aircraft strikes. The high frequency single side band (HF SSB) was available to enter the corps air support operations net. The commander of the aviation unit used the helicopter's integral FM and UHF radios to control his aircraft. If space allowed, a man with a PRC-25 radio was carried in the C&C helicopter to permit the commander, while on the

RIGHT: *Concertina wire is attached to the cargo hook of a UH-1D of Company A 'Little Bears' of the 25th Aviation Battalion on a supply mission to the 196th Infantry Brigade (Light) near Tay Ninh in September 1966. (US Army/Military Review)*

ground, to maintain communications with his fire support co-ordinators.

The techniques of employment of the 'Charley-Charley ship' varied according to terrain, weather and mission but it usually flew at about 2,000 feet AGL, from where the commander controlled all the available forces and had voice contact with virtually every one of his subordinate commanders. Despite the unprecedented perspective and rapid communications which the C&C helicopter provided, it did have some limitations. Bad weather forced it to fly at lower altitudes where it was more vulnerable to ground fire and, if it were shot down with the complete command group on a single helicopter, the operation was stymied. Furthermore, airborne commanders sometimes failed to appreciate the problems on the ground because distances appeared shorter, terrain smoother and situations simpler from the air. Nevertheless, the Helicopter Command Post proved to be an effective and indispensable command and control vehicle for the type of warfare conducted in Vietnam.

ABOVE: *Fitted with a Model
3090 agricultural sprayer, a
UH-1H 'Warrior' slick of the
336th Assault Helicopter
Company undertakes a
defoliation mission in the
Mekong Delta on 26 July
1969. Through the use of
agents Blue and Orange,
helicopter defoliation
operations were conducted to
clear vegetation around bases,
to maintain 'Rome-plowed'
areas and to prevent ambush
sites along lines of
communication. (US Army)*

The combat service support rôle of the Huey embraced resupply, medical evacuation, aircraft recovery and many other general duties. All these missions were classed as combat sorties, but not all were in direct contact with the enemy as was the case for combat support. The majority of these were of a logistical nature for the resupply of all the paraphernalia of war to units in the battle zone. Aviation units developed standard type loads for the Huey which saved time and detailed planning. The loads were adjusted according to the factors of weather, density altitude and fuel requirements of the helicopter to perform its mission. Many Huey units had a Standard Operating Procedure (SOP) whereby the first load was limited to 1,500 pounds and each successive one to a maximum of 2,000 pounds until refuelling became necessary. On occasions, this procedure wasted valuable cargo space if the conditions permitted a heavier payload; but it did reduce the tendency to load the aircraft over gross weight limitations which was the cause of many helicopter accidents in Vietnam. Although the majority of these flights were routine, there were few more hazardous missions than the emergency resupply of a unit under fire at night.

Numerous field expedients and improvised weapon systems were fitted to Hueys in order to enhance their capabilities both in the offence and in support of other helicopters or ground forces. Some of those that proved successful in combat were produced in kit form as a limited production item and were issued generally to Huey units. Among these was the Mortar Air Delivery or MAD system—a simple wooden container holding up to a couple of dozen 81mm mortar bombs, which were rolled down a chute through the cabin doorway on command from the pilot, who sighted the target through the chin bubble. Thus an innocuous looking helicopter flying overhead out of small arms range was actually a 'bomber' whose lethal load could be unleashed on an unsuspecting enemy. Some

Hueys were fitted with various types of spraying equipment to dispense riot agents or defoliation chemicals, as well as foam for fire-fighting. Others were equipped with loudspeakers for psychological warfare operations. One limited production item was the XM-19 flare dispenser which ejected MK-24 (later MK-45) flares from a Huey acting as a 'flareship' during night operations. The XM-19 system contained twenty-four flares and was mounted on a jettison plate attached to the cargo floor of a Huey. In an emergency the entire XM-19 flare dispenser was jettisoned out of the right-hand cargo door in eight-tenths of a second by compressed gas from a nitrogen bottle.

In 1966, experiments were conducted to dispense smoke from a low-flying helicopter so as to obscure the enemy's view of an LZ during an assault landing. The first system used a UH-1C gunship with its XM-3 rocket launchers mounted rearwards to eject smoke grenade canisters. This was superseded by the XM-52 smoke generator which comprised a fifty gallon self-sealing fuel bladder under the troop seat of a Huey, a pump and flexible hoses running to a ring with twenty-four nozzles fitted around the engine exhaust cowl. When injected into the hot exhaust gases, the SGF-2 fog oil immediately vaporized and thick white smoke billowed to the rear. Flying as low and slow as feasible, the 'smoker' was very vulnerable to ground fire and, due to its effectiveness, it became a priority target to enemy gunners. In consequence, smoke ship crews mounted .50 calibre machine guns or miniguns in the doorways for heavy suppressive fire, and were often teamed with a gunship as close escort when undertaking their hazardous mission.

As a variation on this theme, inventive crew chiefs attached white smoke grenades to the helicopter landing skids with a pull-wire from their position to the grenade pin. When receiving hostile fire, the grenade was activated and the pilot put the helicopter into a tight

TOP RIGHT: *A 'Blackhorse' UH1D/H Huey of the 11th Armored Cavalry Regiment stands by in a revetment during 1969. Precise identification between the D and H model Hueys is difficult—the data stencil on the side of this helicopter states that it is a UH-1D, but its Bureau Number indicates a UH-1H. (John Graber)*

MIDDLE RIGHT: *Members of the 1st Australian Task Force load supplies aboard a UH-1H of No. 9 Squadron, Royal Australian Air Force at Luscombe Field in Vung Tau during 1969. With a complement of eight Hueys, No. 9 Squadron operated in Vietnam from 12 June 1966 to 8 December 1971 providing airlift, medical evacuation and subsequently gunship support to 1ATF throughout Phuoc Tuy Province. (Australian War Memorial)*

BOTTOM RIGHT: *A trooper from Charlie Company, 2/8th Cav., 3rd Brigade, 1st Cavalry Division (Airmobile) guides a Huey into a landing zone blasted and cut out of dense jungle. (US Army/Military Review)*

ABOVE LEFT: *A UH-1D of Company A, 101st Aviation Battalion drops C-rations to members of the 1st Brigade, 101st Airborne Division during a search-and-destroy operation north of Ben Cat in December 1965. (US Army/Military Review)*

ABOVE RIGHT: *A member of the Aero Rifle Platoon gets into difficulty while rappelling from a Huey slick of B Troop, 1st Squadron, 9th Cavalry Regiment, 1st Cavalry Division (Airmobile). Rappeling was a rapid method of inserting troops into dense vegetation where the helicopter was unable to land. (US Army/Military Review)*

spiral or other manoeuvre indicating a loss of control. It was hoped that on seeing the smoke the enemy would be deceived into thinking that the helicopter was hit, and so stop firing to watch the expected crash. Besides such improvisations, all Hueys carried a selection of smoke grenades in various colours to mark targets for other aircraft, as well as fragmentation and riot agent grenades.

The third category of Huey missions was administrative sorties, which encompassed all non-combative flying duties. Described disparagingly as 'ash and trash', they included training, maintenance test flights, command and liaison, courier flights, Red Cross support, patient transfer, transport of personnel from forward areas for Rest and Recreation, support of civil activities, VIP flights over the combat zone, and myriad others. Although the use of helicopters on these missions detracted from support of the other two categories, it was nevertheless necessary because of training and maintenance requirements, as well as the factors which prevailed in Vietnam such as terrain, weather and the limited and often insecure road network. These missions constituted approximately twenty per cent of the total helicopter sorties and hours flown in Vietnam.

Whatever the mission, the adaptable and reliable Huey performed it day after day. At the height of US Army aviation activity there were 2,406 Hueys flying in the hot and humid skies of Vietnam. The UH-1 was produced in greater numbers than any other utility aircraft since World War 2 except the Soviet Antonov-2 biplane. It is perhaps fitting, therefore, that the first aerial victory ever by a helicopter was achieved when a Huey shot down an AN-2 Colt. On 12 January 1968 an Air America Huey was delivering 105mm howitzer ammunition from a US navigation station perched on a high pinnacle in northern

Laos to an artillery unit nearby. As it approached, the Huey observed two AN-2 biplanes strafing and bombing the artillery positions. After radioing for fighter support the Air America pilot decided to pursue the intruders, which were engaged by the crew chief with an AK-47 assault rifle. One Colt was shot down at the scene, and the other crashed into a hillside some thirteen miles away.

The distinctive blue and white livery of the CIA's own airline, Air America, was ubiquitous throughout South-East Asia during the years of conflict. The final helicopter sorties of the Vietnam War were flown by Air America Hueys from the roofs of apartment buildings during the last desperate hours before the fall of Saigon in April 1975.

'Happiness is a cold LZ'—Airmobile Combat Assault

The principal purpose of helicopter-borne airmobility was to place combat rifle units and supporting troops on or within close assault distance of their tactical objectives. Furthermore, airmobile assault made it possible to deliver fresh riflemen at the decisive point in the battle zone unwearied by long ground approach marches, while maintaining tactical cohesion irrespective of time, distance and terrain factors.

Airmobile operations in Vietnam were conceived in a reverse sequence known as 'backward planning'. Firstly, the 'ground tactical

BELOW: *Huey slicks of the 229th Assault Helicopter Battalion, 1st Cavalry Division (Airmobile) land at a PZ to embark troops. (US Army/1st Cavalry Division)*

plan' was prepared including the assault tactics to seize objectives, artillery and aerial fires to be employed, resupply, medical evacuation, and the extraction by air or other means of the manoeuvre elements at the completion of the mission. Secondly, a 'landing plan' was devised to place the troops on the ground in the right order and location, integrated with their own fire support scheme. Next, an 'air movement plan' was prepared to ferry troops and supplies by air to the 'Landing Zone' (LZ). A 'loading plan' was then developed to put troops and equipment on the correct aircraft in the right sequence at the designated 'Pickup Zone' (PZ). Finally the 'staging plan' insured that all the elements of the 'Airmobile Task Force' (AMTF) arrived at the PZ on time and in the proper condition to begin loading.

The majority of airmobile combat assaults were organized at battalion level with a command group comprising the AMTF commander (the ground commander who exercised control of all elements of the airmobile force); the air mission commander (controlling the aviation elements participating in the operation); and the fire support co-ordinators (both artillery and air force). Together, they devised the detailed plans that incorporated each other's contributions and requirements in the support of the ground commander's mission. During execution, the command group rode in a Command and Control helicopter which was not normally integrated in the tactical flight formation but was free to move wherever the two commanders could best control the operation. If time and security considerations allowed, an aerial reconnaissance was carried out to determine approach and departure routes, the size and state of the landing zone and the most appropriate flight pattern.

The first important phase in the execution of an airmobile

operation was the loading plan. Loading was essentially a matter of having troops and equipment organized into individual helicopter loads and waves so that helicopters could land directly beside each load, take troops and equipment aboard and take off in the minimum time. Once airborne, the AMTF assumed its flight formation. Dependent on the size of the force and, as importantly, the size and shape of the LZ, the formation most often adopted was a stepped 'V' or a variation with 'heavy left' or right echelon, these being the most versatile and easy to control. Others included diamond and arrowhead formations. The helicopters flew at forty-five degrees to the side and rear of the lead ship. Flying as level as possible, helicopters in close formation were separated by one rotor diameter, in normal formation by two diameters, and in open formation by three. Flight routes were selected to minimize interference by enemy forces and to maintain cover and concealment.

Since it had to be assumed that the enemy was defending every landing zone, it was highly desirable that airmobile landings be made within range of supporting artillery. As a rule, all combat assault landings were preceded by preparatory artillery bombardment and airstrikes or, on occasions, by small reconnaissance parties acting as 'pathfinders' to mark the landing zone. The security thus gained for the assault force outweighed any attendant loss of surprise. The enemy offered three main threats to airmobile assault forces. Firstly, claymore mines and improvised explosive devices were placed in the landing zone itself and in the adjacent treeline, to be detonated either electrically or by pressure on the approach of helicopters and troops. Secondly, enemy personnel and weapons were located in prepared positions around the edge of the landing zone and several yards back into the surrounding vegetation. Thirdly, enemy forces positioned several hundred yards from the landing zone could deploy to attack the assault forces during or immediately after the landings.

Direct fire support was crucial to deal with each of these potential threats and included mortar, artillery, naval gunfire, tactical aircraft, strategic bombers and armed helicopters (the latter to be discussed later). During a specific operation the AMTF could be supported by any or all of these means which were controlled by the command group in the 'C&C' helicopter. A combination of air strikes and artillery was used on enemy emplacements around the perimeter of the landing zone to a depth of fifty to seventy-five yards back into the vegetation. Medium and heavy artillery was preferred because 105mm rounds were largely ineffective in destroying well-built bunkers. Similarly, bombs weighing at least 500 pounds were necessary to destroy landing zone defences, while 750- or 1,000-pounders were better. Aircraft also flew runs perpendicular to the treeline dropping napalm to splash back under the jungle canopy and into the embrasures and firing apertures of enemy bunkers. These same fires often disrupted the mines and explosive devices placed in the treeline. The deeper targets located in areas several hundred yards from the landing zone were engaged by artillery.

Air strikes and artillery had to be planned and co-ordinated so that both forms of attack were employed simultaneously and continuously. The standard and simplest method was to divide the landing zone through its centre—the fire support co-ordination line—and to assign airstrikes to one side and artillery to the other. All

LEFT: *Over the LZ threshold— slicks of the 'Crusaders', the 187th Assault Helicopter Company, approach the LZ carrying troops of the 3rd Battalion, 22nd Infantry, 25th Infantry Division during a CA in January 1970. (US Army/Infantry)*

the while consideration had to be given to the artillery gun target lines (it was not uncommon for several artillery units to be firing on the target from more than one fire support base), and also to the direction of attack and break-away of the tactical air support aircraft, so as to prevent the helicopter formation from flying through its own artillery barrage or the flight pattern of high-performance aircraft which required considerable airspace to manoeuvre. Preparatory barrages around the landing zone were usually brief but intense, typically of five to ten minutes duration, and ended with a last WP (White Phosphorous) round to signal artillery 'tubes clear' one or two minutes prior to the troop lift transports crossing the LZ threshold. The armed helicopter gunships then made rocket and strafing runs and marked the landing points for the lead helicopters with smoke.

As the landing zone was approached, the helicopters of the AMTF moved into close formation and dropped in altitude. In most combat assaults the preferred approach was a 'high speed letdown' (for maximum rate of descent) with a right turn into the landing zone, which allowed the flight leader to observe the LZ throughout the manoeuvre. This straight-in approach was most frequently used to effect the initial landing in the minimum space and time. A spiralling approach in formation was considered the least desirable for an assault landing because it could less effectively be supported by gunships, but was sometimes necessary, especially in hilly terrain.

During final descent further suppressive fire was delivered to the edges of the LZ by the door gunners of the troop transports. If space

65

permitted all aircraft attempted to land simultaneously, with the lead helicopter well forward on the landing zone. Landings were effected with the minimum of hovering so as to allow each helicopter to move in as undisturbed air as possible, thus deriving maximum lift at minimum power under the existing circumstances—especially important when operating under critical load conditions. Furthermore, when landing troops, they and their equipment were less affected by rotor wash and the resulting wind-blown debris.

While on the landing zone and prior to take-off, the flight commander issued a typical radio message—'Lift off in fifteen seconds'. The other pilots were thus prepared to depart the LZ at the same time so as to reduce the possibility of fire being concentrated on a single helicopter. On take-off, the flight commander radioed 'Lift-off, breaking right' or 'breaking left' if different from the briefing. This allowed the transport helicopters to anticipate the manoeuvre and also notify the gunships of the flight's intention. Any terrain features that might conceal enemy positions such as villages, river banks or ridge lines were avoided, whenever possible, during departure. Military power was used until a safe altitude was reached.

A typical combat air assault mission as described by Robert Sisk, formerly a warrant officer with C Company, 229th Assault Helicopter Battalion, 1st Cavalry Division (Airmobile), took place on 1 August 1966, when the First Team provided support to the 3rd Brigade, 25th Infantry Division during Operation 'Paul Revere II' when it made contact with four NVA regiments. It was the fiftieth operation for the Air Cavalry since its arrival in Vietnam:

'My company, "Charlie" or C Company, 229th Assault Helicopters, was despatched to Landing Zone 'Oasis', a forward firebase southwest of Pleiku. Our area of operations extended from Pleiku to the Cambodian border and included the Chu Pong Mountains and the Ia Drang Valley, all covered by thick, triple-

RIGHT: 'Up!'—the cryptic communication from the crew chief to the pilot once the infantry had disembarked. The helicopter then lifted off and hovered at a few feet until the complete flight was up. It then departed the LZ in formation. Here, riflemen of the 'Big Red One' leap from a UH-1D Huey of the 'Champagne Flight', Company A, 1st Aviation Battalion, 1st Infantry Division. (US Army/Military Review)

ABOVE: *Among the methods devised to allow troops to land in jungle areas was the 'Jungle Canopy Platform System', shown here under test by a UH-1D of Company A, 227th Assault Helicopter Battalion, 1st Cavalry Division (Airmobile). The equipment comprised two stainless steel nets and a platform laid on them on which the helicopter landed; however, commanders were reluctant to use the system in combat and it was discontinued. (US Army/1st Cavalry Division)*

RIGHT: *At the conclusion of an operation in Phuoc Thanh Province, a UH-1H of the 1st Cavalry Division (Airmobile) lands to extract members of Bravo Company, 2nd Battalion, 7th Cavalry on 20 January 1971, just prior to the departure of the division from Vietnam. (US Army/Infantry)*

canopy jungle. At LZ 'Oasis', the first battalions of the 7th and 12th Cavalry plus units of the 2nd Battalion, 7th Cavalry, were massing for air assaults.

'During our briefings, we were told all of the landing zones would probably be "hot" and booby-trapped. The weather was exceedingly bad: torrential rains, low-lying clouds and ground fog. This was to be my first combat air assault. I was nervous and excited.

'The door gunners and crew chief made last minute checks on their machine guns and loaded belts of ammo into the gun chutes. The infantrymen were busy writing letters and preparing for the air assaults, checking packs, cleaning weapons and hooking hand grenades to their belts.

'Several LZs were to be assaulted simultaneously. Slicks from the 227th and 229th Assault Helicopter Battalions were to air-assault the grunts into the LZs while the big Chinooks of the 228th would sling the artillery into place once the LZs were secured.

'We lifted off in flights of four. Once airborne, the helicopters joined up in a diamond formation. Chief Warrant Officer Neil Stickney was the aircraft commander; I was the co-pilot. Our flight would be the second wave into the landing zone, following four slicks from the 1st Platoon of Charlie Company. We were to maintain a one-minute spacing between formations. Behind us were two more flights of four ships each, for a total "gaggle" of sixteen helicopters. On each side of the gaggle, B-model Huey gunships from Delta Company flew shotgun for the assault helicopters.

'Each helicopter was assigned a color code with a number—small plates on each side for easy identification. This helped the infantrymen find their assigned helicopter and it also determined the position in the formation we would be flying. "Wagonwheel Six" was designated the code name for Maj. Williams, who was flying the lead ship, Yellow One. He gave orders to the aircraft commanders to have

their door gunners test-fire the M-60 machine guns. From the open doors of the ships ahead, I could see short bursts of tracer rounds spewing from the guns. Stickney told our gunners to fire a burst. The rapid chatter of each weapon was reassuring.

'"Two minutes out", the flight leader said on the UHF radio. Up ahead I could see smoke and explosions in the intended landing zone. The dark smoke and bright reddish-orange flashes of the explosions stood out against the low clouds and patches of fog. An artillery battery from a distant firebase was pounding the landing zone with high-explosive rounds.

'"Last round on the way", a voice suddenly blurted over the UHF. One ship in the flight was usually assigned to monitor the artillery FM radio frequency to advise the flight leader when the barrage was ended. The last round was "Willie Peter" [white phosphorous].

'The WP burst in the center of the clearing, a billowing cloud of thick, white smoke. "One minute out", the flight leader said. Two aerial-rocket-artillery helicopters suddenly appeared and made firing runs down both sides of the landing zone. The ARA ships broke off their rocket runs and went into a daisy-chain holding pattern, west of the LZ. The first wave of slicks touched down. I could see the door gunners raking the jungle with machine-gun fire. Soldiers spilled out both side of the choppers and crawled for the nearest cover.

'The gunships had made the initial approach with the first flight, firing machine guns and rockets. They then swung around and escorted the next flight into the LZ. One of them was fitted with an M5 grenade launcher, and I could see it firing into the tree line. It looked like a fat kid spitting watermelon seeds.

'"White flight short final", the platoon leader of our flight said. The first flight of slicks were still holding in the LZ while more grunts exited. Timing was critical because the following flights were on final approach.

ABOVE: *A South Korean soldier disembarks from a UH-1D/H of the Republic of Korea Capital Division Aviation Section during an operation in Binh Dinh Province. (US Army/Infantry)*

'"If they don't get the hell out of there, we'll have to make a go-around", said Stickney. Then the flight on the LZ lifted slowly and began to accelerate straight ahead and away. I locked my shoulder harness and lowered the visor on my helmet. A few weeks earlier, another assault helicopter company had lost an aircraft when the windshield was shot out. Neither pilot had his visor down; the shredded plexiglass blinded them both. The helicopter crashed, killing the crew chief.

'"We're in contact; the LZ is hot, the LZ is hot", an excited voice suddenly blurted over the FM radio. As we touched down I could see grunts lying flat behind rotting trees and giant ant hills. To the north-east of the clearing a steady stream of tracers poured from the dense tree line of the jungle.

'"We've got automatic-weapons fire east side", the same excited voice said. "We're pinned down. Wagonwheel Six, can we get those ARA ships back in here?"

'"Affirmative, Blue Fox. Do you want just the east side hit?", Wagonwheel Six asked.

'"Roger, for now. We've got a heavy machine gun in the north-east corner and small-arms fire all along the east side", replied Blue Fox.

'"White flight is up", Stickney said, meaning all of the grunts were clear of the helicopters.

'"Lifting", the platoon leader replied. All four helicopters lifted off, still in diamond formation.

ABOVE: 'Hotel' Hueys of the 174th Assault Helicopter Company disembark soldiers of the 1st Battalion, 6th Regiment of the ARVN 2nd Infantry Division on LZ 'Kala' prior to an attack on the old Special Forces camp at Kham Duc on 26 July 1970. (US Army/Infantry)

'A long stream of tracers arced up at White Two, the helicopter on the right point of the diamond. "We're taking a lot of fire", the aircraft commander of White Two said in a calm, matter-of-fact voice.

'"Green and red flights, go to a staggered trail formation. We've got room in the LZ to do it. It will give you better coverage", Wagonwheel Six said.

'"Blue Fox, this is Black Knight Six. Do you want your reserve platoon brought in?", asked the battalion commander, orbiting in the command-and-control helicopter. Normally the C and C helicopter would orbit high over the LZ. But because of the low clouds, it had to remain low-level, well off to one side of the battle.

'"If we can get that heavy gun knocked out, I think we'll be okay", Blue Fox replied.

'"Blue Fox, this is Hog One; we're starting our run now", the ARA flight leader said. "We've got enough fuel for about two runs apiece", he added.

'"Okay, concentrate on the north-east side", said Blue Fox.

'White Flight made a left 180-degree turn and I could see the next flight of helicopters lifting from the landing zone. Streams of tracers continued to pour from the dense foliage on the east side.

'The first ARA ship was just pulling up after its rocket attack on the heavy machine gun. As the helicopter broke to the right, I saw a flash of fire from the right rocket pod. Smoke trailed from the pod and the

flames were getting bigger. "We've got a pod on fire and I can't jettison it", said the pilot of Hog One. "I'm going to put down on the LZ". The ARA ship continued in a right turn. The last flight of slicks was just lifting off as the burning ship rolled out level and approached the landing zone. Suddenly, the flaming rocket pod exploded. The helicopter rolled violently to the left. A large piece of rotor blade broke off as the ship went inverted. Losing forward momentum, it plummeted straight down.

'"We've bought it", the pilot of Hog One said just before the ship hit the ground. It lay partially on the LZ, its broken tailboom sticking out of the heavy jungle growth. The whole aircraft was in flames. Several soldiers ran in a low crouch toward the wreckage. They were still being fired at from the tree line. "I'm going to land", said the pilot of the other ARA ship.

'"Negative; stay on station. We've got people on the ground that will get the crew out", said the battalion commander.

'"Black Knight Six, three of the crew are dead. The fourth one was thrown clear but he's hurt real bad", said Blue Fox.

'"Okay, we'll get Dust Off in there to get him out", replied Black Knight. "Also, I'm going to send your reserves in. Wagonwheel Six, pick up the ready reaction force at 'Oasis' and assault them into the same landing zone", he added.

'"Roger", said Wagonwheel Six.

'"We can't get a medevac right now; they're all busy", Black Knight said a minute later. "Wheel Six, can you send one of your ships in to get that crewman out?"

'"Affirmative, sir. Green Four, break out of formation and do the medevac. Keep both gunships with you", said Wagonwheel Six.

'Green Four broke from the formation and made a left turn back into the landing zone. The two gunships continued to make firing runs on the east side of the clearing. The remaining ARA ship had knocked out the heavy machine gun and was returning to 'Oasis' with its fuel critically low.

'We returned to Landing Zone 'Oasis' and picked up the ready reaction force. We air-assaulted them into the same LZ, this time receiving very little ground fire.'

Helicopter Combat Service Support

The success of airmobile combat assault operations in Vietnam depended to a considerable degree on the rôle of the combat service support helicopter for resupply, medical evacuation, artillery movement, aircraft recovery and the unceasing transport of troops, equipment and civilians, for both administrative and combat purposes. The use of helicopters in the logistic support rôle was fundamental to the concept of airmobility. Not only did helicopters free combat units from a complete dependence on surface transportation, but they also forged the link to their forward elements in virtually any area of operation, irrespective of the prevailing conditions. The majority of logistical missions were undertaken by the UH-1 Huey, CH-47 Chinook and CH-54 Tarhe helicopters which delivered an extraordinarily diverse variety of stores to

forward areas, including all the grim essentials of war such as ammunition, medical supplies, water, food, fuel and weapons as well as that indispensable item for the fighting soldier—mail. As a rule, the Chinook transported bulk supplies to battalions and companies, whence they were distributed in smaller loads down to platoon level by Huey. The CH-54 'Flying Crane' was primarily employed to lift heavy items of equipment to otherwise inaccessible locations and for the evacuation of damaged aircraft from the combat area.

'Shithook'—the CH-47 Chinook

The Boeing-Vertol CH-47 Chinook was designed as a 'battlefield mobility' helicopter to replace the piston-engined CH-37 Mojave, and entered service with the US Army in August 1962. Powered by two Lycoming T-55-L-7 turboshaft engines with a combined normal rating of 4,400shp, the CH-47A soon proved its effectiveness during exercises with the 11th Air Assault Division (Test). Its capacious, watertight fuselage accommodated thirty-three fully equipped troops or a payload of 10,000 pounds, and carried them at a speed of 140 knots. In September 1965 the first Chinooks arrived in Vietnam with the 1st Cavalry Division (Airmobile), when the fifty-six aircraft assigned to the 228th Assault Support Helicopter Battalion were flown from the deck of the carrier USS *Boxer* anchored off Qui Nhon to the division's base at An Khe. On 28 November 1965 the 147th Aviation Company (Assault Support Helicopter) arrived at Vung Tau, from where its Chinooks were initially used in direct support of the 1st Infantry Division. In the first two years of operations, Chinook units flew over 238,000 sorties transporting over 610,000 tons of cargo and 671,000 passengers in over 88,000 flying hours at an average of more than forty-four hours per month per helicopter. During the same period, over 1,350 downed aircraft were recovered by Chinooks.

RIGHT: *A rigger of the 173rd Airborne Brigade stands atop a load of supplies, ready to hook the 'doughnut ring' of the cargo net to a CH-47A of the 179th Assault Support Helicopter Company—'the Hooks'—during Operation 'Greeley' in June 1968. During the first two weeks of this operation in the Dak To area the Chinooks of the 'Hooks' airlifted an average of 300 tons a day. (US Army/News Features)*

RIGHT: *With a drag chute deployed and rotor blades lashed down to aid stability, an AH-1G Cobra is recovered by a CH-47A Chinook to a safe area for repair after being shot down. Note that all the ordnance has been removed from the gunship prior to lifting. (US Army/Aviation Digest)*

FAR RIGHT: *A bulldozer driver shelters behind his Caterpillar D-7 from the eighty-knot rotor downdraft of a CH-47A of B Company, 228th Assault Support Helicopter Battalion, as it delivers an M-102 105 mm howitzer to the 1st Cavalry Division (Airmobile) at LZ 'Carolyn' north-east of Tay Ninh on 19 April 1969, during Operation 'Montana Raider'. (US Army/Infantry)*

77

The hostile operating conditions of high temperatures and high density altitude had a predictably detrimental effect on the Chinook's performance with regard to payload and airspeed. This was compounded by the necessity to carry almost a ton of combat equipment, including suppressive fire weapons, an extra crewman as gunner, armour plate for vital components, armoured seats, personal body armour and survival gear. Under these conditions a typical payload was reduced to 7,000 pounds in the Highlands and 8,000 near the coast, at an airspeed of ninety-five knots for a 100 nautical mile radius mission. As early as December 1965 the 1st Cavalry Division (Airmobile) submitted an urgent request for improved hot weather performance, and for remedies for the many teething troubles that required extensive inspection and maintenance time. As with any new piece of equipment, and particularly one deployed in battle before field testing had been fully completed, there were a host of problems: brakes jammed when applied, causing the tyres to skid and blow out; the 'droop stop' sometimes failed, which caused the blades to strike the fuselage during shut-down; and considerable difficulties were encountered with the engine transmission gearboxes and the Stabilization Augmentation System. Many of these problems were resolved in the field; and in May 1967 an improved model, the CH-47B, was introduced which incorporated uprated engines and an aerodynamically improved 'droop snoot' rotor blade, providing a forty-five per cent increase in payload and speed under typical Vietnamese conditions. Despite these problems, the CH-47A exceeded the Department of the Army availability requirement of fifty per cent: between September 1965 and September 1970 this figure increased from 53.7 to 77.9 per cent, with an accumulative average availability of 66.8 per cent.

BELOW: *A fifty-five-gallon drum of CS tear gas drops from a CH-47A of C Company, 228th Assault Support Helicopter Battalion, 1st Cavalry Division (Airmobile) onto suspected VC emplacements on 21 July 1967 during Operation 'Pershing'. Acting in the 'bomber' rôle, Chinooks dropped 29,600 pounds of riot agents during the course of this operation in Binh Dinh Province. (US Army)*

In all logistic resupply missions the Chinook made extensive use of the external sling load technique, which required only the time to fasten standard type loads to the cargo hook suspended beneath the aircraft. Typical loads included 200 rounds of 105mm howitzer ammunition or two 500 gallon fuel bladders. By this method it was commonplace for a Chinook to airlift 100 tons of supplies a day within a ten mile radius. Although aerial resupply and the transportation of passengers were its basic functions, the Chinook was put to many other uses, even including an improvised 'bomber' rôle against specific targets where other means of tactical air support could not be economically employed. In particular, the Chinook delivered large quantities of riot agents and napalm against the extensive underground fortifications and tunnel systems developed by the Viet Cong, with the intention of driving the enemy into the open. Packed in fifty-five gallon drums, the napalm or bulk CS was rolled out of the rear of the Chinook with a fusing system activated by a static line which armed the drum after it was free of the aircraft. By this method a single CH-47 could accurately drop two-and-a-half tons of napalm or up to thirty drums of tear gas on an enemy installation. The main targets for such drops were known or suspected base camps, rest areas and infiltration routes.

An additional major Chinook rôle was the movement of artillery units which were needed to provide constant fire support during fast-moving, airmobile operations. In effect the Chinook became the 'airmobile prime mover', capable of displacing a complete 105mm howitzer battery with a basic load of ammunition in as few as eleven sorties. With uprated engines, the CH-47 was able to lift the M-102 105mm howitzer externally with sixty rounds of ammunition slung below while the seven-man crew rode inside. This capability was

BELOW: *As dusk falls, troops of the 1st Battalion, 46th Infantry of the Americal Division disembark from a CH-47B Chinook of the 178th Assault Support Helicopter Company at Landing Zone 'Professional', west of Tam Ky, after an operation on 21 November 1969. The B-model Chinook features spoilers on the forward pylon to aid directional stability, together with other modifications. (US Army/Infantry)*

exploited to move an artillery battery deep into enemy territory to bombard locations which were beyond the range of prepared field artillery positions. For this so-called 'artillery raid', the battery was emplaced by Chinook at a point from which suspected targets identified by intelligence could be engaged with rapid fire, and the unit was then extracted by air before the enemy could react. During Operation 'Irving' in October 1966 one such artillery raid was conducted by A Battery, 2nd Battalion, 19th Artillery of the 1st Cavalry Division (Airmobile). Four 105mm howitzers with crews, 280 rounds of ammunition and fire direction personnel were airlifted by Chinooks of the 228th Assault Support Helicopter Battalion into an area that the enemy had long thought to be secure. The 280 rounds were fired on previously selected targets in less than seventeen minutes, after which the artillery was extracted by Chinooks. Based on up-to-the-minute intelligence, these artillery raids were often planned and executed in under three hours.

However, the majority of field artillery units remained in prepared positions at fire support bases located throughout the battle area within range of the supported manoeuvre forces. In consequence, infantry battalions in Vietnam were rarely required to operate beyond the protective umbrella of friendly artillery. Many fire bases were established on high ground for maximum fields of fire throughout the area of operation and for ease of defence against ground attack. At the outset of many operations such fire bases had to be constructed from scratch in order to provide fire support to the manoeuvre battalions. This was the rôle of the combat engineer, and special air-portable construction equipment was developed to be airlifted to forward areas by CH-47 Chinook and CH-54 Flying Crane.

Once the location of the FSB had been determined, an engineer

ABOVE: 'Running Scared', a CH-47A of the 242nd Assault Support Helicopter Company—'The Muleskinners'—hovers over an M113 APC stuck in the mire as a crew member attaches a sling to the Chinook cargo hook. This spectacular technique for recovering bogged vehicles was devised by Major General Ellis W. Williamson, Commanding General of the 25th Infantry Division. APCs trapped in the mud up to the tops of their hulls could be extracted by the more powerful CH-54 Flying Crane. (US Army)

RIGHT: Engineers of the 3rd Platoon, Company C, 1st Engineer Battalion, 1st Infantry Division clamber down a 'troop ladder' from a CH-47A Chinook to clear a helicopter landing pad in the jungle with chainsaws and explosives on 8 January 1967 during Operation 'Cedar Falls'. The landing pad was then expanded to accommodate six helicopters and subsequently a fire support base, as required. (US Army)

squad was inserted by Chinook supported by armed helicopters. If the area was not large enough for a conventional landing, the engineers were inserted by rappelling or 'troop ladder' through the jungle canopy, and their clearing equipment—machetes, brush hooks, axes, demolitions and chainsaws—was lowered to them. Infantry troops were inserted at the same time to provide local security. The first priority was the clearing of a landing pad for a single helicopter by means of C-4 explosive, bangalore torpedoes and chainsaws—the eighteen inch Remington and the thirty-six inch McCulloch 895 chainsaws being the most suited for rapid clearing because of their light weight and ease of handling. With the landing pad cleared, a helicopter brought in more engineers, demolition equipment, chainsaw spare parts and POL to expand the landing zone until large enough for a Chinook to insert a light-weight bulldozer, such as the Case 450 or the Caterpillar D-4A, and additional engineer equipment. Larger dozers such as the Caterpillar D-5 were airlifted in two loads and re-assembled on the site for land clearing and to prepare artillery gunpits, ammunition bunkers and defensive berms. As soon as feasible, field fortification materials and prefabricated shelters for the command post and fire direction centre were flown in, as well as an airportable tractor with backhoe attachment, such as the Case 580 or the International Harvester C616, to dig trenches and foxholes for the infantry. Even while construction was underway the artillery was inserted by Chinooks, so that by the end of the day the fire base was capable of its own defence and ready for action in support of infantry units.

Of all the multifarious missions undertaken by the Chinook, that of aircraft recovery was the most spectacular and, in terms of monies saved, highly cost effective. From the outset of helicopter operations in Vietnam the necessity of recovering aircraft downed in hostile

BELOW: *A CH-47C of the 101st Airborne Division (Airmobile) deposits an M-101 105mm howitzer on a hilltop position during the construction of a fire support base. Introduced in October 1968, the C model incorporated T-55-L-11 engines with a combined rating of 6,000shp which, with other improvements, almost doubled the payload of the CH-47A. The blunt trailing edge of the aft pylon and body strakes on the fuselage and rear ramp, for improved directional stability, are the identifying features of the B and C models. (US Army/Aviation News)*

ABOVE, FAR LEFT: *Rigged for recovery, a UH-1D 'Bushranger' gunship of No. 9 Squadron, Royal Australian Air Force lies in the shallows on the shoreline near Vung Tau as a CH-47B comes to the hover to effect recovery. (US Army/News Features)*

ABOVE LEFT: *A 'Dust Off' UH-1D of the 159th Medical Detachment (Helicopter Ambulance) is recovered by a CH-47A Chinook on 21 May 1966 during Operation 'Wahiawa', a search-and-destroy mission conducted by the 25th Infantry Division north-east of Cu Chi. (US Army)*

LEFT *A crew member of a UH-1H 'recovery ship' of the American Division connects a sling between the Huey cargo hook and the main rotor hub of a disabled Loach at LZ 'Siberia' for recovery back to a safe area at Chu Lai on 26 May 1970. (US Army/Infantry)*

territory, rather than destroying them in place to prevent their equipment from falling into enemy hands, became apparent. Originally performed by the CH-37 Mojave, the technique was perfected and became a standard operating procedure with the advent of the CH-47 Chinook. Year after year, the Chinook recovered hundreds of aircraft which were returned to service instead of becoming combat losses. Although the majority were UH-1 Hueys, the Chinook also recovered fixed-wing types such as the C-7 Caribou and the A-1 Skyraider, as well as other helicopters including on occasions other Chinooks—a task more suited to the CH-54 'Skycrane'.

When an aircraft was forced down, whether by enemy action, equipment failure or pilot error, the unit maintenance officer flew to the site and determined whether it could be repaired on the spot or needed to be evacuated to a safe area. If the latter, a recovery team was summoned comprising a Chinook and the UH-1 Huey 'recovery ship' of an aviation maintenance unit, which had a crew of six—pilot, co-pilot, crew chief, and three riggers who prepared the downed aircraft for lifting. It usually took only about ten minutes to rig an intact aircraft; the guns and radios were removed, the cyclic and collective were tied down, the rotor blades were secured along the long axis of the aircraft, and a six-foot nylon strap was fastened to the lifting eye on top of the rotor mast. The Chinook orbited the area out of range of ground fire until these preparations were complete, when it came to a hover over the downed aircraft to effect the hook-up.

The Chinook then took off with its sling load and the recovery ship followed, its crew informing the Chinook pilot all the while of any unusual behaviour of the slung aircraft, which could be jettisoned in an emergency. An intact Huey was normally carried at an airspeed of sixty to seventy-five knots, but if its windshields were broken or the tailboom was missing it tended to oscillate and was carried at about forty knots. At higher airspeeds the load could yaw violently and strike the Chinook. When the two recovery aircraft were close to their destination, the Huey proceeded ahead and landed. It was then in a position to guide the Chinook into the landing site to deposit the recovered aircraft safely at the desired spot.

'Flying Crane'—the CH-54A Tarhe

Variously known as 'Flying Crane' or 'Skycrane', the CH-54A Tarhe was a heavy lift cargo helicopter with a payload, externally carried, of ten tons. It was powered by two Pratt and Whitney JFTD-12A turbine engines of 4,050shp each (later 4,620shp) giving a speed of ninety-five knots. With a crew of four, one of whom faced aft and operated the limited-authority flight controls during lifting operations, the CH-54A had a 20,000 pound capacity crane and 100 feet of cable for winching loads from areas of dense woodland or other obstacles, a capability which proved of great value in Vietnam.

Four CH-54As of the 478th Aviation Company were deployed to Vietnam with the 1st Cavalry Division (Airmobile) in September 1965. The primary mission of the CH-54A was the lifting of heavy items and equipment beyond the capabilities of other helicopters,

RIGHT: *A Case 450 bulldozer is airlifted into Khe Sanh by a CH-54A 'Flying Crane' of the 355th Aviation Company (Heavy Helicopter) to assist in the refurbishment of the former USMC Combat Base as a forward staging area for 'Lam Son 719', the ARVN incursion into Laos in February 1971. (US Army)*

BELOW: *A CH-54A 'Skycrane' of the 478th Aviation Company (Heavy Helicopter) recovers a badly damaged CH-47A of the 228th Assault Support Helicopter Battalion to the 'Golf Course'—the base of the 1st Cavalry Division (Airmobile) at An Khe. (US Army)*

such as bulldozers, bridging, 155mm artillery pieces and damaged aircraft. Its capacity to lift the M-114A1 155mm howitzer without breaking it down into two separate loads—as was necessary for the CH-47 Chinook—was of special significance to the field artillery, because it expedited the positioning of medium artillery in areas not readily accessible by road. The 155mm was airlifted for the first time by CH-54 during Operation 'Masher-White Wing' conducted by the 1st Cavalry Division (Airmobile) around Bong Son in January 1966.

The Skycrane was also used for logistical resupply, flying ammunition pallets, 500 gallon fuel bladders or blivets (three to the Chinook's two) and other bulky loads in support of combat operations. However, it rarely ventured into contested landing zones: at a unit cost of $2.2m it was too valuable to be needlessly exposed on hazardous missions. On 19 April 1968, during Operation 'Delaware' in the A Shau Valley, CH-54A (66-18205) was struck in the cockpit by an RPG (Rocket Propelled Grenade) while on short final into a landing zone with a bulldozer. The aircraft exploded in flight, crashed and burned, killing the crew of four. A further eight Skycranes were lost due to operational causes during the war.

The majority of loads carried by the Skycrane were by sling, but an enclosed container designated the Universal Military Pod was

developed, which the helicopter straddled with its widespread tricycle landing gear. This 'people-pod' was used for troop-carrying, casualty transfer, the movement of stores, or as a mobile command centre. A 'medical pod' was also designed as a mobile field surgical unit by the commanding officer of the 15th Medical Battalion, Lieutenant Colonel Jueri Svjagintsev—who for obvious reasons was known as 'Dr Alphabet'. Principally employed by the 1st Cavalry Division (Airmobile), these pods were found to be difficult to emplace in Vietnam and, once installed, immobile. After the division moved north in January 1968 their use was discontinued as impractical.

On occasion, the CH-54A also conducted spectacular 'bombing' missions when it carried an M-121 10,000 pound bomb which was dropped by parachute and detonated by an extended fuse so that it exploded at a height to clear dense vegetation without cratering the ground. In this way an instant landing zone was created for the insertion of helicopters, or else engineers were airlifted in to extend it to the desired configuration. Three heavy helicopter companies served in Vietnam with CH-54A Skycranes; the 273rd, 355th and 478th Aviation Companies of the 1st Aviation Brigade.

BELOW: *Ground troops scurry for shelter as the 100-knot rotor downdraft of a CH-54A sends air matresses and broiling dust lashing across the drop-point for an M-114A1 155 mm howitzer being delivered by a 'Flying Crane' during a 1st Cavalry Division (Airmobile) operation near Song Be in 1969. Note the rearward-facing perspex bubble behind the cockpit, where a crewman operates the limited-authority flight controls during the final moments of such a manoeuvre. (US Army/Infantry)*

4 US ARMY HELICOPTER GUNSHIPS IN VIETNAM

Teeth for the Gunships—Helicopter Armament Subsystems

Despite the success of the armed helicopter concept as demonstrated by the Utility Tactical Transport Helicopter Company and the Assault Helicopter Companies which followed, the UH-1B gunship suffered several shortcomings—including its slower speed than the troop transports it escorted, and its short loiter time and reduced ordnance load when operating in hot and humid conditions. Following the recommendation of the Howze Board, the US Army had identified the need for a purpose-designed attack helicopter and an industry design competition was proposed in 1964. However, due to Air Force opposition on the grounds that the armed helicopter mission duplicated an existing Air Force capability, and a consequent restriction of funds as well as a number of other pressures for delay, a contract for the Advanced Aerial Fire Support System (AAFSS) was not awarded until March 1966, when the Lockheed AH-56A Cheyenne was chosen for development. Unfortunately the Cheyenne programme was plagued from the outset by problems due to its complexity and revolutionary configuration, which rendered the design prohibitively expensive and unsuited to mass production at a time when gunships were sorely needed in combat.

Meanwhile, the Bell Helicopter Company was continuing its extensive research and development of the UH-1 series, as well as pursuing a privately funded design for an attack helicopter using proven components of the Huey. In the spring of 1965, under conditions of strict secrecy, the company began the construction of a prototype, the Model 209. This was based on a previous design, the Sioux Scout, which had incorporated a tandem seating arrangement for the pilot and gunner. The new aircraft was flown for the first time on 7 September 1965 and began service trials in December. Two further pre-production prototypes of the HueyCobra were ordered on 4 April 1966; and nine days later a contract was awarded for 110 production aircraft as an interim measure, given the difficulties of the AAFSS.

Even so, despite such a rapid and unprecedented procurement procedure, the HueyCobra was not scheduled to enter service until 1967. In the meantime the existing UH-1B and an improved model, the UH-1C, had to continue to fulfil the gunship rôle. Among the progressive improvements to the Huey, Bell had devised a rigid rotor head which was stronger, simpler to maintain and gave increased performance. Known as the 540 'door hinge' rotor hub, it allowed larger twenty-seven inch chord rotor blades and the more powerful T53-L-9 engine to be fitted, which yielded more lift, greater speed, and an increase in payload of 1,000 pounds. With other refinements

ABOVE: *A trio of UH-1B gunships of Company A, 501st Aviation Battalion line up at Bien Hoa on 30 October 1965, displaying their armament systems and ordnance, including the M-16 to either side and the XM-3 in the middle. Note the rattlesnake and bird insignia on the doors and nose: subsequently the 71st AHC, the slick platoons were called 'Rattlers' and the guns 'Firebirds'. Many early Huey gunships adopted a snake motif, giving rise to the generic nickname of 'Cobras'. However, with the introduction of the AH-1G—which was officially named HueyCobra—confusion arose, and the latter was commonly called 'Snake'. (US Army)*

Combinations of weaponry carried by armed Hueys. (The Cobra Company)

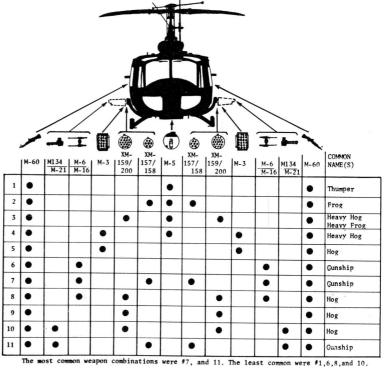

	M-60	M134 / M-21	M-6 / M-16	M-3	XM-159/200	XM-157/158	M-5	XM-157/158	XM-159/200	M-3	M-6 / M-16	M134 / M-21	M-60	COMMON NAME(S)
1	●						●						●	Thumper
2	●					●	●	●					●	Frog
3	●				●		●		●				●	Heavy Hog / Heavy Frog
4	●			●			●			●			●	Heavy Hog
5	●			●						●			●	Hog
6	●		●								●		●	Gunship
7	●					●		●					●	Gunship
8	●			●						●			●	Hog
9	●				●				●				●	Hog
10	●	●			●				●			●	●	Hog
11	●	●				●		●				●	●	Gunship

The most common weapon combinations were #7, and 11. The least common were #1,6,8,and 10.

the 'Charlie' model went some way to resolve the speed differential between the 'slicks' and gunships, and its increased fuel capacity and ordnance load allowed it to remain on station longer during fire missions. Deliveries of the 766 UH-1Cs built began in June 1965, and they first saw service in Vietnam during 1966.

Developments of helicopter armament subsystems had continued apace in Vietnam and at Fort Rucker, Florida—the home of US Army Aviation. In Vietnam, Chief Warrant Officer Clemuel Womack of UTTHCO had adapted a seven-tube 2.75 in. FFAR pod to the M-6 system to give a multi-weapon capability. Other variants featured six- or eight-packs of the 2.75 in. 'Mighty Mouse' rockets which were attached either to the helicopter landing skids or to the Universal External Stores Mount that incorporated the M-6 'flex guns'. Subsequently, a standardized version emerged in 1964 designated the M-16 Armament Subsystem, which became the most common weapon combination on helicopter gunships during the early years in Vietnam.

Weighing 1,294 pounds, the M-16 comprised the standard M-6 armament subsystem and two seven-tube rocket pods (either XM-157 or XM-158) suspended from 14-in. bomb racks, MA-4A, attached to the Universal Mounts by means of the XM-156 Helicopter Mount, Multi-Armament. From late 1965 the XM-158 rocket launcher pod superseded the XM-157. The latter's rocket tubes were not individually replaceable, making repairs difficult and time-consuming. The XM-158 obviated the problem as it comprised a cluster of seven separate, removeable 53½-in. aluminium tubes with safer rear loading. The M-16 Armament Subsystem allowed the gunner to fire the M-6 subsystem in its flexible mode, and the pilot to aim and fire the 2.75 in. rockets by means of the XM-60 reflex infinity sight mounted on the windshield frame above his seat. A rocket

RIGHT: *A UH-1B of the 'Razorbacks', the 120th Assault Helicopter Company, unleashes a rocket during an attack run west of Saigon. Fitted with the M-16 Armament Subsystem, this gunship retains on the fin the 'mortarboard' marking of the 57th Transportation Company, one of the original two helicopter companies to serve in Vietnam. (US Army/Military Review)*

armament panel installed on the aircraft control pedestal allowed the pilot to select the number of pairs of rockets to be fired, from one to seven, with up to six pairs per second to a maximum effective range of 2,500 metres. Machine gun fire was automatically interrupted when the rockets were launched.

Another area-neutralization rocket launcher was the XM-3 Armament Subsystem, which was an earlier interim design intended as a direct fire area weapon against troops, lightly armoured vehicles and other soft targets. Introduced into Vietnam in May 1963, it comprised a launcher pod containing twenty-four rocket tubes attached to the universal mount on each side of the UH-1B/C helicopter. It was capable of selective fire from one pair (i.e. a single rocket from each pod) or multiple pairs up to a full discharge of all forty-eight rockets delivering 480 pounds of high explosive, with a rate of fire of six pairs per second. The system was aligned by a Mark VIII reticle sight mounted on the instrument panel, and was fired by a switch on the cyclic control. The weight of a fully loaded system, with ten-pound warheads, was 1,439 pounds which, combined with crew and stores, taxed the UH-1B severely. Due to their frequent reluctance to become airborne and to their ungainly appearance, aircraft so equipped were nicknamed 'Hogs'. A 'Hog' was normally attached to a 'Light Fire Team' of two gunships equipped with M-16 subsystems, which then became a 'Heavy Fire Team' or 'Heavy Team'.

When the XM-3 system of the 'Hog' was combined with the M-5 Armament Subsystem, Helicopter Grenade Launcher, the gunship became a 'Heavy Hog'. The M-5 was designed to fire 40mm grenade

projectiles as a direct fire weapon against area or point targets. The system included a nose-mounted, flexible turret; the M-75 grenade launcher; ammunition booster; ammunition feed chuting and stowage box; sighting station; and associated electrical components and controls. Through the use of the flexible sight, the co-pilot/gunner directed the weapon through its flexible limits of fifteen degrees elevation, thirty-five degrees depression and sixty degrees right or left of the nose. It could also be fired in a fixed-forward mode by either the pilot or co-pilot/gunner. The M-5 was capable of firing its total ordnance load of 150 rounds at a rate of 220 rounds per minute to a maximum effective range of 1,500 metres. A later version doubled the number of rounds to 302, stowed in a rotary ammunition drum located over the cargo hook hole. The M-5 was type classified on 25 July 1964. Its total weight when fully loaded was approximately 335 pounds or, for the later model, 484 pounds.

Late in 1966 the M-16 'flex guns'/rocket launcher combination was superseded by the M-21 Armament Subsystem. The primary difference was the replacement of the four M-60C machine guns by two M-134 7.62mm high-rate-of-fire automatic guns (or 'miniguns', as they were known) which doubled the firepower. The complete 'M-21 Armament Subsystem, Helicopter, 7.62mm Machine Gun–2.75 Inch Rocket Launcher: Twin High Rate Machine Gun' comprised two remotely controlled, power-operated, flexible pylons, each mounting one M-134 and provision for the rocket pods, each containing seven 2.75 in. FFAR. Linked 7.62mm ammunition was stowed inboard with a capacity of 6,000 rounds with an additional 400 rounds in the flexible chuting that fed the guns. A flexible sighting system enabled the co-pilot to aim and fire the miniguns remotely, while the pilot could fire either the rockets or the machine guns when in the stowed position, using a fixed sight. The electrically-driven, air-cooled, six-barrelled miniguns had a cyclic

ABOVE: *A 'Ruthless Rider' UH-1C of 7th/17th Cav. initiates a gun run with its M-21 Armament Subsystem and XM-158 rocket launchers. Note the full-length wind baffle on the trailing edge of the door post, which lessened the buffeting that door gunners were subjected to during flight. (US Army/Aviation Digest)*

rate of fire of 4,000 rounds per minute—2,000 r.p.m. per gun. The flexible mounts allowed the guns to move ten degrees up, eighty-five degrees down, seventy degrees outboard and twelve degrees inboard. If either gun reached the twelve degrees inboard limit it ceased to fire, but the opposite gun then accelerated from 2,000 to 4,000 rounds per minute. A three second 'limiter' prevented the gunner from firing extended bursts, to prolong the life of the guns and preclude unnecessary expenditure of ammunition. An additional safety feature cleared the guns completely after each burst: every time a minigun ceased to fire, a minimum of six live rounds was ejected overboard.

Although there were numerous improvised and experimental weapon combinations fitted to helicopters, including .50 calibre AN-M2 Browning machine guns and 20mm cannons, few were standardized for quantity production. The above-mentioned armament subsystems were the principal ones employed by UH-1 gunships, the M-21 being the most widespread in Vietnam from 1967 onwards.

One other standardized helicopter gunship armament used in limited numbers was the M-22 anti-tank guided missile subsystem. This comprised six AGM-22B missiles mounted on UH-1B and UH-1C Hueys to provide point fire support against small hard targets such as tanks, AFVs, pillboxes and bridges. With a maximum range of 3,500 metres, the sixty-four-pound missile was launched and guided by the co-pilot/gunner using a small control stick and an XM-58 anti-oscillation sight. In flight, guidance commands were transmitted to the missile by means of two wires trailing from its aft end to the control mechanism. The system was first used in Vietnam by 2/20th Artillery in October 1965 to destroy a series of bunkers, and subsequently against the booby-trapped and barricaded gates of a village, some five miles east of Duc Co Special Forces Camp.

However, the need to neutralize such pin-point targets was relatively uncommon in Vietnam, whereas area targets suitable for the XM-3 were widespread. Since it took some three hours to exchange these armament subsystems, it proved uneconomical to have M-22-dedicated aircraft. Chief Warrant Officer Robert Maxwell of 'B' Battery, 2/20th Artillery tackled the problem by devising a combination of the two systems with an AGM-22B missile mounted outboard of the XM-3 rocket pods, which were sometimes reduced to twelve tubes each to reduce weight. The M-22/XM-3 configuration was termed the 'Maxwell System' and was first used in combat in December 1965 to attack a VC command post located in a cave, and a second one masked behind a waterfall. Both targets were destroyed. It was not until May 1972 that the M-22 was used in its intended anti-tank rôle, when six UH-1M helicopters fitted with the system achieved two confirmed kills, one against a T-54A and the other against a PT-76.

TOW versus T-54: Strella versus Snake

The 'Mike' model Hueys armed with the M-22 Armament Subsystem were deployed to Military Region I (formerly ICTZ) following the experiences of LAM SON 719, which saw the first widespread encounter between gunships and NVA armour. During the battle air cavalry teams sighted sixty-six tanks but, since they lacked suitable ordnance with which to engage them, most of the targets were turned over to fixed-wing attack aircraft. A 2.75 in. High Explosive Anti-Tank (HEAT) rocket was available, the Mark V; but it suffered from a high failure rate, having been developed during the Korean War and stored since, and it also required a direct hit to disable an AFV. Accordingly, gunships adapted their tactics to use whatever ordnance was on board. In a typical engagement, the target was attacked with flechette rockets to eliminate supporting infantry and to force the crew to close the hatches of their tank, which was then attacked by a combination of HE and WP rockets and 20mm cannon fire, the latter being particularly effective. By these means, six tanks were destroyed and eight others were immobilized.

Subsequently a dual-purpose anti-tank and anti-personnel rocket was developed; but with the accelerating withdrawal of US troops from Vietnam interest waned. However, on 30 March 1972 the NVA swept across the DMZ, and for the first time in the Vietnam War the enemy attacked in force with armour. Simultaneously another offensive was launched from Cambodia into Military Region 3, overrunning Loc Ninh and encircling the city of An Loc. The first tank destroyed by Cobra gunships was hit early on the morning of 13 April when three AH-1Gs of F Battery, 79th AFA, 3rd Brigade of the 1st Cavalry Division (Airmobile) engaged six T-54s attacking An Loc. Using old Mark V HEAT rockets, a Cobra struck one tank in the engine decks from a high angle of attack of thirty to thirty-five degrees. On the same day, another tank was destroyed by a seventeen-pound HE rocket.

With the increased threat of NVA armour on the battlefield, the requirement for the dual-purpose 2.75 in. rocket under development

ABOVE RIGHT: *An AH-1G 'Snake' of 1st Squadron, 1st Cavalry is re-armed during the battle for Quang Tri in April 1972. During the Easter Invasion at least thirteen NVA tanks were knocked out by gunships armed with 2.75in. FFAR. (US Army/Aviation Digest)*

BELOW RIGHT: *A 'Charlie' model UH-1 gunship of the 7th/17th Air Cavalry armed with the M-22 Armament Subsystem is refuelled at Dak To during 1968. The AGM-22B missiles were commonly referred to by their French designation of SS-11, although strictly this only applied to the ground fired version—'sol-sol' being ground to ground, whereas these are AS-11, 'air-sol'—air to ground. (Robert Steinbrunn)*

Colour Section

3

4

5

6

7

8

9

I

12

13

16

17

became urgent. Through extraordinary efforts at Picatinney Arsenal a production line was set up immediately after the invasion. Within four days, 1,000 rockets were manufactured and ready for shipment to Vietnam, where they arrived on 15 April. Of longer range and greater accuracy, the XM-247 warhead was a potent addition to the Cobra's firepower. By 11 May, Cobras equipped with only the 2.75 in. rocket system destroyed ten T-54s, three PT-76s and damaged six other T-54s. The number of rockets expended on any tank varied from a minimum of six to a maximum of fifty-six.

In April 1972 a totally new weapon system, destined to alter profoundly the doctrine both of attack helicopters and of armoured warfare, was deployed to the battlefields of Vietnam. The experimental Tube-launched, Optically-tracked, Wire-guided (TOW) anti-tank missile, then undergoing development for the AH-56A Cheyenne attack helicopter, was airlifted to Tan Son Nhut where it arrived on 24 April. At the time, the XM-26 airborne TOW system was fitted to two superannuated UH-1B gunships which were redesignated NUH-1B. With three crews, most of whom were civilians, the 1st Airborne TOW Team immediately began intensive equipment checks and training of Army aviators.

On 28 April the team moved to Camp Holloway, near Pleiku in MR2, to counter an expected attack on Kontum. After further gunnery training with the 'Package', as the system was also known, daily flights were flown in search of enemy armour. During the morning of 2 May a captured M41A3 tank was spotted on the approaches to Kontum as ARVN forces were falling back to the city. It was engaged by CW2 Carroll Lain and destroyed with a single missile; later in the morning three other enemy tanks were knocked out. Thereafter, numerous missions were flown in support of the city's defenders by the NUH-1B TOW Hueys escorted by two AH-1G Cobras of the 7th Squadron, 17th Air Cavalry, and a UH-1H C&C helicopter. On 26 May another concerted attack against Kontum began, and the two TOW helicopters were in action from 0640. By late morning they had flown three sorties each and had fired twenty-one missiles, which destroyed nine tanks—five T-54s and four PT-76s—and a number of other point targets.

During the first month of combat the TOW system destroyed twenty-four tanks, seven trucks, two artillery pieces and four APCs, as well as numerous other targets. A further two tanks were destroyed by ground-launched TOW missiles (XM-151); subsequently, ten others were knocked out by tripod- or jeep-mounted launchers, including nine during a single engagement near FSB Nancy, north-west of Hue on 25 June. In the same period, the six M-22-armed UH-1M gunships fired a total of 115 SS-11 missiles—ninety-five of which were in training, because it was a more difficult system to operate than the TOW and required a larger number of firings to qualify personnel. Of the twenty fired in action, a T-54A was destroyed on 21 May after being engaged by nine missiles, a PT-76 was destroyed by another six, and the remaining five damaged a second PT-76. Throughout the campaign the airborne TOW team fired 101 missiles in action and destroyed fifty-seven targets to give a kill ratio of over fifty per cent, which was almost five times more effective than the SS-11. The two NUH-1Bs remained in Vietnam until the withdrawal of US forces.

The Easter or Nguyen Hue Offensive of 1972 also saw the introduction by the NVA of the SA-7 'Strella' anti-aircraft missile. First encountered during June, the shoulder-fired, heat-seeking missile caused the loss of at least four AH-1G Cobras; it usually struck near the battery compartment below the exhaust outlet, severing the tailboom and sending the aircraft into an uncontrollable spin. Two crews were killed but, through a combination of airmanship and luck, two crews survived the ensuing crashes. Within weeks Cobras were fitted with an exhaust cowl which vented the hot gases upwards into the main rotor downwash and thus dissipated the focus of heat on which the Strella's guidance system locked. Subsequently, most helicopters were fitted with infra-red suppression kits; and high intensity flares were ejected from aircraft, which frequently caused the missile to track the flare and explode at a harmless distance. Despite these measures the Strella remained a potent weapon, and the threat forced helicopters either to operate at much lower altitudes where they were more vulnerable to ground fire, or else to adopt far steeper attack angles from high altitude, which diminished the effectiveness of their weapons and wing stores.

'Guns A-Go-Go'—the Flying Tank

Although the Bell HueyCobra was selected as the interim gunship design in 1965 due to delays with the AAFSS, the US Army also

expressed an interest in the Boeing-Vertol proposal of an armed and armoured CH-47A Chinook medium helicopter in accordance with a requirement established in February 1964 for a heavily armed helicopter. After some prevarication, the Army ordered four of these modified Chinooks on 30 June 1965, and these were delivered by the end of the year.

Designated A/ACH-47A, the aircraft was armed with an M-5 40mm grenade launcher in the nose, and on each side pylon an M-24A1 20mm cannon together with either an XM-18 minigun pod or an XM-159 nineteen-shot 2.75 in. FFAR rocket launcher. In addition, five machine guns—either AN-M2 .50 calibre or M-60D 7.62mm—were mounted in the cabin, two on each side and one on the rear ramp. With 600 40mm grenades (four times the load of the standard Huey Hog), 1,600 rounds for the 20mm cannons, 38 rockets and 3,500 rounds of .50 calibre ammunition, the A/ACH-47A had a 360-degree fire capability and an expendable ordnance load of some one-and-a-half tons.

As a protective measure the aircraft incorporated 2,681 pounds of dual-layer steel armour to protect vital components, not least of which was the eight-man crew. The pilot's and co-pilot's armoured seats provided complete torso protection from front, sides, back and below, while the remainder of the crew had personal body armour. The flight performance of the A/ACH-47A was comparable to that of a standard Chinook but depended largely on the armament load, which itself was related to the weapons fitted. With the above-mentioned load the aircraft weighed about 31,000 pounds, having a radius of operation of 100 nautical miles with a mission duration of two hours at an average airspeed of 120 knots.

Of the four A/ACH-47A gunships, three (serial numbers 64-13149, 64-13151 and 64-13154) were despatched to Vietnam in May 1966 to form the 53rd Aviation Detachment, for combat evaluation under the auspices of ACTIV which lasted from June to October. Employing standard gunship tactics, the A/ACH-47A Chinooks normally operated in fire teams of two aircraft with one acting as a base of fire while the other manoeuvred into an advantageous attack position. However, due to equipment malfunction (the M24-AI 20mm cannon proved troublesome) and combat damage, single-ship missions were sometimes flown which rendered the aircraft more vulnerable to ground fire. It was on such a mission that the first significant combat damage was incurred when, on 9 July, '149' sustained two .50 calibre hits at 850 feet while in support of Task Force Dragoon of 1st Squadron, 4th Cavalry during an ambush on the Minh Tanh Road in War Zone C. Three of the ten men aboard were wounded and the aircraft was forced to land, resulting in severe airframe damage.

For a period, the two remaining aircraft '151' and '154' supported the 1st Australian Task Force in Phuoc Tuy Province, escorting UH-1s of No.9 Squadron, RAAF during the insertion and extraction of patrols and combat assault landings. On 6 August, 64-13151 was lost in an accident during take-off at Vung Tau; although the crew

BELOW: *The ACH-47A Chinook gunship was armed with a nose-mounted M-5 Armament Subsystem, M-159 rocket launchers and/or minigun pods, two M-24A1 20 mm cannons (XM-34) and five .50 calibre or M-60 machine guns in the fuselage. Note the additional armour plating under the nose and on the rotor pylons. (Private collection of Shelby L. Stanton, from* Vietnam Order of Battle*)*

ABOVE: *Although the pilots' seats of most helicopters in Vietnam were armoured, those of the ACH-47A Chinook provided the most comprehensive protection, with hinged armour sections covering the frontal torso area while the avionics equipment behind the seat was also extensively protected by a lightweight, high-strength steel armour plating developed by the Aeronautronics Division of Philco Corporation. (Republic Steel Corporation/Military Review)*

survived, the aircraft was damaged beyond repair. During September the 53rd was assigned to 1st Cavalry Division (Airmobile) at An Khe, coming under the control of division artillery, with support provided by the 228th Assault Support Helicopter Battalion. At the end of the month Chinook 64-13145 arrived from the United States to replace '151', and '149' rejoined the detachment after repairs, bringing unit strength up to three aircraft once more. It was with the Cavalry that the A/ACH-47A was most effectively employed. With the Chinooks operating from a higher altitude, which reduced the risks of ground fire, the stand-off range of their rockets and cannon was fully exploited. After the completion of the evaluation programme the unit was redesignated 1st Aviation Detachment, and remained with 1st Cavalry under the operational control of 2/20th ARA. The A/ACH-47A Chinooks, now nicknamed 'Guns A-Go-Go' or 'Go-Go Birds' by cavalry troopers, participated throughout the Bong Son campaign that continued into 1967, performing various tasks ranging from harassment and interdiction missions to the extraction of reconnaissance teams, and all the while providing heavy fire support—as indicated by this after-action report:

'On 14 February a "Go-Go" firing section (one aircraft) responded to a fire mission for Topkick 18 and provided approximately forty minutes of sustained fire on a target that had friendly elements heavily engaged and pinned down in an open rice paddy within fifty meters (150 feet) of the hostile fire. Attempts to disengage were made with tube artillery, TAC Air and ARA; however, the Armed Chinook was the only system which was successful in silencing the positions and disengaging the troops during the two-hour time frame in which attempts were made.

'The target area contained bunkered automatic weapons positions, tree snipers and a vegetation-covered ditch line protecting the bunker area. On the initial firing pass, the 20-mm. cannon partially uncovered the ditch line and the rockets and M-5 (40-mm. grenade launcher) gun system knocked out the main bunker. Successive runs completely uncovered the remaining portion of the ditch and disabled other bunkers. Continuous .50-caliber suppressive fires worked the tree sniper positions and the open ditch. After all forward firing weapons had been expended, a low, slow flight procedure was initiated which enabled the .50-caliber machine guns to continue to work the target as the troops and their wounded repositioned themselves. The ground commander credited the Armed Chinook with saving his unit.'

On 5 May 1967 Chinook '145' suffered a catastrophe when, during an attack, a forward mounting pin sheared and caused one of the 20mm cannons to fire upwards, destroying the rotor blades. The aircraft lost control and crashed, killing all those on board. The two remaining aircraft continued operations throughout 1967, being employed to good effect in ARA raids, road reconnaissance, convoy escort and LZ preparation. The saga of the 'Go-Go Birds' ended in February 1968 during the Tet Offensive when the 3rd Brigade of the division undertook Operation 'Hue City'. On the 22nd, '149' (by now nicknamed 'Easy Money') and '154' ('Birth Control') were flying a mission near the Citadel when '154' was hit by heavy ground fire and was forced to land near the walled city. The downed crew were

rescued by 'Easy Money', but '154' was subsequently hit by a mortar bomb and destroyed. Without another Chinook for mutual support, it was deemed unsafe for '149' to fly further combat missions. The last A/ACH-47A was returned to the 1st Aviation Brigade in April and became a crew trainer with 17th Aviation Group.

In almost two years of combat, three 'Go-Go Birds' were lost, one to hostile action and the others due to operational failures. The ACTIV submitted a favourable report on their effectiveness on operations in Vietnam; but no further versions were ordered by the Army, due primarily to the introduction of the AH-1G Cobra—which fulfilled the same basic mission—and to the fact that the CH-47 Chinook was too important as a transport for production to be diverted to the manufacture of heavy gunships.

'Snakes'—the HueyCobra

While the first batch of HueyCobras was being manufactured, the Army established the AH-1G New Equipment Training Team (NETT) at St Louis, Missouri on 1 August 1966. Subsequently assigned to the Bell Helicopter plant at Fort Worth, Texas, the AH-1G NETT familiarised themselves with the two pre-production models and the first production aircraft. Throughout the training period, NETT members were able to recommend improvements to aircraft on the assembly line, while passing on their knowledge to 300 Army personnel who were to become AH-1G instructors at Army flying schools.

With its narrow, low-drag airframe, the AH-1G HueyCobra was designed specifically as a tactical aerial armament platform capable of carrying a wide assortment of weapons to meet particular mission requirements, while incorporating many of the proven structural and dynamic components of the prior UH-1C. The principal difference lay in the rotating control system, which was modified to accept the Stability Control Augmentation System in place of the standard Bell stabilizer bar. The high degree of commonality between the AH-1G and the UH-1 series minimized the training and logistic requirements on its entry into service.

The configuration of the cockpit, with its tandem seating arrangement for the pilot and gunner, yielded an aerodynamically sleek fuselage which resulted in an armed helicopter capable of 140 knots in level flight and, when attacking targets in a shallow dive, a speed of 190 knots. The gunner was located in the forward seat and had an almost unobstructed field of view to aim and fire the turret-mounted weapon system. Early models of the AH-1G were equipped with the TAT-102A (Tactical Assault Turret) mounting a single 7.62mm M-134 Gatling-type minigun, with 8,000 rounds of ammunition. Subsequent aircraft incorporated the XM-28A1 Armament Subsystem which consisted of a power-operated chin turret mounting either one 7.62mm minigun and one 40mm M129 grenade launcher, or two of each. The system thus provided area and point fire weapons for attack on personnel and lightly armoured and unarmoured *matériel* targets. The weapons had an elevation of twenty degrees, depression of fifty degrees and traverse of 110 degrees left and right of the aircraft's longitudinal axis.

The pilot was positioned above and behind the gunner, from where he flew the helicopter, commanded the mission and fired the wing-mounted weapons or the turret in the stowed position. The short, detachable stub-wings, mounted below the transmission, provided four hard points for a variety of external stores such as XM-157, XM-158 and XM-159 rocket pods, XM-18 7.62mm minigun armament pod or XM-35 20mm automatic gun. The wings also acted to unload the rotor in high-speed forward flight to enhance manoeuvrability. Two smoke grenade launchers were mounted in the aft belly of the AH-1G, each containing six coloured smoke grenades which were ejected downwards by springs to mark targets for other helicopters. Through his control panel the pilot managed all the armament subsystems. He was able to override the gunner's controls to return the turret to the stowed position, enabling him to fire either the turret weapons, the inboard or the outboard stores in any combination including all together. As on previous systems, when rockets were launched a safety interlock interrupted the turret gun firing circuits to preclude the possibility of hitting one of them if the guns were aimed to one side.

Although its smaller size, speed and agility increased the survivability of the AH-1G, it was further protected by armour for the crew and critical components, by self-sealing fuel tanks and by the suppression of infra-red radiation. The pilot's and gunner's seats were constructed of composite armour with the back and bottom made of dual-property steel armour and the side panels of a ceramic/fibreglass composite. In addition, both crew members wore ceramic chest protectors. Composite armour weighing forty-six pounds protected the most vulnerable parts of the engine including the compressor, fuel control, oil filter and fuel filter: in total, the AH-1G incorporated 223 pounds of armour protection. If the pilot was incapacitated, the gunner had sidearm cyclic and collective controls to fly and land the aircraft.

The AH-1G HueyCobra was the first true armed helicopter capable of carrying different types and combinations of weapons to suit various mission requirements. As was the case with the earlier gunships, the HueyCobra's principal missions were escort, troop support, reconnaissance and direct fire support. On a typical mission the AH-1G could reach the target area in about half the time taken by the UH-1 gunships, and could deploy twice their firepower while remaining on station for almost three times as long.

On 28 August 1967 six AH-1G HueyCobras and their attendant NETT departed Fort Worth for Vietnam, where they were based at Bien Hoa. At 1707 hours on the 31st the AH-1G made its first flight in Vietnam, and four days later, on 4 September, its first combat sortie. Although officially on a test flight, HueyCobra '66-15263', flown by Major General George Seneff Jr., commander 1st Aviation Brigade, and CWO J.D. Thomson, received its baptism of fire when it happened upon an engagement between UH-1 gunships and an enemy force on a small island. After several firing runs by the gunships the Viet Cong attempted to flee the island in small boats. One vessel became the target for the HueyCobra and was attacked by rockets and minigun fire. The crew was later credited with the HueyCobra's first kill of the war—one sampan destroyed and four Viet Cong dead. In late September the first combat unit to be

ABOVE: *A 'Heavy Frog' UH-1C of the 'Thunder Chickens', the 195th AHC, armed with the M-5 Armament Subsystem and XM-159 rocket launchers, bombards the village of Khu Gia Vien on 31 January 1968 as the Viet Cong attack US installations near Long Binh during the Tet Offensive. (US Army/Military Review)*

equipped with the HueyCobra was the 334th Armed Helicopter Company, when 1st Platoon—the 'Playboys'—exchanged their UH-1Cs for AH-1Gs. The first official combat mission was flown on 8 October when two 'Playboy' HueyCobras, piloted by Captain Kenneth Rubin and CWO Robert Bey with gunners CWOs John Ulsh and Richard Wydur, escorted ten UH-1 slicks of the 118th AHC during a combat assault. Later that day the same aircraft destroyed four enemy bunkers and fourteen sampans.

Despite its greatly improved performance, some gunship pilots had a number of reservations about the AH-1G, most notably the lack of side gunners and the totally enclosed cockpit. On UH-1 gunships the door gunners provided protective fire to the sides and rear and, just as importantly, acted as observers to locate enemy positions and warn of hostile fire. Lacking these extra crew members, the AH-1G was more susceptible to fire from the flanks, compounded by the virtually soundproof cockpit which made it extremely difficult for the crew to determine when they were under fire until incoming rounds passed uncomfortably close or struck the aircraft. Early production HueyCobras suffered from inadequate ventilation, resulting in temperatures often over 100 degrees Fahrenheit inside the cockpit. This problem was resolved by installing an Environmental Control Unit which acted as a powerful air conditioner.

From late 1967 onwards the AH-1G began replacing the UH-1B/C to become the standard helicopter gunship in Vietnam, although 'Charlie' and 'Mike' model Hueys continued to serve until the end of the war. With the increased speed and greater agility of the AH-1G, pilots were able to refine their attack procedures. Adopting a steeper target approach dive angle and varying the target approach speed, the HueyCobra, with its narrow frontal aspect, was a much more difficult target for the enemy gunners, who sometimes did not engage it at all for fear of its tremendous firepower. Most engagements were initiated from an altitude of 1,500 feet, but the accuracy of the weapon systems permitted effective fire from as high as 4,000 feet where aircraft were far less vulnerable to ground fire.

Gunship Tactics

Armed helicopters were assigned to five types of US Army aviation units in Vietnam: Assault Helicopter Companies (nondivision), Armed Helicopter or Aerial Weapons Companies (nondivision and airmobile division), General Support Companies (infantry and airmobile division), Aerial Rocket Artillery Battalions (airmobile division), and Air Cavalry Troops (nondivision, airmobile and infantry division, armoured cavalry regiment). Non-divisional aviation assets came under the command of the 1st Aviation Brigade. Although performing most of the missions and employing similar gunship tactics to those outlined below, the rôles of aerial rocket artillery and air cavalry are discussed separately.

The task of the armed helicopter was primarily to support the ground forces, and this was achieved by four types of mission: escort, troop support, armed reconnaissance and direct fire support. Often these functions overlapped, but for the sake of simplicity the operational concept of gunships can be divided into these four

BELOW: *The gunner aims through his N8 sight as a 'Centaurs' AH-1G of D Troop, 3rd Squadron, 4th Cavalry fires rockets from its XM-159 pods in the ARA role in support of the 25th Infantry Division during an operation in 1968. (US Army)*

categories, since Army statistics reveal that they flew these missions in approximately equal proportions.

The armed helicopter was conceived to fulfil a need to escort troop lift helicopters throughout combat assault missions, and for this task the standard ratio was a fire team of two gunships to every five slicks, though this depended on the size of the formation. Similarly, a minimum of two gunships was required to escort a single-ship mission such as medical evacuation, aircraft recovery, combat resupply or search and rescue. During a combat assault the escorting gunships of the fire teams flew on each side of and close abeam the troop transports. Normally these fire teams of two aircraft each were armed with flexible machine guns (M-6, M-16, M-21) with the fire team leaders in a position to place immediate fire on the terrain beneath the lead helicopter in the slick formation. Their wingmen flew positions that enabled them to cover the body of the formation and the terrain beneath. Gunship platoon leaders generally flew to the rear of the lead fire teams so as to observe the entire formation. Also to the rear came the special weapons helicopters (M-5, XM-3, XM-159, M-22) of the aerial artillery whose rôle was direct fire support—to be discussed later.

If ground fire was received by a slick aircraft flying at low altitude, the door gunner immediately dropped a smoke grenade and communicated the location of the threat to the gunships so that suppressive fire could be applied. This was rarely done by UH-1 gunships because they had insufficient speed to catch up with the slicks later. On approach to the LZ the gunships were positioned aft and below the troop transports. Around thirty seconds before the lift crossed the LZ threshold, the escort gunships opened fire down the sides of the slicks into the LZ ahead. Usually three or four pairs of rockets were fired along each edge of the LZ and, as the lift crossed the threshold the gunships ceased rocket firing and completed the

BELOW: 'Squatter Swatter', an AH-1G of D Troop, 1st Squadron, 4th Cavalry flies over terrain devastated by B-52 'Arclight' bomb strikes during 1969. This aircraft was flown by 1/Lt Hugh Mills, who exemplified the new breed of officer and warrant officer required as helicopter gunship pilots; during two tours in Vietnam, Mills flew 3,300 hours in combat during 1,019 missions, and was shot down sixteen times. (US Army/Armor)

pass firing their flexible guns. They then climbed to a low orbit at about 500 feet AGL over the LZ, searching for enemy activity as the slicks disgorged their infantry. After the slicks had taken off, the armed escorts usually remained in the area of the LZ to provide suppressive fire cover for succeeding transports and the troops on the ground. Armed helicopters also escorted vehicle convoys, river craft and other ground elements.

Troop support embraced a host of missions in support of ground unit operations. These included reconnoitring the area of advance— often a helicopter fire team was assigned to cover the flanks of an advancing unit; sweeping for ambushes and booby traps; detecting, engaging and holding the enemy until greater firepower was brought to bear to destroy them; giving immediate fire support to a unit in contact; providing emergency medical evacuation and resupply; and providing reactive fire support to bases and installations under attack. Although reconnoitring was more suited to the capabilities of light observation helicopters, gunships were effective in screening large areas, especially semi-open terrain and where rules of engagement allowed immediate return fire, as in a 'free fire zone'.

Reconnaissance missions were divided into four categories: day visual, day sensor, night visual and night sensor. The widespread use of helicopters at low level for visual reconnaissance was an innovation of the Vietnam War. The concept was developed by Air Cavalry Troops employing light observation helicopters supported by gunships, and is discussed later. However, when such aircraft were unavailable gunships were sometimes used for this mission.

A variety of heliborne sensors for the detection of concealed enemy

BELOW: *A 'Stinger' gunship of the 116th Assault Helicopter Company circles overhead as 'Hornet' slicks of the lift platoon land infantrymen of the 2nd Battalion, 14th Infantry, 25th Infantry Division during an operation in the Hobo Woods in 1970. (US Army/Infantry)*

activity were employed in Vietnam, most of them experimental. One that did see service was the Airborne Personnel Detector (APD) or 'people sniffer', an electromechanical instrument that sensed microscopic particles suspended in the air. There were two types of 'sniffers': one was sensitive to combustion particles such as campfires, cigarettes or the burning of jungle scrub prior to cultivation, and the other to ammonia as present in human sweat, urine or faeces. A sniffer flight usually comprised a UH-1 mounting the apparatus and two escort gunships, with one closely accompanying the sniffer aircraft for immediate suppressive fire while the second remained high to control the flight and support the other two aircraft as required. Used primarily in wooded and uninhabited terrain, the device had the capability of detecting the current or recent presence of personnel in a given area, providing valuable and timely information which permitted the commitment of firepower against an elusive enemy. However, the APD could not differentiate between friendly or enemy forces or even animals, and the VC often confused the system by hanging bags of buffalo excrement in trees. Through systematic and repeated usage some units, notably the 9th Aviation Battalion, achieved considerable success with the equipment.

By and large during the Vietnam War, friendly forces controlled the land by day but 'the night belonged to Charlie'. To deny the cover of darkness to the Viet Cong, pyrotechnic flares delivered from helicopters, fixed-wing aircraft and mortars were widely used; but they suffered from the disadvantages of short burning time and the tendency to drift downwind, and their parachute suspensions created a collision hazard for aircraft in the area.

BELOW: *An AH-1G of the 334th Armed Helicopter Company flies over III CTZ on 30 March 1970. It is armed with XM-158E1 rocket pods, XM-28A1 chin turret and the XM-35 Armament Subsystem which comprised one XM-195 20mm, six-barrel rotary cannon, a shortened version of the USAF M-61A1 Vulcan gun, on the inboard station of the left stub wing. (US Army)*

In May 1965 the Helicopter Illumination System was devised by ACTIV. Originally called 'Lightning Bug' and subsequently 'Firefly', it comprised a cluster of seven C-123 Provider landing lights on a tubular framework which was clamped to the cargo tiedown rings on the deck of a UH-1. It was normally mounted in a UH-1B gunship armed with the M-16 Armament Subsystem, accompanied by two 'Heavy Hogs' with the M-5/XM-3 combination. The 1.2 million candle power lights could be adjusted from pinpoint to wide beam, and from an altitude of 900 feet provided illumination equivalent to that of a floodlit football field. Once the target was bathed in light the other gunships engaged the enemy. Contrary to expectations, the Firefly did not prove especially vulnerable. Due to the intensity of the light source, range estimation and target lead proved very difficult for the enemy and simultaneous attack by the gunships tended to discourage any ground fire. Firefly was extensively employed against VC sampan traffic on the waterways in III and IV Corps Tactical Zones. Later, it was often mounted in a UH-1D/H Huey armed with a .50 calibre machine gun, which proved to be a most effective 'sampan perforator', again accompanied by two gunships. Firefly was superseded by a Spectrolab Xenon 20,000 watt searchlight called the Nightsun FX150 which was almost five times more powerful and allowed the 'light ship' to fly at higher and therefore safer altitudes.

The need to deny the enemy freedom of movement during the hours of darkness led to the development of a variety of helicopter night sensors, which gave rise to a series of Huey 'night fighters'. The most widespread was known as 'Nighthawk'. The system comprised an AN/TVS-4 Night Observation Device (NOD) or 'starlight scope' mounted above an AN/VSS-3A Xenon searchlight with both infrared and white light capability, which equipped the M-551 Sheridan Airborne Armored Reconnaissance Vehicle. Together with an M-134 minigun, the system was fitted in a UH-1D/H which operated in conjunction with one or two gunships, flying between 500 and 1,000 feet AGL at about 50 knots with the gunships to the rear at about 1,500 feet. When the Nighthawk detected a target by means of the NOD and IR it could either illuminate the area with white light, open fire with the minigun, or both, with the accompanying gunships then firing into the minigun's tracer pattern.

The Nighthawk proved very effective in areas of sparse vegetation and along canals and waterways, especially for the interdiction of sampan supply traffic. Nighthawks were also employed as a reaction force to exploit targets acquired by ground surveillance radar such as the AN/TPS-25 in what were known as 'Night Hunter' operations. The moving target radar operated from a secure area, usually a fire support base, and when a suitable target had been sighted and plotted the Nighthawk team was alerted. The aircraft then flew to the target area, which was illuminated by artillery at the moment Nighthawk arrived at the scene. Once the enemy were located and marked by the light ship, gunships engaged them with rockets and minigun fire.

In May 1966 four UH-1C gunships equipped with low-level-light television (LLLTV)—known as the Remote Image Intensifier System—were deployed to Vietnam. Tests were undertaken between 5 June and 5 November in the Mekong Delta; but the equipment proved unreliable, and the five 'Batships' were returned to their

The shield and sword insignia on the transmission 'dog house' identifies the 'Crusaders', 187th Assault Helicopter Company, whose gun platoon was known as the 'Rat Pack'. Here, an AH-1G armed with XM-157B and XM-159C rocket launchers fires on a target (US Army/Armor)

original configuration as standard gunships. In the following year a refined version was developed by Hughes Aircraft as the AN/ASQ-132. After extensive testing in the United States, three INFANT (Iroquois Night Fighter and Night Tracker) systems were assigned to the 1st Air Cavalry Division (Airmobile) for combat evaluation in November 1969. Each INFANT comprised a UH-1H with an M-21 Armament Subsystem and the AN/ASQ-132 night vision image intensification equipment. Eventually, four INFANT platoons equipped with UH-1M Hueys were deployed to Vietnam. Another experimental system fitted to the UH-1M was the AN/AAQ-5 FLIR (Forward Looking Infra-red Fire Control System). This included a passive type infra-red sensor mounted in a stabilized gimbal on the nose which presented a television type picture of the viewed image (based on the thermal radiation characteristics of both target and background) on monitors to the pilot, co-pilot and rear seat observer. As with INFANT, FLIR was integrated with the M-21 Armament Subsystem and both enabled the helicopter crews to detect, identify and direct fire upon ground targets at night.

With the introduction of the AH-1G HueyCobra similar night fighting equipment was developed under the ENSURE (Expedited Non-Standard Urgent Requirement for Equipment) programme. CONFICS (Cobra Night Fire Control System) utilized a LLLTV system for target acquisition and fire control of the AH-1G's armament during night operations. It was integrated with the optical sighting station of the XM-28A1 Armament Subsystem by means of a monitor for use by the gunner but not the pilot. Operations at night were possible in light levels equivalent to overcast starlight. The final and most sophisticated system was SMASH (South-east Asia Multi-Sensor Armament Subsystem for HueyCobra), which comprised a modified AH-1G helicopter with an AN/APQ-137 Moving Target Indicator Radar in a pod attached to the outboard right wing hard point, and a Sighting Station Passive Infra-red, AN/AAQ-5, mounted on the nose of the aircraft. These sensor systems provided the helicopter crew with the capability of detection, identification and attack of ground targets during night search and destroy missions. Both CONFICS and SMASH were deployed only on an experimental basis. Furthermore, the effectiveness of the Huey night fighters was compromised because the noise of the helicopters warned the NVA/VC of their approach and afforded them time to seek cover.

Direct Fire Support was one of the most important attack helicopter missions and was undertaken to support friendly forces who were in contact with the enemy. Comparable in concept to Close Air Support provided by fixed-wing aircraft, direct fire support differed in that attack helicopter ordnance was delivered considerably closer to friendly units. By day, the rule of thumb was machine gun fire at fifty yards under normal circumstances and twenty-five in an emergency; rockets at seventy and forty yards respectively, and 40mm grenades at sixty and forty—whereas for fixed-wing aircraft the rule was one yard for every pound of ordnance, e.g. a 250 pound bomb would be dropped 250 yards from friendly troops. At night ranges were increased by two-thirds, but again, in an emergency, fire could be brought to bear as close as the ground commander deemed fit. Since sixty per cent of all ground engagements were within 100 yards, the importance of attack helicopter direct fire support becomes self-evident; indeed, many strafing runs of UH-1 and AH-1 attack helicopters were delivered as close as ten yards. Such close fire support was all the more important because the enemy often employed 'hugging' tactics to place themselves near to allied ground forces at ranges too close for the effective use of heavy weapons, such as cannon artillery and airstrikes.

A request for armed helicopters could be initiated down to any level including the squad. It was forwarded to the battalion TOC (Tactical Operations Center) and, after appraisal, to the brigade where, if approved, the mission was relayed to any armed helicopters under its control. Once notified, the gunships were 'scrambled' and the time taken for them to become airborne was typically between two and seven minutes, the average being four and a half minutes. While airborne *en route* to the target area the fire team leader contacted the unit, advised them of his arrival time, and in turn was briefed on the tactical situation. To preclude flying through friendly artillery fires the fire team leader radioed the AWCC (Artillery Warning Control Center) and was informed of any artillery barrages which could affect the flight path. By day, the majority of gunship pilots flew around, over or under artillery so as not to compromise the fire plan; but at night they invariably interrupted artillery fires, since it was extremely difficult to confirm the exact location of the aircraft in relation to the artillery gun target line during darkness. The average time from the airfield to the target area was usually fifteen to twenty minutes and, if friendly artillery was firing on the target at the time the aircraft arrived, the fire team leader normally requested it to cease to give the gunships more freedom to manoeuvre.

In daylight the device most often used by friendly forces in contact to indicate their position was the smoke grenade. As the gunships arrived on station the ground elements released their smoke without stipulating its colour. The fire team leader then identified the colour, by which means the enemy was precluded from releasing similar-coloured smoke grenades and confusing the situation. During darkness units used a variety of means including strobe lights and flares.

The most usual method of indicating the target was by means of a

clock code giving the distance and direction from a common point, such as the smoke grenade or a prominent topographical feature. However, the target could not be engaged until the dispositions of the friendly forces on the ground, including their front lines, flanks and those of adjoining units, had been positively identified. This vital requirement was one of the primary factors contributing to long orbit times prior to target engagement which, in difficult terrain, could take as long as twenty minutes, but on average took around nine minutes: the majority of the times recorded were seven minutes or less. Once the friendly unit was located, the gunships' fire was adjusted in the same manner as artillery fire using the target's relationship either to a known point, to the gun target line or to the observer target line. The adjustment time was from the firing of the first ordnance until the target was engaged with effective fire: this averaged one and a half minutes, while some adjustments were as fast as thirty seconds and others as long as ten minutes.

Direct fire support was also employed to supplement artillery and fixed-wing fire plans during landing zone preparations for air combat assaults. As indicated previously, artillery and TAC air ended their fire plans approximately one minute before the troop lift helicopters crossed the LZ threshold. During the next thirty seconds rocket-firing helicopters (not the transport escort gunships) struck in and around the LZ, at points not eliminated by TAC air or artillery and at likely enemy locations or possible targets. This saturation fire was intended to detonate mines and booby traps and to suppress the area in general. The gunships fired approximately fifty per cent of their ordnance in this thirty-second pass, and then climbed to an orbit about 1,500 feet above the LZ to cover the landings. The continuous application of fire support from artillery, TAC air and gunships was designed to keep the VC/NVA from the immediate vicinity for a sufficient period to allow the lift transports to land, disembark troops and take off before the enemy could take up defensive positions, many of which would have been destroyed in the process.

'Gun Run'—An Attack Helicopter Firing Pass

The factors pertaining to an attack helicopter firing pass included the covering patterns flown prior to engagement, the firing run itself, and the disengagement or 'break' manoeuvre to leave the target area. Normally, specific attack patterns were not pre-planned but certain considerations applied to all of them. The flight leader adjusted each attack to take advantage of the terrain and weather, to exploit enemy weaknesses and to employ his combat elements to the maximum advantage. Important considerations included the number of attack helicopters, target characteristics, helicopter weapons capabilities, friendly forces in the immediate area, the dispositions of enemy defences and the immediate tactical situation.

The description of a typical 'gun run' which follows applies to an AH-1G on a 'Hunter-Killer' mission in conjunction with a 'Loach', an OH-6A Light Observation Helicopter. In this example the AH-1G Snake was armed with thirty-eight 2.75 in. FFAR (two XM-159 rocket pods), 4,000 rounds of 7.62mm ammunition and 300 40mm grenades.

The AH-1G flew large orbits in a covering pattern around the low reconnaissance helicopter at an altitude out of small arms range. The speed of a gunship in a covering pattern ranged from thirty to ninety knots. By increasing airspeed the gunship reduced its vulnerability to ground fire, especially when flying a regular orbit which aided observation of the 'low bird'. However, higher speeds increased the time it took to align the aircraft with the target and thus the Loach's exposure to enemy fire. On the other hand, at low speeds, due to its low forward flight speed and predictable flight path, the gunship became more vulnerable to ground fire, especially from enemy anti-aircraft weapons. A compromise was therefore sought between response time, smoothness of flight and safety. Orbit speeds were most commonly between sixty and seventy knots. When taken under fire, the Loach marked the target with a smoke grenade and left the area. On receiving the Loach's call that it was taking fire, the Snake dropped its nose and rolled into a dive. Most gun runs in daylight were initiated between 1,500 and 2,000 feet AGL, though on certain escort and night missions lower altitudes were adopted. Attack dive angles were classified as shallow (five to ten degrees), medium (ten to twenty degrees), and steep (twenty to thirty degrees). Steep dive angles were commonly used for point targets while shallow dive angles were more suited for area fire. In general, pilots used a steeper attack angle when firing rockets than firing guns. An attack from normal altitudes was rarely made at over forty-five degrees, because the high speed of the dive reduced the time to fire at the target and induced the helicopter to overfly the target, which greatly increased its vulnerability to enemy fire.

On achieving rough alignment with the target, the Snake released the first pair of 2.75 in. rockets to distract enemy gunners from the Loach. The speed of the gunship in a firing run depended on its orbit speed. With an initial speed of sixty knots, the Snake achieved 120 knots at the break, which in a typical firing run of 1,000 yards allowed a firing time of 21.5 seconds. A firing run was commonly initiated at a slant range of 2,000 yards with the break occurring before the 500 yard mark, and at an altitude of 500 feet AGL to keep the gunship

ABOVE RIGHT: *The classic scout helicopter of the Vietnam War was the OH-6A Cayuse whose universal nickname of 'Loach' derived from its official designation as a Light Observation Helicopter or LOH. Here, an OH-6A of the 11th Armored Cavalry Regiment stands by for its next mission as the eyes and ears of the formation commander. (John Graber)*

BELOW RIGHT: *An OH-13G Sioux (nicknamed 'Possum' by the Australians) of 161 (Independent) Reconnaissance Flight lands the CO of the 1st Battalion, 5th Royal Australian Regiment at FSB 'Polly' on 9 August 1969. Used primarily for command and control, the Possums performed a variety of tasks within IATF including reconnaissance, navigational assistance to units operating in difficult terrain, radio relay and artillery adjustment, as well as emergency resupply or casualty evacuation. (US Army)*

beyond the range of most enemy small arms and automatic weapons ground fire and to avoid overflying the target. During a firing run the Snake did not attempt to achieve maximum speed because this reduced firing time on the target. Full power was only used in flying to the target area and in returning to altitude to initiate another gun run.

In a typical firing pass, six rockets in three pairs were fired into the target area, followed by a 4.58-second discharge of 40mm grenades (thirty-one rounds at 400 rounds per minute), and finally a 2.76-second burst of 7.62mm minigun fire (184 rounds at 4,000 rounds per minute). With the ordnance load described above, this allowed six rocket passes, ten grenade passes and twenty-one minigun passes. This number of passes was considered reasonable for a typical contact and, assuming no gun jams or rocket 'hang-ups', a light fire team of two gunships could make twelve firing passes on a target. The rate of firing obviously depended on the nature of the situation: in a light contact or when it was necessary to conserve ammunition, ordnance was 'dribbled out' with one or two pairs of rockets per pass; in a typical firefight three to four pairs were fired, and in a heavy contact five to seven pairs, with a corresponding higher rate of 40mm grenade and minigun fire. For saturation fire the ARA fired as many as thirty pairs of rockets per pass.

When flying in support of troops in contact one other cardinal rule of attack helicopter employment applied, in that gunships avoided attacking over the heads of friendly units. Since the enemy was often on line when deliberately opposing friendly ground forces, it was inadvisable to attack over the latter's heads because this was to fly into the cone of fire of the greatest number of enemy weapons. Furthermore, such an approach did not effectively employ the beaten zone of the helicopter's armament against the long axis of the enemy positions. Finally, cartridge cases and expended rocket caps falling on the heads of friendly units were most disconcerting if not actually dangerous, and could be mistaken by unseasoned troops for incoming fire.

As in all flying operations in Vietnam, weather was a constant consideration and constraint. Customarily, gunship pilots desired at least a minimum ceiling and visibility of 1,000 feet and one mile respectively; however, if the need arose, pilots flew in far worse conditions. On critical missions, such as Dust Off and emergency resupply, pilots flew with a 100-foot ceiling and a half-mile visibility. At night, flying conditions were commensurately more difficult.

Air Cavalry

Air cavalry operations in Vietnam added a new dimension to land warfare. Originally deployed as a component of the airmobile division in September 1965, air cavalry squadrons and troops eventually supported every division and major formation serving in RVN. With their variety of helicopters, air cavalry provided ground commanders with heretofore unattainable capabilities for reconnoitring large expanses of terrain, locating fleeting enemy targets and destroying them by bringing overwhelming firepower to bear, either

The original OH-13Es deployed to Vietnam in 1962 with the 8th and 57th Transportation Companies were returned to the US without seeing action. In September 1965 the OH-13S arrived with the 1st Cavalry Division (Airmobile) and saw extensive service as a scout helicopter prior to the introduction of the OH-6A. During the first two years of operations, scout helicopters flew over 500,000 sorties and were a significant factor in the development of Air Cavalry tactics. Here, an OH-13S alights on a landing pad hacked out of the jungle. (Tim Page)

from their own assets or those of the parent organization. Against a cunning and elusive enemy good intelligence was paramount, and the air cavalry troops became the eyes and ears of the formation commander. 1st Squadron, 9th Cavalry (Aerial Reconnaissance) of 1st Cavalry Division (Airmobile) was the first air cavalry unit in Vietnam, and it initiated the majority of engagements fought by the division, from its first major action at Plei Me on 1 November 1965 during the Ia Drang campaign until the division departed Vietnam after 2,056 days overseas. The stated doctrine of the First of the Ninth Cav. was: 'The primary rôle of the air cavalry troop is to find and fix the enemy for its supported unit. In this process, the troop is frequently able to kill or capture and destroy enemy facilities. Large areas can be swiftly and easily reconnoitered using the troop organic aero scout and aero weapons platoons, allowing the manoeuver element commander to place the preponderance of his force in other critical areas.'

One air cavalry troop was integral to the armoured cavalry squadron of the infantry division and to the armoured cavalry regiment, and three to the air cavalry squadron of the airmobile division; several separate air cavalry troops also served with the 1st Aviation Brigade. Each troop consisted of three tactical platoons: an aero scout platoon equipped with nine light observation helicopters, an aero rifle platoon with six UH-1D/H utility helicopters, and an aero weapons platoon with nine attack helicopters. The platoons were divided into teams, each with a colour code to denote its function. Thus, a 'white team' comprised two armed light observation helicopters—originally OH-13S Sioux and OH-23G Raven, then OH-6A Cayuse, and finally, on a limited scale, OH-58A

BELOW: *With a maximum capacity of five passengers, this Loach is being crammed with female Vietnamese detainees on 18 June 1969 during Operation 'Dirty Devil' in Hau Hghia Province. First deployed to Vietnam on 15 February 1967, there were 591 Loaches in the country by the time of this operation. (US Army)*

Kiowa. These helicopters shared similar characteristics in that they were small, agile, highly manoeuvrable, made low maintenance demands, had good crash survivability, and were relatively inexpensive. The last two features were of considerable consequence because the rôle of the aero scout was one of the most hazardous of all flying duties in Vietnam, only equalled by that of Dust Off pilots. During 1969 the pilots of the aero scout platoon of Troop D, 1st Squadron, 4th Cavalry, with a complement of fifteen, suffered thirty-two killed or wounded in action, and this level of casualties was not exceptional.

The OH-6A Cayuse, nicknamed the 'Loach' from the initials LOH of Light Observation Helicopter, was the principal scout helicopter employed in Vietnam. It was armed with the XM-27 Armament Subsystem comprising an M-134 minigun with 2,000 rounds of ammunition. With the system installed passenger space was reduced, and the crew comprised a pilot and an observer with a Colt CAR-15 rifle or M-60 machine gun for protection and smoke grenades to mark targets. White teams of two Loaches were usually only employed for reconnaissance in areas where significant contact with the enemy was not expected as they lacked sufficient firepower for self-defence. One aircraft flew low to attain close visual reconnaissance, while the other remained at altitude to provide cover and navigation and to act as a radio relay for information gleaned by the 'low bird'. In support of ground troop operations, white teams screened the front and flanks of units and assisted navigation by plotting their current dispositions in jungle or difficult terrain. They also directed airstrikes, adjusted artillery and naval gunfire support, and maintained radio contact between friendly forces as well as assisting fire control between units.

The 'blue team' was used to complement the aerial reconnaissance capabilities of the air cavalry troop by providing an infantry rapid reaction force to exploit any situation that developed on the ground. The 'blues' of the Aero Rifle Platoon, or ARP, were employed on a variety of missions; but with an average insertion strength of thirty personnel carried in the integral UH-1D/H helicopters of the lift platoon, timely reinforcement was essential, and a rifle company from one of the battalions in the area was usually designated as a 'ready reaction force'. One platoon was on immediate call to be flown in by the six ARP Hueys if contact was established, while the other two platoons remained on standby to be employed if necessary. Typical tasks for the 'blues' included ground reconnaissance, reinforcement of Ranger patrols in contact, the securing of downed aircraft, and many others.

A 'red team' consisted of a pair of attack helicopters of the aero weapons platoon which provided the principal firepower of the troop. It was strictly an offensive weapon used for direct fire support, aerial rocket artillery raids, and artillery fire during operations beyond the range of ground-based cannon artillery. More often than not an attack helicopter of a red team was combined with a Loach of a white team—this pair, through the mixture of colours, being known as a 'pink team'. Pink teams were the basic tool of the air cavalry troop and were used extensively by all air cavalry units throughout Vietnam, although methods of employment differed between squadrons and even among troops within each squadron. Pink teams

ABOVE: *'Bravo Blues'*
disembark from 'Darlin' Jenny
II', a UH-1D of B Troop, 1st
Squadron, 9th Cavalry of the
1st Cavalry Division
(Airmobile) on 24 April 1967
during Operation 'Oregon' in
Quang Ngai Province. (US
Army)

were devised as a means of providing armed cover to the vulnerable Loach and the capability to exploit immediately any situation encountered by the observation helicopters.

Used primarily in the economy-of-force rôle, a pink team was normally employed on visual reconnaissance missions, known as 'Hunter-Killer'. Additional pink teams could be employed as required by the size of the area of operations to be covered and the extent of enemy activity therein. These missions were more effective in unpopulated areas where signs of activity were more likely to be enemy and where reconnaissance by fire was permissible. Such missions were often generated by other less positive forms of intelligence such as agent reports, SLAR, Red Haze and other airborne sensors. Even so, visual reconnaissance by pink teams was the most effective technique devised for finding and fixing the enemy in Vietnam. Through its use, large portions of an area of operations were searched daily to determine enemy presence.

The normal method of operation of the pink team was for the Loach to fly at reduced speed and altitude to detect signs of enemy activity. Normally it flew at sixty to eighty knots when entering an area. Subsequent passes were made more deliberately at twenty to thirty knots, followed by a careful yard by yard search of suspicious areas. Even in dense vegetation, Loaches were able to locate enemy positions. Once the enemy was detected, often by the Loach being fired upon, the target was marked by a smoke grenade and the aero scout moved out of the vicinity while the gunship dived to attack. If the location appeared productive, the aero rifle platoon was inserted to investigate while the Loach screened escape routes and the gunship provided fire support, augmented by other pink teams if necessary. If heavy contact was made or conditions warranted it, the

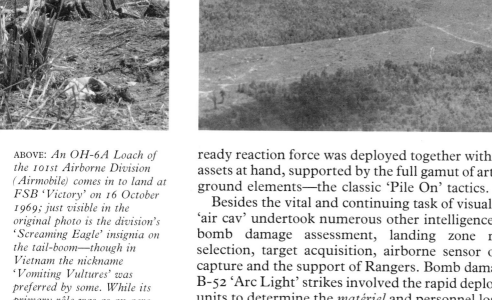

ready reaction force was deployed together with any other airmobile assets at hand, supported by the full gamut of artillery, airstrikes and ground elements—the classic 'Pile On' tactics.

Besides the vital and continuing task of visual reconnaissance, the 'air cav' undertook numerous other intelligence missions including bomb damage assessment, landing zone reconnaissance and selection, target acquisition, airborne sensor operations, prisoner capture and the support of Rangers. Bomb damage assessment after B-52 'Arc Light' strikes involved the rapid deployment of air cavalry units to determine the *matériel* and personnel losses inflicted, and to capture any demoralised and shell-shocked enemy forces caught in the blast. LZ reconnaissance and selection entailed finding and mapping suitable sites for airmobile operations, and the insertion of Pathfinders to mark an LZ for following helicopters. Target acquisition involved the location of targets for supporting arms such as TAC air, artillery and gunships, as well as patrolling the vicinity of base areas alert for mortar and rocket flashes from enemy weapons so that immediate counter-battery fire (known as Quick Fire) could be initiated to destroy them. The capture of prisoners, or 'body snatch', was a special operation to apprehend suspected enemy personnel, often employing the aero rifle platoon to accomplish the task while aero scouts screened the area and gunships provided armed cover. Rangers (formerly Long Range Reconnaissance Patrols) operated within each division and separate brigade area. These specialized troops were qualified for airborne operations and trained to rappel from helicopters into difficult terrain. Air cavalry frequently supported Rangers with Hueys for insertion and extraction, command and control, and the aero rifle platoon as a reaction force, while gunships provided direct fire support.

Aerial Rocket Artillery

ABOVE: *A 'white team' of three OH-6A Loaches lands in a rice paddy to confer with ARVN Special Forces (LLDB). The left-hand Loach is fitted with the XM-27 Armament Subsystem comprising a single M-134 minigun and 2,000 rounds of ammunition. (Tim Page)*

One of the major innovations of the airmobile division was the incorporation of an aerial rocket artillery battalion within divisional artillery. Commonly referred to as 'ARA', two such battalions served in Vietnam: 2nd Battalion, 20th Artillery (Aerial Rocket)—known as 'Blue Max' or simply '2/20th'—with the 1st Cavalry Division (Airmobile); and 4th Battalion, 77th Artillery (Aerial Rocket) with the 101st Airborne Division (Airmobile). Each battalion comprised a headquarters and service battery of three UH-1B/C gunships—subsequently, UH-1D/H—for reconnaissance and command and control; and three ARA batteries (A, B and C) which were each organized into three platoons, each of two sections. A section comprised a fire team of two aircraft, UH-1B/C and from late 1968 AH-1G. Within each firing battery, four gunships were armed originally with the M-22 Armament Subsystem and the remainder with XM-3 rocket launchers; but after the introduction of the AH-1G the gunships were equipped with four XM-159 nineteen-tube 2.75 in. FFAR rocket pods, although they were often unable to carry the full complement of seventy-six rockets because of maximum gross weight limitations when operating in the higher reaches of Vietnam.

Aerial Rocket Artillery was employed to provide aerial fire support to manoeuvre forces throughout an area of operations, and was assigned any of the standard tactical missions for field artillery. It was especially effective in support of airmobile forces beyond the range of cannon artillery. The four basic missions of ARA were direct fire support (forty-seven per cent); preplanned fire missions, for instance LZ preparation (thirty per cent); reconnaissance (seventeen per cent); and escort (six per cent). The battalion was under operational control of the division artillery and each ARA battery was commonly coupled with one of the three divisional direct support artillery battalions, with platoons or sections located at fire support bases throughout the area of operations for maximum effectiveness and speed of response. The latter was the hallmark of the ARA, since each battery maintained at least one section on twenty-four hour alert with crews remaining close to their combat-loaded gunships.

When a fire mission was received, crews on alert were scrambled and another section assumed the same status. Scramble times were commonly one to three minutes, with ninety-six per cent of missions 'off the pad' within two and a half minutes—as compared to five minutes for standard armed helicopters. Because of their forward location in many instances, *en route* flying times averaged only eleven minutes. Once over the target area the ARA section checked or shifted artillery fire, located friendly units and identified the target—a period known as 'on station time', which for the ARA averaged five minutes and for standard armed helicopters, nine. This achieved, the ARA gunship fired two rockets on its initial pass and received corrections from the forward observer to move the burst onto the target. All adjusting volleys consisted of two rockets until the target was struck and the ARA then fired for effect with a full salvo. This period was known as the 'adjustment time', and for the ARA averaged three minutes as against one and a half for other gunships. Thus, the total response time for a fire mission for the ARA was twenty-three to twenty-four minutes, as compared to thirty-two to thirty-seven for other armed helicopters.

5 DUST OFF – US ARMY HELICOPTER AMBULANCES IN VIETNAM

'The Originals'—57th Medical Detachment (Helicopter Ambulance)

In support of the increasing numbers of US military personnel in Vietnam, the 8th Field Hospital was established at Nha Trang in April 1962 to provide a full range of medical services. Later in the same month the hospital was augmented by the arrival of the 57th Medical Detachment (Helicopter Ambulance) comprising five HU-1A Iroquois helicopters: the first of a long line of Hueys to see service in Vietnam. However, although alleviating the logistics problem of overcrowded Saigon 200 miles to the south-west, the 57th's location at Nha Trang placed medical support far from most of the US military units then in-country. On 8 May the 57th flew its first mission to evacuate from Tuy Hoa a US Army adviser suffering from a high fever.

Under the command of Captain John Temperelli Jr., the 57th spent most of the summer sitting in Nha Trang with little to do: it was unable to support the US personnel fighting far to the south, while they, in consequence, did not appreciate the capabilities of the new unit. The problem was compounded by the lack of replacement parts for the newly arrived Hueys and, by August, two of the five were out of commission because the 57th had no spare rotor blades. The situation was exacerbated by the demands of other aviation units for the 57th's few remaining parts. During November a major air assault codenamed Operation 'Boondodge' was launched into War Zone D, and the Hueys of the 57th were cannibalized for tail rotor gearboxes and starter generators to keep the armed Hueys of UTTHCO flying. With the promise that these vital parts would be returned, the 57th reluctantly agreed to the arrangement; but only one ever was, and the unit was totally grounded from 17 November to 15 December. Its integrity was further compromised by political machinations when suggestions were made to remove the red crosses from the helicopters and assign them general support duties under the command of the Army Transportation Corps.

All in all, the Year of the Tiger was not an auspicious start for the 57th; but the Battle of Ap Bac in January 1963 was to alter the situation dramatically. The high casualties incurred persuaded Army commanders that the helicopter ambulances might be better employed nearer the fighting, and on 30 January the 57th was deployed to Tan Son Nhut airport in Saigon with its one flyable aircraft. During February command of the unit passed to Major Lloyd Spencer, and in the following month the last of its grounded UH-1As was replaced by five new UH-1Bs. On 23 March 1963 the 57th declared itself fully operational again, but the requirement to provide medical evacuation throughout South Vietnam with only

ABOVE RIGHT: 'The Originals', the name adopted by the 57th Medical Detachment (Helicopter Ambulance), adorns the nose of this UH-1H on stand-by at Camp Blackhorse of the 11th Armored Cavalry Regiment in 1969. With a personnel rescue hoist fitted, the 'Hotel' model Huey was the definitive medical evacuation helicopter employed in Vietnam. (John Graber)

BELOW RIGHT: One of the first Hueys in Vietnam, an HU-1A of the 57th Medical Detachment (Helicopter Ambulance) takes off during a mission in 1962. Originally based at Nha Trang, far from the major fighting in the Delta, the 57th was under-used at first, evacuating only twelve American and fourteen ARVN personnel in its first two months of operations. By 1967 helicopter ambulances were evacuating 5,000 casualties a month. (US Army/Aviation Digest)

five helicopters was a daunting task. To achieve this objective, two machines were despatched to Pleiku in the Highlands; subsequently one of these moved to Qui Nhon to provide wider coverage of II Corps Tactical Zone, while the three in Saigon covered III and IV Corps Zones.

With its assets spread so thinly, the 57th still worked without any sort of tactical call sign beyond the basic 'Army' and the tail serial number of the aircraft. Similarly, the unit communicated internally on any vacant radio frequency it could find. Major Spencer decided that this situation was unsatisfactory, and paid a visit to the Navy Support Activity in Saigon, which controlled all the callsigns used in Vietnam. Most of them, such as 'Bandit', 'Avenger' or 'Dragon', were more suited to assault units; but one, 'Dust Off', caught his eye, since it epitomized the conditions of a helicopter pick-up in the dry and dusty countryside. By adopting the call sign 'Dust Off', the 57th not only achieved unit recognition and therefore a more defined status, but also introduced into the lexicon of military jargon a new phrase that became synonymous with all aeromedical evacuation units in Vietnam—and which, indeed, has survived the war.

'Mad Man' Kelly and the Birth of a Tradition

Following the annual rotation of personnel in January 1964 the 57th was commanded by Major Charles Kelly, an officer who, by his actions and valour, was to set an example that Dust Off pilots tried to emulate for the remainder of the war. It also earned him the nickname of due respect—'Mad Man' Kelly. On 1 March 1964 the two aircraft operating in II CTZ were recalled to the south and, as Detachment A, 57th Medical Detachment (Helicopter Ambulance), Provisional, operated from the airfield at Soc Trang. The number of evacuees

RIGHT: *A wounded ARVN soldier who stepped on a mine during an operation in the Plain of Reeds, west of Saigon, is carried to a UH-1B of the 57th Medical Detachment (Helicopter Ambulance) on 18 May 1963. (US Army)*

ABOVE: *Troopers of Company C, 2nd Battalion, 8th Cavalry, 1st Air Cavalry Division (Airmobile) load a wounded companion on to a UH-1D 'Medevac' helicopter of the Air Ambulance Platoon at Plei Me during the Battle of Ia Drang Valley on 4 November 1965. (US Army)*

immediately increased by over 100 per cent, from 193 to 416 in that month. Living in crude huts and bunkers, Detachment A was joined by Major Kelly who chose flying rather than ground duty in Saigon, where the rest of the 57th struggled along with air conditioning, private baths and a bar, although most of the pilots preferred Soc Trang. Soon the 57th was receiving more than enough requests to keep all of them busy in their ageing UH-1Bs, which had clocked up an average flight time of over 800 hours each. The pilots themselves flew excessive hours, and some stopped logging their flight time at 140 hours so that the flight surgeon would not ground them for exceeding the monthly ceiling.

Night flying became standard and, in April 1964, the detachment flew 110 hours at night while evacuating ninety-nine casualties. During one such mission, Major Kelly heard on the radio that a VNAF T-28 Trojan had been forced down and, after joining the search, he soon located the aircraft. As he circled the area the Viet Cong opened fire, and one round passed through the open cargo door, slamming into the cabin roof. Unruffled, Kelly landed beside the T-28, taking fire from all sides. Once on the ground, he and two crew members jumped out and engaged the Viet Cong with sub-machine gun fire as they rescued the VNAF pilot. The helicopter left the area without further damage. The major and his Dust Off crew flew more than 500 miles that day.

For Kelly this was not exceptional, and when further pressure was applied for the 57th to place removable red crosses on its aircraft and accept general purpose assignments, his characteristic response was to seek more missions. He himself flew around IV CTZ almost every night on a circuit of 450 miles, calling in at several bases to evacuate casualties who otherwise would have to wait until daylight for treatment. Known as 'scarfing', the stratagem worked—the monthly totals of evacuees rose, and there were no further demands for the 57th to be anything else but a medical evacuation unit.

Night or day, fine weather or foul, Kelly allowed nothing—not even enemy fire—to thwart his determination to evacuate casualties. On one mission fire was so intense that he was forced away, only to return within the hour and shoot a landing through the fusillade. Indifferent to its red crosses, the Viet Cong unleashed a barrage of rifle, machine gun and mortar fire on the hapless helicopter while the crew chief and medical corpsman loaded the wounded. One round struck the main fuel drain valve, and Kelly took off with the aircraft spewing JP-4. Losing fuel rapidly, he radioed the Soc Trang tower for a priority landing. With emergency vehicles at the ready, the tower operator enquired whether anything else was required. Kelly replied, 'Yes, bring me some ice cream.' Moments after landing the engine spluttered and died, the fuel tanks empty. The base commander drove up and handed Kelly a carton of ice cream. The casualties were safe.

Apart from the Viet Cong, the 57th's principal problem was a shortage of pilots. The Aviation Branch had assigned some newly qualified Medical Service Corps pilots to non-medical helicopter units in Vietnam. Thus, as the fighting intensified in the Mekong Delta, the unit could not respond to every evacuation request. In consequence, other helicopter companies were obliged to maintain some of their aircraft on a stand-by basis for medical evacuation, but without the benefit of a medical corpsman or specialized equipment. With no immediate prospect of new aviators from the United States, Kelly and his Dust Off pilots continued to fly round the clock and to fulfil as many missions as humanly possible.

BELOW: *A casualty injured during Operation 'Cedar Falls', is carried from a UH-1D of the 283rd Medical Detachment (Helicopter Ambulance) on 12 January 1967. Note the hoist fitted in the cabin doorway. (USAF)*

On the morning of 1 July 1964 the major received a call from an ARVN unit in contact near Vinh Long. An American adviser and several infantrymen were injured. Kelly and his crew flew to the area, where the fighting continued unabated as the helicopter came to a hover. As Kelly floated the aircraft back and forth searching for the casualties the Viet Cong turned their fire on the helicopter. One adviser radioed Kelly to clear out of the area, but he replied calmly, 'When I have your wounded'. The helicopter was hit repeatedly before one round passed through the open door and struck Kelly in the heart. He murmured, 'My God', and died; the helicopter pitched out of control and crashed. Shaken but not seriously injured, the rest of the crew crawled from the wreckage, pulling Kelly's body with them. They and the other casualties were later evacuated by their Dust Off companions. Major Kelly was posthumously awarded the Distinguished Service Cross and the South Vietnamese conferred on him several decorations for gallantry. More important than the medals he earned was his legacy to the Dust Off pilots who followed. It ensured that the Kelly ethos, that the wounded must be saved above all else, was to endure until the end of the war.

Escalation

As US involvement in Vietnam mounted, five more helicopter ambulance units were alerted for assignment to South-East Asia. The 82nd Medical Detachment (Helicopter Ambulance) arrived in Saigon on 5 October 1964, and became operational on 7 November from the base at Soc Trang. With the influx of new pilots and aircraft it was no longer necessary to fly looking for casualties, and the system became formalized to a degree whereby Dust Off acquired its own radio frequency over which American advisers could call or relay their mission requests directly to the helicopter ambulance units via FM radio.

The arrival of the 1st Cavalry Division (Airmobile) in September 1965 heralded the deployment of a new type of medical evacuation

ABOVE: *In an emergency, any helicopter could be used for medical evacuation. Here, a UH-1D of the 'Black Cats', the 282nd Assault Helicopter Company operating from Marble Mountain, comes in to pick up wounded and dead of 3rd Battalion, 4th Marines after an ambush on 18 May 1967 during Operation 'Hickory'. Unlike Dust Off Hueys, however, standard helicopters did not have the benefit of trained medical personnel on board. (USMC)*

unit—the air ambulance platoon. As part of the division's 15th Medical Battalion, this comprised twelve UH-1D Hueys with a medical evacuation section of eight helicopters and a crash rescue section of four, three of which were equipped with Kaman 'Sputnik' fire suppression systems to enable firefighters to enter burning aircraft. Unfortunately, with the system fitted and a full crew of two pilots, two firemen, a crew chief and a medical corpsman, the helicopter could not take off in the Central Highlands unless the fuel tanks were drained to 400 pounds or less, which reduced its range to an unacceptable degree. Accordingly, the system was abandoned and the crash rescue aircraft reverted to standard helicopter ambulances.

The platoon adopted the callsign 'Medevac', and was soon heavily involved in the Battle of the Ia Drang Valley. Of its twelve aircraft, one was destroyed on 10 October, four were usually undergoing maintenance, two were required for base coverage at An Khe and two supported Republic of Korea (ROK) forces on the coast, leaving only three helicopters to support the nearly 3,000 men of the division's 3rd Brigade during Operation 'Silver Bayonet' in the Ia Drang. The

average number of casualties was seventy to eighty per day, with 280 on the worst. The unit was hard pressed to meet such a commitment and, on occasions, troop lift ships were employed to carry the less seriously injured casualties from the landing zones. In the first three months of operations the platoon lost two pilots killed, one crew member wounded and nine helicopters shot up by enemy action.

During this period two more Medical Detachments (Helicopter Ambulance), the 254th and 283rd, were deployed to Vietnam, as well as another new type of medical evacuation unit, the 498th Medical Company (Air Ambulance). With twenty-five UH-1Ds, the latter unit was based at Nha Trang to cover operations in II CTZ with separate platoons at Qui Nhon, Pleiku and Ban Me Thout. Although this provided excellent medical evacuation for the tactical combat units, it posed considerable command and maintenance problems; but the system proved workable, and the 498th was soon in the thick of the fighting. On 11 November one helicopter flew from Qui Nhon to evacuate a wounded ROK soldier. As he was being loaded aboard, the enemy opened fire on the helicopter and the pilot was shot through the neck. The co-pilot grabbed the controls and, just as the NVA were about to surround the aircraft, he pulled pitch with no regard for the torque meter, making a low-level take-off straight through the enemy soldiers while the crew chief leaned out of the cargo door and clubbed them with his M-14 rifle. The helicopter successfully returned to Qui Nhon where the pilot received emergency treatment. His life was saved.

By 1967 there were sixty-four helicopter ambulances operating in RVN but, with the massive influx of troops as the war escalated, the theatre required at least 120 to provide adequate coverage. Throughout the year more medical evacuation units were deployed, including the 54th MDHA at Chu Lai to support the 'Americal' Division; the 159th MDHA at Cu Chi to support the 25th Infantry Division; the 571st MDHA joined the 254th at Nha Trang; and the 50th MDHA was based at Phu Hiep to support the 173rd Airborne Brigade and the other units operating in the south of II CTZ. By the end of the year US troop strength in RVN had reached half a million, and most of the medical evacuation units that would serve in Vietnam had been deployed. The Dust Off system had been proven in battle and the Kelly tradition prevailed. To the troops in a cruel and frustrating war, one certainty remained: if wounded, they knew that a Dust Off helicopter would fly through thick and thin to evacuate them rapidly to hospital for immediate medical treatment. In many cases a casualty was on the operating table within an hour of being wounded.

'Contact! Stand-by Dust Off'

One of the basic design specifications for the Bell UH-1 was the requirement by the Aviation Section of the Surgeon General's Office for the Army's utility helicopter to carry at least four litter cases; hence the Huey had a maximum width of ninety-eight-and-a-half inches to accommodate stretchers sideways. However, the -A and -B model Hueys often lacked sufficient power to perform their

139

evacuation rôle in the heat and high altitudes of South Vietnam. Even the UH-1D, with its more powerful engine and longer rotor blades, lacked the lifting power necessary in the high density altitudes encountered in the northern part of the country and in the Central Highlands, where the 498th Medical Company and the Air Ambulance Platoon of the 1st Cavalry Division (Airmobile) operated. The problem was only resolved with the introduction of the UH-1H, the first of which arrived with the 45th Medical Company (Air Ambulance) in July 1967. Its Avco-Lycoming T-53-L-13 engine was rated at 1,400shp, as against the 1,100 shp of the L-11 in the UH-1D, while consuming ten per cent less fuel; this enabled the 'Hotel' model to lift five casualties by means of a hoist. Thus, on a normal ninety-five-degrees Fahrenheit day in the western Highlands, a UH-1H hovering out of ground effect could lift 1,063 pounds, while the UH-1D could manage only 184 pounds or—possibly—a single casualty.

From the outset of operations in Vietnam, many medical evacuation missions were compromised by the helicopter's inability to get to the site of the casualties because of the nature of the terrain. This was especially evident in dense jungle where the wounded had to be carried long distances to open ground, or else a landing pad had to be laboriously hacked out of the trees. In either case the delay in providing treatment for the casualties could prove fatal. A solution was found in fitting a 'personnel rescue hoist' in the cabin doorway of the Huey. Fitted to the end of the hoist cable were several types of rescue devices, the most common being the 'jungle penetrator'. Developed by the Kaman Corporation, the penetrator was lowered through the jungle canopy and the casualty was strapped on to its folding extensions. For the seriously wounded a rigid wire basket, the 'Stokes litter', was substituted. On 17 May 1966 the electric hoist was first used in Vietnam, and the 'jungle penetrator' in the following month. Although this system proved successful and many lives were saved, a hovering Dust Off helicopter presented an easy target to enemy gunners and a hoist mission was always the most dangerous to perform.

The fundamental purpose of the helicopter ambulance was to bring the combat casualty from the battlefield to the operating table in the shortest possible time. Dust Off helicopters were tasked with either 'area support' to cover all allied units in a defined region, or 'direct support' to cover a particular unit during a specific operation. The majority of medical evacuation missions arose during area support. Missions were received either in flight, at the unit base, or at a stand-by area usually near the headquarters of the formation supported. Precise information had to be given to the Dust Off crew to effect evacuation, such as co-ordinates of location, nature and number of wounded, the tactical security of the Pickup Zone, *et al*. Casualties were classified as either 'urgent', 'priority' or 'routine'. 'Urgent' demanded immediate response from any helicopter ambulance in order to save life or limb, while 'priority' were those casualties who had serious but not critical wounds and were likely to remain stable for up to four hours. In practice many casualties were understandably overclassified as 'urgent'. Similarly, the security of the PZ was often exaggerated by ground units anxious to evacuate their casualties.

The Dust Off aircraft commander had to consider all these factors as the PZ was approached while the pilot in the right-hand seat flew the helicopter. All flights were undertaken with two pilots in the cockpit, both to aid navigation and to enable one to take over the controls if the other was incapacitated. During a hoist mission the pilots alternated at the controls every five minutes to keep the helicopter in a hover. The other crew members were the crew chief who maintained the aircraft, and the medical corpsmen who provided emergency first aid in flight. At the PZ, the latter two loaded the casualties or, if the hoist was used, one operated the winch while the other stood in the opposite door to suppress enemy fire and inform the pilot of hazardous obstacles nearby.

Once airborne with the casualties, the corpsman identified the most serious patient, applied first aid and reported the nature of his wounds to the aircraft commander. He in turn radioed the local medical regulating officer, who advised him of the nearest hospital with the necessary surgical capability to deal with the condition. Since most pick-ups were made within range of a surgical, field or evacuation hospital the helicopter ambulances usually bypassed the battalion aid and division clearing stations, which could offer little better emergency treatment than that available in the helicopter, and flew directly to whatever facility offered the most appropriate medical care. Although the less seriously injured casualties were often evacuated too far back, the practice saved thousands of wounded who required immediate life-saving surgery.

These, then, were the basics of a routine medical evacuation mission; but the reality was often different, as the following recollections by Alfred Nichols graphically portray. Formerly a pilot with the 82nd Medical Detachment (Helicopter Ambulance), he also served with the Special Forces for five years; for his valour in this mission Nichols was awarded the Silver Star. On 8 January 1968 he and his crew were sipping cold drinks at Dong Tam hospital, and

RIGHT: *Perched on the helipad of an ATC(H) 'Tango boat', a UH-1D of the 45th Medical Company (Helicopter Ambulance) evacuates casualties from a US Navy Monitor of River Assault Flotilla One during a Mobile Riverine Force operation in the Mekong Delta on 12 August 1967. The wounded soldier on the cabin floor is lying in a 'Stokes litter' which was used in conjunction with the hoist to extract the seriously injured from areas where the Dust Off was unable to land. (US Navy)*

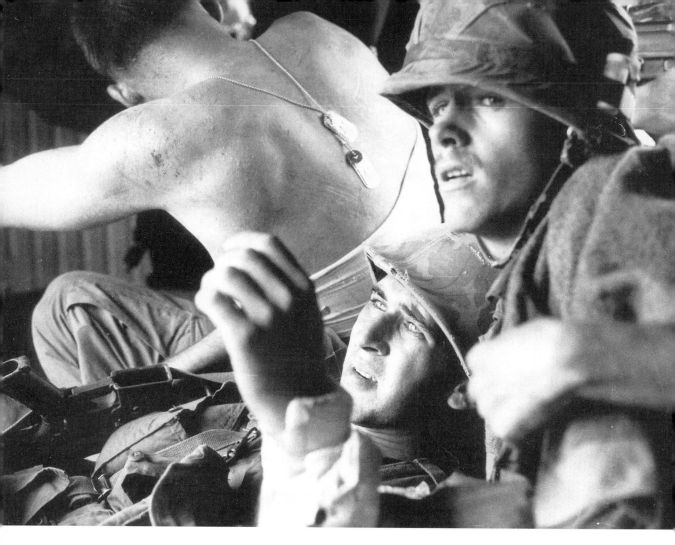

ABOVE: *Marine casualties undergoing the terror of a 'hot LZ' south of Da Nang; the medevac helicopter, trying to fly them to the safety of 'Charlie med', was fired on by NVA machine guns on 1 September 1967. (USMC)*

joking about their last evacuation mission in support of an ARVN unit, during which they had purloined a Thompson sub-machine gun:

'Our laughter stopped when the RTO from operations rushed in. We had another mission. We had to pick up six wounded 9th Division infantrymen in the rice paddies north-east of the city, between Dong Tam and Tan Tru, about fifteen minutes away. The area had been called in as secure.

'We scrambled out the door and were airborne in about four minutes. As we neared the area, I tried to call the platoon with the wounded on the FM radio. I could only get the company's commander. The company was about 500 or 600 meters from the platoon and they'd lost contact with it, the CO told us, "But I can throw smoke and direct you".

'We spotted his smoke and began our approach to a paddy along tree line. Suddenly the CO yelled, "Stop! You're flying into the enemy's position!"

'We were already receiving automatic-weapons fire, and mortars and grenades were exploding on the ground where we'd be touching down. The CO had given us the direction for our approach, but he was about 180 degrees off. I broke off the approach and got the hell out, climbing to about 2,000 feet so we could survey our damage. We'd been hit several times. A funny "swoosh-swoosh" noise indicated that our blades had been hit and the smell of fuel meant that our fuel cells had been hit as well. I called, "Mayday", on the guard radio frequency, giving our location.

'A new voice came up on our radio. It was the platoon leader. "We're pinned down", he said. "Everyone's wounded or dead. Whenever we try to move the VC start shooting. They're in the L-shaped tree line and we're about 75 to 100 meters away in the paddy. We'll try to give you as much fire support as we can and we'll try to throw smoke."

'Just then a Sting Ray gun ship team came up on our channel, telling us they were working the area: "We have you spotted and we'll give you one gun run over the enemy position." [Stingray was B Company, 9th Aviation Battalion 'Condor'.]

'The four of us had a quick conference. We'd give it one more try. The Sting Rays made their gun run, placing machine gun and rocket fire on the enemy position. The platoon leader threw smoke to mark the pick-up position. "You're going to die on this one", I told myself, "but you've got to try to do it." Having made up my mind, a feeling of calm washed over me. The decision had been made and my fate determined. I knew that the other crew members felt the same way. We'd all do our best until we went down. We started our approach.

'The Sting Rays, their gun run over, told us, "Go in, Dust Off. The area's secure." Having used up their ammo, they had to turn back to refuel and re-arm. They received no hostile fire as they left. We were on our own.

'As the ground rose to meet our prop wash, we could see the wounded scattered about across a seventy-five-yard area. Fifty yards short of touch-down all hell broke loose. Automatic weapons fire from the tree line hit us from the left and rear of the Huey.

'The other three were returning fire from the door and window as I brought us down. We could plainly see crouching black-clad figures firing at us from among the trees. The medic and crew chief, who was standing on the skid, jumped out.

'Several of the wounded infantrymen dived into the open door. I heard the dull thud of bullets hitting them while they were scrambling aboard. Bullets zipped and ricocheted through the pilot compartment but I kept control of our bird. All this time, Robbie was firing out the left window at the muzzle flashes. His M-3 grease gun jammed just as the crew chief shouted, "I'm hit!" Shot through the legs, he sprawled on the ground. Robbie threw his M-3 out the window, jerked open the left pilot's door and ran back to the crew chief. He dragged him inside with the other wounded, and jumped back into his seat, yelling, "Take off!"

'But I'd seen another wounded GI in front of us. He was on his knees, screaming, "Don't leave me!" and clawing at the air. Blood was running from the corner of his mouth and it covered his chest. Robbie saw him too. He darted out into the crossfire and picked up the wounded man, shoving him in the back with the others, before he jumped back aboard.

'I knew it was time for us to take off. We'd been on the ground for about two hour-long minutes. But try as I might, the collective would not move. I had to yell because our communications system was shot out.

'"Robbie!" I screamed, "The skid's stuck in the mud. Help me with the controls!" He helped me to pull, yelling, "We've lost our

hydraulics too." Then we concentrated on pulling on the collective power controls and I manipulated the pilot's cyclic controls. We were getting airborne—after a fashion.

'We wallowed and bounced through the air, getting translational lift. Our full load of wounded kept up a steady stream of fire out the doors, as we plowed our way through banana and coconut trees, knocking out the lower chin bubble on the way up.

'Our hydraulics were gone, and the radios and intercom were shot out. All the gauges looked inoperative and the engine and transmission warning lights were lit up like a Christmas tree. Robbie told me to head for Tan Son Nhut airport. We could make a running landing there.

'I motioned to the fuel gauge. It showed we had only 250 pounds of fuel. We'd just gone in with 850 pounds. If we could trust the gauge, we were losing fuel fast and only had a few minutes to fly.

'Someone screamed behind me. I jerked around in my seat. The soldier with the chest wound had rolled out of the open door and was hanging half in and half out. The medic had grabbed him by the arms but the soldier was so weak he couldn't pull himself up. Another soldier reached over and together they got him back in.

'"We've got to put down!" I yelled to Robbie, and pointed to a paved road below us. We'd moved about four miles away from the enemy contact. He nodded. "Do you want to take over?" I asked. He flashed a determined, confident grin in reply and signalled for me to keep the controls.

'We made a long shallow approach to the road, passing over an ARVN outpost, and landed about a mile away. We hit the road and slid about 150 feet in a straight line, still upright.

'As we stopped, Robbie jumped into the back to help the wounded and I ran to our front to set up security. I spotted a Vietnamese coming down the road at us on a motorcycle, and fired a warning burst up in the air from my M-16. With ten wounded and a disabled helicopter I didn't want anybody around us except Americans. He stopped and turned, heading back down the road.

'Within five minutes several ARVN vehicles pulled up. Their American adviser was with them. They set up a defensive perimeter for us. A few minutes later, a slick ship from the Greyhounds [240th AHC] and two Dust Off choppers that had heard our "Mayday" landed and loaded the wounded aboard. As I walked past the right side of my helicopter to board the rescue craft, I saw the blood. The red cross painted on the cargo door was streaked pink and red from where the soldier had been hanging.

'Going back I rode in the right "hell hole" (the right passenger seats up against the transmission compartment facing outward) with the platoon leader I'd just rescued. He had been shot along the side and I could see his rib.

'"All of my radio men were shot", he told me. "I had to crawl to a radio to reach you. It was awful. Every time one of us moved, the VC shot us. I thought I was going to die until I heard 'Dust Off' on the radio."

'I smiled at that: about the time he was feeling good again, we'd been sure we were going to die.

'The rescue 'copter landed at the hospital pad at Dong Tam. I walked beside the stretcher carrying our brave crew chief into the triage area. He grinned up at me. "Keep the Thompson", he said. "I won't be needing it in the hospital."

'I turned, dragging myself back to the pad to check the rest of the crew. A young soldier approached me and asked, "Sir, will I be court-martialled?"

'Confused and tired, I just stared at him for a minute before I thought to ask, "What did you do?"

'"Sir, I got on your helicopter when you landed to pick up the wounded back there. I'm not wounded."

'I chuckled to myself and spoke gently. "No, you won't be court-martialled. Son, did you really think we'd leave you there by yourself?" I think he was the only person in his unit who wasn't wounded or killed. All of the wounded we'd carried out made it, even the soldier with the chest wound. There were about ten or eleven of them.

'I looked at my watch when I walked back into the club. I'd been gone about an hour. I began to shake. Fear had finally caught up with me. My thumb and forefinger were throbbing—I must have sprained them while I tried to hold the helicopter steady during that last emergency landing. It was weird. I'd started the afternoon having a Coke in an air-conditioned club with an American radio and TV. Then we'd moved out into Indian country, come under heavy fire, been shot down and taken our own wounded. I'd flown a severely damaged aircraft out of a hot LZ with a full load of wounded and crash-landed. Now I was back at the same table drinking another Coke.

'I was to have another eight months of this bizarre life. My comrades were other Dust Off crews, gun drivers, slick-ship pilots, scouts and bird dog pilots. During this time, thirty-eight more 82nd Medical Detachment aircraft were hit. I was flying eight of them. I was forced down twice more by enemy fire and once by aircraft equipment failure. We lost nearly all of our aircraft when the 1968 Tet offensive began. But I remember that afternoon best. For what we'd done, the four of us were awarded Silver Stars.'

The Tradition Upheld

During the Tet Offensive in 1968 the helicopter ambulance units suffered severe losses in both men and machines. Across the length and breadth of the country, the Dust Off system had to deal with thousands of casualties; and it was not found wanting. The techniques of aeromedical evacuation had been honed to a perfect edge, but Dust Off flying remained a highly dangerous mission. Although pilot error and mechanical failure accounted for more aircraft and crew losses in Vietnam than did enemy fire, Dust Off pilots were more concerned about the latter than any other danger. For helicopter ambulances the rate of loss to hostile fire was 3.3 times that of all other types of helicopter missions in the Vietnam War. When compared to non-medical helicopters on combat sorties, it was still 1.5 times as high; only aero scout units suffered comparable losses. Approximately 1,400 Army personnel served as helicopter ambulance pilots during the war, of whom about forty were killed and 180 wounded by hostile fire, while a further forty-eight were killed and 200 injured as a result of other crashes. Consequently, almost a third of Dust Off aviators became casualties, as did the crew-chiefs and medics who flew with them.

In accordance with the Geneva Convention, helicopter ambulances did not carry arms or ammunition at the outset of the Vietnam War, but the enemy showed no compunction in firing on aircraft clearly marked with red crosses. Accordingly, crews soon carried personal sidearms and sometimes M-79 grenade launchers for self-protection. With the advent of hoist missions the helicopter ambulances became even more vulnerable, since they had to remain in a high hover for minutes on end; and the rate of aircraft losses and crew casualties grew alarmingly. Gunship escorts were increasingly sought for such missions, but they remained hard to obtain throughout the war. Some units responded to the danger by carrying a fifth crew member as gunner with an M-16 rifle. Only the Air Ambulance Platoon of the 1st Cavalry Division (Airmobile) went so far as to mount M-60 machine guns on their aircraft.

None of these measures reduced the loss rate dramatically, but they did prevent it from reaching a prohibitive level. Late in the war a scheme was devised whereby helicopter ambulances were painted white overall to make them more distinctive. At the same time, ten million leaflets were dropped over enemy-occupied territory explaining that the unarmed helicopters were solely employed for medical evacuation of both friend and foe. The test programme for white helicopters began on 1 October 1971 and continued until the following April, but the result was inconclusive. However, since there was no marked increase in the loss rate, the remaining helicopter ambulances in RVN were painted white and retained their prominent red crosses.

At the height of American involvement in the Vietnam War there were 140 helicopter ambulances operating in the country. In March 1969 the number of US troops reached its peak, and thereafter the gradual withdrawal began. Nevertheless, the courage displayed by Dust Off pilots was undiminished, few examples being more striking than that of CW3 Michael J. Novosel, a pilot of the 82nd Medical Detachment (Helicopter Ambulance).

In 1964 Novosel had forsaken a safe and lucrative career as an airline pilot to fly Army helicopters in Vietnam. Forty-eight years old and a father of four, Novosel served two tours of duty in Vietnam, and evacuated 5,500 casualties. On his second tour he was joined by his son, Michael Jr., who evacuated a further 2,500 casualties, giving a family total of 8,000. Four times a day he had to apply medication to his eyes to treat glaucoma, a condition which the Army waived to allow him to fly a Dust Off helicopter once again. Standing only five foot four and weighing less than 150 pounds, he hardly presented the image of the stereotypical military hero; but he possessed greater qualities, as this official account of a remarkable action reveals:

'On the morning of 2 October 1969 the right flank of a three-company ARVN force came under intense fire as it moved into an enemy training ground right on the Cambodian border in the Delta province of Kien Tuong. During the next six hours US Air Force tactical support and Army gunships tried several times to enable the stranded soldiers to escape. Most of the uninjured soldiers managed to retreat some two thousand meters south, but others, finding their retreat blocked by high waters in swamps and rice paddies, could not get out. Several who had been wounded lay scattered about where they had been hit, near a group of bunkers and two forts used by the enemy in training exercises for simulated attacks on South Vietnamese installations.

'In the mid-afternoon a US Army command-and-control helicopter above the battleground radioed for a Dust Off ship. Operations control of the 82nd Detachment relayed the request to Dust Off 88, whose aircraft commander, Mr. Novosel, and pilot, WO1 Tyrone Chamberlain, had already flown seven hours of missions that day. The crew chief was Sp4c. Joseph Horvath and the medical corpsman was Sp4c. Herbert Heinold. Novosel immediately headed toward the border. Since the wounded ARVN soldiers did not show themselves on his first two hotly contested approaches to the area, Novosel

RIGHT: *Clutching the hoist, the crew chief of a UH-1H of the 237th Medical Detachment (Helicopter Ambulance) leans out to warn the pilot of overhanging branches during a mission on 16 October 1969. (US Army)*

RIGHT: *A medical corpsman of the 45th Medical Company (Helicopter Ambulance) tends two soldiers wounded by mortar fragments at FSB 'Mace' as the 'Long Binh Dust Off' helicopter prepares to lift off. (US Army)*

circled at a safer range to signal the wounded to prepare for an evacuation. Finally one soldier had the nerve to stand up in the elephant grass and wave his shirt overhead. Novosel dropped his ship into the area again and skidded along the ground toward him. The crew scooped up the soldier and took off.

'After that, by ones and by twos, the ARVN soldiers waved to the circling helicopter that continued to draw enemy fire. Four soldiers stood up, and Dust Off 88 picked them all up on one approach. Enemy machine guns killed at least one other soldier as he signaled. At 1730, Dust Off 88 dropped the first load of casualties off at the Special Forces camp at Moc Hoa, refuelled, and headed back to the fray. While Chamberlain monitored the instruments and tried to spot the casualties, Horvath and Heinold hung out both sides of the aircraft on the skids, grabbing people when they could and pulling them inside the ship. Where elephant grass was so tall that it prevented landing, Horvath and Heinold hung onto litter straps to reach far enough down to grab the men below.

'During the second series of lifts, while Novosel hovered at a safe range, Air Force F-100's roared down on the enemy, dropping 500 pound bombs and firing 20mm cannon. But when Dust Off 88 went back in for the wounded, enemy fire was still extremely intense.

'The second group of ARVN soldiers were seriously wounded. One had a hand blown apart; another had lost part of his intestines; another was shot in the nose and mouth. As soon as the ship left the area for Moc Hoa, Heinold began tending the more seriously injured, applying basic lifesaving first aid to make sure the wounded were breathing and that the bleeding was momentarily staunched. During the fifteen-minute flight back he also managed to start intravenous injections on those he thought were low on blood or going into shock.

'Although the enemy fire knocked out the VHF radio and airspeed indicator early in the mission, Novosel continued to fly. At least six times enemy fire forced him out of the area. Each time he came back in from another direction, searching for gaps in the enemy's fixed field of fire from the fort and numerous bunkers. Between his three trips to the area Novosel used his craft to guide the withdrawal of stragglers around the swamps and rice paddies.

'On the last of his trips, with dusk approaching, a pair of AH-1G Cobra gunships gave the helicopter some covering fire. At 1900, when nine casualties were already on board, Horvath told Novosel that a man close to the bunker was waving at them. Suspecting that something was awry, Novosel told his crew to stay low in the ship while he hovered backwards towards the man, putting as much of the airframe as possible between the bunker and his men. As soon as the soldier was close enough, Horvath grabbed his hand and started pulling him into the ship. Before he could get him in, an enemy soldier stood up in the grass about thirty feet in front of the ship. He opened fire with his AK47, aiming directly at Novosel. Bullets passed on either side of him. One deflected off the sole of his shoe, and plexiglass fragments from the windshield hit his right hand. Shrapnel and plexiglass buried in his right calf and thigh. Both in pain and disgust, and to warn the co-pilot, Novosel shouted, "Aw hell, I'm hit." The aircraft momentarily went out of control and leaped sixty feet into the air. The ARVN soldier Horvath had been pulling aboard slipped off the ship, but Horvath kept his grip and pulled him back in.

LEFT: *A wounded paratrooper of 1st Battalion, 506th Infantry (Airmobile), is helped aboard an 'Eagle Dust Off' UH-1H of the 326th Medical Battalion during a 'Screaming Eagles' operation in 1969. (US Army)*

As he did so, he fell backwards on some of the men already there and cut his neck on their equipment. Chamberlain got on the aircraft controls with Novosel and they flew back to Moc Hoa. They shut down the engine, unloaded the wounded, and inspected their ship. Despite several hits to the rotor system and the cockpit, the aircraft could fly. The crew returned to Binh Thuy, ending their work after eleven hours in the air. They had evacuated twenty-nine wounded ARVN soldiers, only one of whom died. For this, Novosel was awarded the Medal of Honor.'

As the withdrawal of US troops continued, a programme was set up to form a VNAF Dust Off service under the process known as 'Vietnamization'; however, it did not reach fruition until March 1971. In the same month the Dust Off system faced its severest test of the whole war during the incursion into Laos. LAM SON 719, the ARVN operation to disrupt the Ho Chi Minh Trail, was launched across the border on 8 February 1971 with massive US air support but no American ground troops. For security reasons medical planners remained unaware of the impending operation until the last few days in January. Because of the minimal resistance expected the initial predictions were for low ARVN casualties, which led to a local shortage of helicopter ambulances. The principal units assigned to the operation were the 237th and 571st MDHA, together with the Air Ambulance Platoon of the 101st Airborne Division (Airmobile), which was known as 'Eagle Dust Off'. Since no US advisers accompanied the ARVN ground troops into Laos, all medical evacuation missions across the border had to have an ARVN interpreter on the aircraft.

At first the operation proceeded according to plan but, as the weather deteriorated and enemy resistance stiffened, the advance faltered and air operations became more difficult. Once the extent of the enemy anti-aircraft defences was realized, all medical evacuation missions required a gunship escort, which led to considerable delays in response time. As the ARVN penetrated deeper into Laos the anti-aircraft fire and indirect fire on landing zones became ever more intense. Many of the weapons were radar-controlled, and Dust Off pilots monitoring their VHF radios came to recognize the 'wheep, wheep' of the radar sweeps which warned them to take evasive action. On the ground the situation went from bad to worse, and finally to débâcle. According to the after-action report of the 61st Medical Battalion: 'During the last phase of Operation LAM SON 719 enemy activity further intensified. Landing zones were dangerously insecure. Air Ambulances landing to pick up wounded were swarmed with fit and able soldiers seeking a way out of their increasingly precarious position. Medical evacuation pilots reported complete lack of discipline during the last few days of the operation, coupled with extremely hazardous conditions.' One Eagle Dust Off Huey, a UH-1H with a normal complement of eleven passengers, landed for a pick-up but had to take off almost immediately because of intense small arms and mortar fire in the landing zone. On its return to Khe Sanh thirty-two ARVN soldiers disembarked, all without weapons or equipment but only one of whom was wounded. In disgust, some crews resorted to coating the landing skids with grease to prevent ARVN soldiers from scrounging a ride to the rear on the sides of their helicopters.

Nevertheless, Dust Off saved hundreds of lives and, in the two-month operation, flew some 1,400 missions to evacuate 4,200 patients. Ten helicopter ambulances were destroyed, which represented almost ten per cent of the helicopters lost during LAM SON 719. Six crewmen were killed and fourteen wounded. For Dust Off pilots this was, thankfully, the last major operation of the war. By early 1972 the number of helicopter ambulances had decreased to thirty; and in February 1973, following the ceasefire, three of the last four Dust Off detachments departed—only the 57th remained. On 11 March it flew the last Dust Off mission in Vietnam for an appendicitis case. Between 12 May 1962 and 11 March 1973, Dust Off helicopters carried almost 900,000 patients, of whom US military personnel constituted about forty-five per cent. Of the US Army's 120,000 personnel wounded in action, approximately ninety per cent were delivered to a medical facility by helicopter ambulance. The speed of response of the Dust Off system was such that the percentage of deaths among wounded admitted to hospital was 2.6 in Vietnam, whereas it was 4.5 during World War 2. Remarkable as these statistics are, it was the soldier on the ground who mattered; and his confidence that, if he was wounded, he would soon be picked up by Dust Off made an immeasurable contribution to troop morale.

BELOW: *In early 1971, a VNAF Dust Off service was formed employing the Hueys of departing US helicopter ambulance units. It served until late in the war but, such was the declining morale of the RVNAF in the final battles, some casualties were only evacuated if they had sufficient funds, preferably in US currency. Here ARVN wounded from the camp at Dak Pek, astride Route 14, are unloaded at a hospital in Pleiku following the NVA attack of 12 May 1974. (US Army/Aviation News)*

6 US NAVY HELICOPTERS IN VIETNAM

'Angels of Yankee Station'

At the time of the Tonkin Gulf incident in August 1964, the aircraft carrier groups of 'Task Force 77' of the US Navy's Seventh Fleet, operating on 'Yankee Station' in the Gulf of Tonkin and on 'Dixie Station' off the shores of South Vietnam, employed a variety of helicopters ranging from the ageing Piasecki HUP-3 (UH-25C) Retriever to the recently introduced Kaman UH-2 Seasprite. The helicopters undertook numerous tasks including reconnaissance, communications, electronic support missions, mine-sweeping, anti-submarine operations, supply, ship-to-shore transport, casualty evacuation, and search and rescue (SAR). Most Navy helicopters were capable of fulfilling several of these rôles but they were employed mainly for one duty or another, such as the Boeing-Vertol UH-46 Sea Knight based aboard Fast Combat Support Ships for 'vertical replenishment' of supplies to ships at sea. Similarly, the Sikorsky SH-3 Sea King was designed primarily for anti-submarine warfare and mine counter-measures but, because these did not pose significant threats in the Vietnam theatre, it was used for general support duties. On the other hand, the Kaman UH-2 Seasprite was conceived as an all-weather, multi-rôle, utility helicopter for a wide range of missions but its principal rôle in Vietnam became search and rescue, both as a 'planeguard' to retrieve the crews of carrier aircraft that crashed on launch or recovery, and for the rescue of crews downed at sea or over enemy territory.

As the air war over Vietnam escalated in 1965 with the advent of 'Rolling Thunder', the latter mission grew in importance in order to reduce the number of aircrews being captured and to sustain their morale in the face of the prospect of an enforced sojourn at the 'Hanoi Hilton' if shot down. In the bombing campaign the mission of Navy attack aircraft was punitive raids or 'Alpha strikes' against North Vietnamese targets, predominantly in the coastal regions and subsequently around Hanoi and the port of Haiphong in the heavily defended area known as 'Route Package 6'. With the expansion of the North Vietnamese air defences after the introduction of Soviet surface-to-air missiles (SAM-2) and the proliferation of anti-aircraft artillery guns, as well as fighter aircraft (MiG-15, -17 and -21), so losses increased; and the Navy formed a Search and Rescue system utilizing Grumman HU-16 Albatross amphibious aircraft, rescue helicopters, and A-1 Skyraiders for escort. Two SAR stations were established to the north and south of the Gulf of Tonkin, and the first overland rescue of a Navy pilot from North Vietnam by a Navy helicopter occurred on 20 September 1965. The principal helicopters for this mission were the UH-2 Seasprite, nicknamed 'Angel', and the SH-3 Sea King. In May 1966 an armed and armoured version of

ABOVE: *A US Navy UH-46A Sea Knight lifts supplies from the USNS* Sacramento *to the carrier USS* Hancock *(CVA19) during a 'vertical replenishment' mission on Yankee Station in 1967. (Boeing-Vertol Helicopters)*

the latter, known as 'Big Mother' and specially configured for SAR, was deployed to 'Yankee Station'. Subsequently, a number of Seasprites were similarly converted to what became the HH-2C variant for rescue missions in hostile areas.

Despite these measures for self-defence the helicopters, either UH-2 or SH-3, were usually escorted by A-1 Skyraiders to provide suppression of enemy ground fire; later A-4 Skyhawks or A-7 Corsairs were used, although the A-1 'Spads' were better suited to the task because of their slow speed, long loiter time and heavy ordnance load. During 'Alpha strikes' the rescue teams remained airborne near the coast and along the flight paths of the returning formations so that any aircrew struggling 'to go feet wet' in a damaged aircraft could 'punch out' over the sea and be rescued as soon as possible. At the same time, the teams were close at hand for immediate rescue missions of aircrew shot down in North Vietnam. It soon became evident that speed of response was vital, because an aircrew's chances of evading capture in the densely populated areas of Route Package 6 diminished rapidly after a period of thirty minutes or so.

One of the most dramatic and intrepid rescue missions of the war took place on 19 June 1968 when an F-4B Phantom II of VF-33 from the USS *America* (CVA-66) was struck by a SAM-2 shortly after midnight. The pilot, Lieutenant Commander John Holtzclaw, and his RIO, Lieutenant Commander John Burns, ejected from the flaming aircraft and landed in a rice paddy field between two villages

south of Hanoi and some twenty miles from the coast. Following standard escape and evasion procedure to seek high ground, they made their way to a nearby hill where dense vegetation promised concealment, their 'beeper' survival radios transmitting a distress signal. The rescue mission was initiated from the southern SAR when 'Clementine 2', a UH-2A Seasprite, lifted off the deck of the destroyer USS *Preble* (DLG-15). The crew comprised pilot Lieutenant Clyde Lassen, co-pilot Lieutenant (Junior Grade) Clarence Cook and crewmen Petty Officers Bruce Dallas and Donald West.

'For the first hour', recalls Commander Holtzclaw, 'we heard no airplanes overhead. We made our way up the hill to an extremely dense section of jungle, where we first heard the sounds of airplanes. We used our walkie-talkies and were told Clementine 2 was on the way to get us. Lieutenant Commander Burns and I tried to find a clear area on the hillside for pick-up, but couldn't find one.'

When Clementine 2 approached the area, two surface-to-air missiles streaked past the helicopter followed by a hail of automatic weapons fire. The burning wreckage of the Phantom was soon spotted and the location of the aircrew was established from their 'beepers' at approximately three miles distance. A landing was attempted in a rice paddy field at the foot of the hill where the pilots were hiding, but intense small arms fire forced the helicopter to take off and orbit the area. Meanwhile, other rescue aircraft had arrived and began dropping flares.

Lieutenant Lassen states, 'The survivors were between two large trees about 150 feet apart and other fairly tall trees were also in the area, but I decided that by the light of the flares I'd try to pick them up from the hillside.' As the Seasprite came to hover among the trees Petty Officer Dallas lowered the hoist; but at that moment the flares burnt out, plunging the area into darkness and leaving the pilot with no visual ground reference.

'Dallas yelled that we were going to hit a tree', Lieutenant Lassen continues. 'I added power and was just starting a climb when I hit it. The jolt was terrific. The helo pitched nose down and went into a tight starboard turn. Then I told the rescue aircraft orbiting overhead that we had struck a tree and were experiencing fairly heavy vibration. We requested more flares and were told that no more were available but some were on the way. Also, I told the survivors that they would have to get down off that hill and into the clearing.' In the rear cabin, PO Dallas had problems in recovering the rescue sling. 'I started retracting the hoist as fast as possible', he recollects, 'and in the process the helo hit a tree on the right side. I was leaning out of the open door at the time and I was hit in the face as the tree went by. As soon as the limb hit me I yelled "Get up! Get up!"—and we were out of there and climbing. Nothing but Mr Lassen's skill and experience saved us from crashing.'

The collision damaged the horizontal stabilizer, the tail rotor, the radio antenna and the door, which caused the helicopter to vibrate violently. Undeterred, Lassen made repeated passes over the area while Dallas and Cook fired at the muzzle flashes below. In the darkness of the jungle-covered hillside Holtzclaw and Burns, the latter hampered by a sprained ankle and an injured knee as a result of aircraft ejection, stumbled downhill toward the paddy field below. As they reached open ground Lassen attempted another landing, but once again enemy fire forced the helicopter to lift off and orbit the area. On the third approach yet another SAM narrowly missed the Seasprite, but Lassen continued down despite the enemy fire and brought the aircraft to a hover with its wheels just touching the soft paddyfield. With its spotlight illuminating the ground, the helicopter hung there for three minutes while Holtzclaw and Burns frantically stumbled across the many dikes criss-crossing the rice paddy. Manning the doorway machine guns, Dallas and Cook returned the

ABOVE: *A crewman fires a 'free 60' from the cabin doorway of a UH-1B of Detachment Three as a 2.75in. FFAR is discharged from the XM-158 rocket pod of the M-16 Armament Subsystem. The hand-held M-60 machine guns were often fired upside down so that the cartridge cases were ejected into the cabin and not into the slipstream where they could hit the tail rotor. Known as 'brassing', the damage incurred by the tail rotor blades presented a serious problem because there was, at times, an acute shortage of spares in HA(L)-3. (US Navy)*

enemy fire which was lashing the helicopter from three sides, and managed to keep the encircling enemy forces at bay until the exhausted survivors clambered aboard.

The damaged and vibrating helicopter immediately lifted off and headed for the sea; it had been overland for fifty-six minutes and under fire for forty-five. Nearing the coast, the Seasprite came under fire again and during evasive manoeuvres the damaged door was torn off. Once over the sea the helicopter was not yet out of danger because its fuel reserves were critically low. With every spare radio in Task Force 77 tuned into the unfolding drama, Clementine 2 finally landed aboard the USS *Jouett* (DLG-29) with only five minutes of fuel remaining. For his conspicuous gallantry, Lieutenant Clyde Lassen was awarded the Medal of Honor.

'The Seawolves'—Helicopter Attack (Light) Squadron Three

After airbases had been established in RVN, the US Air Force assumed the responsibility for tactical air support in South Vietnam, and the need for aircraft carrier groups on 'Dixie Station' diminished. Accordingly, they moved north to expand air operations from the Gulf of Tonkin. However, this was not the end of the US Navy's involvement in the fighting in South Vietnam.

Throughout the war the VC/NVA made extensive use of junks and coastal shipping to reinforce the insurgents with men and supplies. In early 1965 the Navy was tasked with the interdiction of enemy infiltration from the sea. Originally codenamed 'Market Place' under the control of Task Force 71 of the Seventh Fleet, the operation was transferred to the US Naval Command in Saigon on 1 August 1965 and redesignated as Task Force 115 Coastal Surveillance Force. The Navy, augmented by the United States Coast Guard, employed a wide variety of patrol vessels for the mission, now called Operation 'Market Time'. As operational experience grew so the need arose to extend the area of interdiction to the numerous inland waterways and canals of the Mekong Delta and the Rung Sat Special Zone—a tract of dense mangrove swamps alongside which the Saigon River flowed to the capital, and a VC stronghold of long standing. On 18 December 1965 Task Force 116 River Patrol Force was established to deny the enemy freedom of movement in these regions under the codename Operation 'Game Warden'.

The principal craft of the Brown Water Navy, as it became known, were the PCF (Fast Patrol Craft) and the PBR (River Patrol Boat). The PCF or 'Swift boat' was based on a standard commercial design for an oil rig support vessel in the Gulf of Mexico. The naval version was armed with twin .50 calibre machine guns atop the pilot house and a combined 81mm mortar and .50 calibre mounting in the deckwell aft. The PBR, which first saw action on 16 May 1966, was a thirty-one-foot, shallow draught boat with a fibreglass hull. It was armed with twin .50 calibre machine guns forward, a single .50 calibre aft and an M-60 machine gun and 40mm grenade launcher mounted amidships. Even this armament proved no match for the heavy firepower of automatic weapons, recoilless rifles, mortars, rockets and command-detonated mines employed by the VC in well-

LEFT: *With .50 cal. machine guns blazing, two PBRs Mark 1 of River Section 523 fire on enemy positions along the Co Chien River as a UH-1B of Detachment Three unleashes a pair of rockets in support. Flying by the book, the Seawolf's firing run is at 45 degrees to the river bank so that its break will be toward the PBRs in order to avoid both their ricochets, and flying over the target itself. (US Navy)*

ABOVE: *Maintenance crews service the UH-1B gunships of Detachment One under typical field conditions. HA(L)-3 was dependent upon the Army's Materials Management Center in Saigon for the supply of spares, and in consequence did not enjoy a high priority. Nevertheless, the squadron's serviceability record, in terms of both cost and availability, was outstanding. (US Navy)*

co-ordinated ambushes from hidden positions on the shoreline.

In order to provide greater fire support and a reconnaissance capability during River Patrol Force operations, the US Naval Command in Saigon proposed the acquisition of armed helicopter gunships for the Brown Water Navy. However, the Navy lacked both suitable aircraft and qualified aircrew for such a mission, so assistance was sought from the Army. As an interim measure eight redundant UH-1B gunships were obtained from the 197th Aviation Company which was being re-equipped with UH-1C Hueys. To provide Navy personnel for these aircraft, the Army's 10th Aviation Group at Fort Benning, Georgia, established a special training programme for detachments drawn from Helicopter Combat Support Squadron One (HC-1) based at Imperial Beach, California, whose usual rôle was SAR from carriers.

The first of these, Detachment 29 under the command of Lieutenant Commander William Rockwell, arrived in Vietnam in July 1966 and began theatre training under the tutelage of the 197th AHC. Originally known as HC-1 Detachment Vung Tau, the unit was nicknamed 'Rowell's Rats', but Army aviators called them 'Seawolves'—a name that was subsequently adopted officially. With its headquarters at Vung Tau, the unit was divided into four elements with detachments at Nha Be in the Rung Sat Special Zone, at Vinh Long in the Mekong Delta, and aboard the USS *Comstock* (LSD-19) patrolling the coastline. On 19 September it assumed the rôle of gunship support to Task Force 116. The first major action occurred on 31 October, when the Navy gunships supported PBRs on the My Tho River in a three-hour engagement against approximately seventy-five enemy sampans. Some fifty were destroyed and a large number of enemy troops killed.

On 11 November the first of four converted Tank Landing Ships (LST) arrived to replace the USS *Comstock* and to serve as a floating base for a squadron of ten PBRs and two helicopter gunships. The

LSTs incorporated living quarters for the aircrews, fuel and ammunition for the Hueys, and a flight deck measuring fifty by seventy-five feet with landing lights to permit helicopter operations at night against the elusive enemy. Lifting off the confined deck in the darkness, without visual references or a radar altimeter and relying only on the pressure-vertical rate and airspeed indicator, was a demanding manoeuvre. Similarly, when returning for a night landing after a fierce firefight and possibly combat-damaged, the landing area appeared as an ill-defined red slot and the helicopter's final approach had to be made with extreme care because, without the aid of a glide-slope indicator or exact reference to the ship's orientation, there was almost no margin for error. At any one time three LSTs were stationed on the waters of the Ham Luong, Co Chien and Lower Bassac Rivers, each with a light fire team aboard, while the fourth underwent maintenance and replenishment.

In early 1967 it was decided to expand the unit and, on 1 April, it was officially commissioned at Vung Tau as the Helicopter Attack (Light) Squadron Three or HA(L)-3, the first US Navy aviation unit ever to be activated in the field. Between May and August 1967 the squadron received some further UH-1B gunships from the 1st Cavalry Division (Airmobile). By the end of the year there was a total of twenty-two helicopters divided among seven detachments, each comprising a light fire team. Detachments -1, -4 and -5 were stationed aboard the LSTs while -2, -3, -6 and -7 were located at Nha Be, Vinh Long, Dong Tam and Binh Thuy respectively. In 9,774 hours of flying, the squadron completed over 7,000 missions in support of Operation 'Game Warden'. Many sorties were flown at night under the most exacting conditions, but the acquired capability to operate on a twenty-four-hour basis was much appreciated by supported units. Night flying was fraught with hazard, and a typical action with its attendant dangers is described by John Andrews, an aircrewman with HA(L)-3:

'At early sunset we would be briefed on our patrol area. This was usually an area of known VC activity and we were out to draw fire, to make contact. We flew a two-ship element, lead and trail. Our lead would fly at about 500 feet with rotating beacon and navigation lights on. We flew somewhat higher, blacked out. If the lead ship was fired upon, the trail ship could drop down and engage the source of enemy fire. On one mission to the north of Vinh Long I was a gunner in the lead ship. We had been at this for some time and were breaking in a new pilot flying in the trail ship for this mission. We received green tracer, we broke our flight pattern and began to circle. Our trail spotted the fire and asked us to place "close covering fire" under him as he made his run. He was on my side and I fired ahead as he made his run. My fire detonated one of his rockets about twenty-five feet ahead of the aircraft and it gave the new pilot quite a scare. We didn't receive any more ground fire after the rocket run, but that particular Lt JG didn't ask for any more "close covering fire" from me.'

During the fierce fighting of Tet 1968, the Seawolves provided much-needed fire support to the Brown Water Navy in several decisive battles that contained the enemy offensive. At Chau Doc on the Upper Bassac River two VC battalions assaulted the town, but were thwarted in its capture by the combined firepower of PBRs and Seawolves. In a thirty-six-hour engagement at Ben Tre the same

ABOVE: *A Seawolf UH-1B is guided on to the landing pad of a YRBM (Repair, Berthing and Messing Barge, Non-Self-Propelled) anchored in the Long Tau River. This gunship is fitted with a .50cal. machine gun, the 'Big Stick', in the right hand cabin doorway. It was a superior weapon to the M-60 against sampans and bunkers, but its effectiveness suffered because of the frequent need to reload from individual 100-round boxes. (US Navy)*

RIGHT: *In late 1966, Task Force 117 was formed in a joint US Navy and Army undertaking to create a Mobile Riverine Force (MRF) for combined operations in the Mekong Delta and the lower portion of III CTZ, particularly in the Rung Sat Special Zone. The 2nd Brigade, 9th Infantry Division provided the ground forces and* (continued opposite)

combination prevented the town from being overrun, and this was repeated across the Delta as the Seawolves responded to numerous calls for gunship support. Following the Tet Offensive, the Seawolves supported 'Game Warden' forces in the eradication of enemy gains and subsequently in operations near Cambodia to stem the flow of supplies across the border.

In early 1969 HA(L)-3 received more UH-1B gunships as the Army began to exchange its UH-1 models for the AH-1G Cobra. This increase in complement coincided with the movement of the squadron from Vung Tau to a new headquarters and maintenance facility at Binh Thuy on the Bassac River in the heart of the Delta region. Later in the year HA(L)-3 assumed the responsibilities of the small Navy flight detachment known as AIRCOFAT, which was based at Tan Son Nhut and performed courier, transport and liaison duties in support of US Navy forces in the Delta. The new detachment was named 'Sealords' and began operating from 'Navy Binh Thuy' in November. On 11 December 1969 it was assigned four new UH-1L Hueys and, on 22 January 1970, a further four. The UH-1L was a limited-production utility variant based on the UH-1E, but with the up-rated T-53-L13 engine, of which only eight were built. Another limited production Huey variant, the HH-1K, was also used by the Sealords. Three examples of the Navy SAR version of the UH-1E were received on 1 November 1970; one was lost on the 26th of the month when it ditched in the Gulf of Thailand, but the crew escaped.

(continued from p.160)
the Navy manned the vessels of River Assault Flotilla One. Helicopters provided the MRF with the capability for command and control, troop lift, reaction force lift, resupply and medical evacuation. To increase the effectiveness of helicopter support a number of 'Tango boats' were modified with a sixteen-foot-square landing pad above the troop compartment, to become the ATC(H): (Armoured Troop Carrier with Helipad). The technique was tested on 4/5 July 1967, and first used in action during Operation 'Coronado I' (1 June—26 July 1967). Here, a UH-1H of the 9th Aviation Battalion 'Condor' lands on an ATC(H) protected by stand-off 'bar' armour, on 26 July 1967. (US Navy)

The Sealords provided logistical support to virtually every Navy unit in the Mekong Delta. During 1970 they carried 7,287 passengers and 254,791 pounds of cargo and completed 6,110 missions. In addition to logistical support duties, the unarmed Sealord aircraft were used as airborne command posts, for emergency casualty evacuation, and to insert and extract ground troops including SEAL units. SEAL operations (Sea, Air, Land—the US Navy's élite Special Forces detachments) were often conducted at night, and usually involved the insertion by Sealord helicopters of four-man teams with a Seawolf light fire team acting as gunship escort. The helicopters then departed and, while the SEALs went about their clandestine activities, awaited the call for extraction—which often demanded immediate response if the SEAL team was in contact.

With its increased number of gunships, HA(L)-3 formed another two Seawolf detachments bringing the total to nine, five of which saw action during the incursion into Cambodia in May and June. For ease of maintenance and command the detachments were stationed circumferentially around the headquarters at Binh Thuy, which also allowed them to provide fire support over as wide an area as possible. During the course of the year 1970, 33,973 hours were flown by HA(L)-3 aircraft; ammunition expended included 18,909,490 rounds of 7.62mm, 108,297 2.75 in. rockets, 41,718 40mm grenades and 1,951,956 rounds of .50 calibre. By the end of the year HA(L)-3 was assigned thirty-five Hueys, including twenty-seven UH-1Bs, two UH-1Cs, four UH-1Ls and two HH-1Ks. During 1970 the Seawolves gave increasing support to ARVN units, and a Vietnamese interpreter was often carried on missions to facilitate communications and obtain target engagement clearance to conform with

political directives. In the following year VNAF personnel were assigned to Seawolf detachments and began flight operations on 19 July.

Throughout 1971, the Seawolves performed their primary mission of providing quick reaction helicopter gunship fire support for Navy and, increasingly, ARVN units operating in IV CTZ and in the lower portion of III CTZ along the Saigon River. Newer aircraft were acquired from 15 June in the form of 'Mike' model Hueys which, because of their increased performance, were assigned to Detachment NINE, the only one still operating from an LST. Unlike the experience of most other US forces then in Vietnam, the Seawolves' pace of operations continued unabated. During 1971 HA(L)-3 helicopters flew for 34,746 hours, and ammunition expended included 16,939,268 rounds of 7.62mm, 96,696 2.75 in. rockets, 32,313 40mm grenades and 2,414,096 rounds of .50 calibre.

After five years of existence, HA(L)-3 ceased operations on 26 January 1972. Due to their rapid response by day or night and the accuracy of their direct fire support, the Seawolves earned the respect of both the units they supported and of the enemy. Captured VC stated the fear they felt for 'the helicopters that strike at night'; while in the words of one PBR crewman, 'They only had one fault. There was never enough of them.'

RIGHT: *The UH1D/H maintenance Huey of the 1st Transportation Corps Battalion (Depot) (Seaborne) rests on the forward landing pad of the Floating Aircraft Maintenance Facility, USNS* Corpus Christi Bay, *at Vung Tau harbour in December 1967. Originally the Navy seaplane tender USS* Albemarle, *the ship was acquired by the Army and modified to perform all the maintenance functions of a depot level repair facility. Anchored off the coast of Vietnam away from the threat of saboteurs, the 370 maintenance personnel on board overhauled and rebuilt all types of Huey components and other aircraft systems. The USNS* Corpus Christi Bay *was normally stationed off Qui Nhon close to the 1st Cavalry Division (Airmobile), the unit it primarily supported. During the Vietnam War the Army was often accused by the Air Force of trying to create its own 'Air Corps' and, with the deployment of the USNS* Corpus Christi Bay, *the Navy looked somewhat askance at the 'Army's aircraft carrier'! (US Army)*

7 US AIR FORCE HELICOPTERS IN VIETNAM

The Early Years of Search and Rescue

The United States Air Force lost its first aircraft in Vietnam on 2 February 1962 when a 'Ranch Hand' C-123 Provider crashed during a crop defoliation mission; the crew perished. Nine days later a 'Farm Gate' SC-47 crashed in mountainous terrain while dropping propaganda leaflets, and all on board were killed. Due to a strict ceiling on personnel and aircraft in Vietnam at the time, there was no USAF rescue capability for downed aircrews beyond a six-man team based at Tan Son Nhut airport. Designated Detachment 3, Pacific Air Rescue Center, it possessed no aircraft and had to rely on Army and Marine aviation units for helicopters on a grace-and-favour basis. Lacking even the most basic equipment, the detachment had to relay requests for assistance to helicopter units by bicycle—which, in the event, proved faster and more reliable than the existing Vietnamese telephone network.

As the scale of aircraft losses rose, it became imperative that specialized helicopters be procured for the search and rescue mission. During the early 1960s the USAF Air Rescue Service (ARS) possessed some 150 helicopters, many of which were ageing models such as the H-19 Chickasaw and the SH-21 Work Horse (Shawnee). The most modern type was the Kaman HH-43 Huskie which was employed for local crash and rescue duties at USAF airbases in the United States and overseas but, on account of its short range of only 220 miles, it was considered unsuitable for the conditions in South-East Asia. Furthermore, since USAF involvement in the region was of a covert nature, the commitment of search and rescue units would only underscore the increasing American participation in the air war. In consequence, the USAF requested a new and more powerful helicopter for the SAR rôle, while the political arguments deferred deployment of the HH-43 Huskie to South-East Asia until June 1964. In the meantime Detachment 3 continued its assignment of organizing *ad hoc* rescue missions, several of which ended in disaster with rescue teams suffering severe losses. Besides the Army and Marine aviation units, Detachment 3 increasingly sought the assistance of commercial companies operating helicopters under US Government contracts in South-East Asia, such as Air America, Continental Air Service and others, most of which were only accountable to an agency based in Langley, Virginia. Their proficient flyers were thoroughly familiar with the terrain and the weather conditions of the region. In the early years their helicopters picked up the majority of those downed aircrew who were rescued, especially in Laos.

In June 1964 two HH-43B Huskies of the 33rd Air Rescue Squadron were deployed to Bien Hoa in South Vietnam from Naha

Air Station in Okinawa; however, because of accumulating losses in Laos, they were transferred to Nakhon Phanom Royal Thai Air Force Base (RTAFB) on the Thailand-Laos border. Following the Tonkin Gulf Incident in August and the commitment of additional USAF units to South-East Asia, further ARS detachments were despatched on temporary assignment to Thailand and Vietnam, with Detachment 1 (Provisional) at Bien Hoa and Detachment 2 (Provisional) at Da Nang. On 20 October these were replaced by Detachments 4 and 5 respectively, which were equipped with the first of the HH-43F combat-modified version of the Huskie. By 1 January 1965 five ARS detachments were operating in South-East Asia, with three helicopters at Bien Hoa, two at Da Nang and two at Pleiku in South Vietnam, and two each at Nakhon Phanom, Takhli and Korat in Thailand.

These thirteen aircraft were responsible for aircrew recoveries throughout South-East Asia, although they only proved really effective in the local rescue missions for which they had originally been designed. In order to increase the range of the Huskies the crews installed extra fuel tanks; and also established refuelling points, known as Lima Sites, at forward locations in jungle clearings and on mountain tops, where fuel drums were stored so that helicopters could leapfrog from one to another during extended rescue operations. Even so, the Huskie's range and loiter time remained inadequate, and a more effective helicopter was required for rescue missions in North Vietnam. Pending the introduction of a specialized rescue model, two Sikorsky CH-3Cs were obtained on loan from Tactical Air Command. On 6 July 1965 they arrived at Nakhon Phanom and, on 10 November, the first pair of the rescue version, the HH-3E, were assigned to Udorn RTAFB. By the end of the year six HH-3Es and a single CH-3C were operating from Udorn; the other had been lost to enemy action on 5 November.

BELOW: *The crew of an HH-43B Huskie run to their rescue helicopter at a base in Thailand at the outset of a mission in 1966. The USAF acquired the Huskie, with the callsign 'Pedro', to carry fire-fighting equipment to the sites of crashes near airfields, but in SE Asia it was also employed for search and rescue missions, pending the introduction of the HH-3 'Jolly Green Giant'.* (USAF)

'Jolly Green Giants'

On 8 January 1966 the ARS became the Aerospace Rescue and Recovery Service (ARRS) and, as part of the new organization, the 3rd Aerospace Rescue and Recovery Group was activated at Tan Son Nhut to act as the principal rescue agency in South-East Asia. The group controlled the activities of three rescue squadrons in South Vietnam: the 37th at Da Nang, the 38th at Tan Son Nhut and the 39th at Tuy Hoa, with detachments at most USAF airbases in Vietnam and Thailand.

The advent of the Sikorsky HH-3E initiated a new era for search and rescue operations. With its extended range, protective armour, defensive armament and large cargo capacity, the HH-3E was well-suited to the aircrew recovery rôle. When operating from Udorn or Da Nang it was able to reach any point in North Vietnam, while its improved communications equipment was compatible with all other allied aircraft operating in South-East Asia. Because of its tan and green USAF South-East Asia camouflage scheme this most welcome sight to downed crews was soon dubbed the 'Jolly Green Giant', in reference to a well-known advertising cartoon character.

The helicopter was also equipped with an external, variable-speed hoist with 250 feet of cable to reach survivors in terrain where the aircraft, was unable to land, such as dense jungle. In such areas the 'jungle penetrator' was attached to the end of the cable so that downed crewmen could be rescued even through triple-canopy jungle growth. The penetrator incorporated spring-loaded arms that parted the jungle foliage as it was lowered; when it reached the ground the survivor strapped himself to it, and released another set of spring-loaded arms at the top to protect his head and shoulders as he was hauled up through the trees. However, on occasion the downed flier was either injured or incapacitated and unable to fasten himself to the jungle penetrator. In such instances a crew member of the rescue helicopter had to be lowered with the penetrator or a Stokes litter to extract the survivor. This was the duty of the pararescueman, known as 'parajumper' or PJ for short.

The Vietnam War generated a variety of élite forces whose specialized skills were mostly dedicated to the taking of human lives by any manner of unspeakable means. The parajumpers were an élite devoted to exactly the opposite purpose. Every PJ was a trained scuba

ABOVE: *An HH-3E flies over the rugged landscape of Thailand during a rescue mission on 9 December 1967, painted in the USAF SE Asia camouflage of tan and green from which its nickname of 'Jolly Green Giant' derived. Note the extendible refuelling probe which increases its basic range of 465 miles. (USAF)*

RIGHT: *Besides the ARRS, USAF helicopters of the Tactical Air Command were also employed in Vietnam for general support duties. Here, a CH-3C 'Big Charlie' of the 20th Helicopter Squadron lifts a Marine M-101A1 105mm howitzer into a firing position on 1 February 1966 during Operation 'Double Eagle'. (USMC)*

diver and parachutist, a specialist in small arms and unarmed combat and, last but not least, a qualified medical technician. At the height of the war this select band numbered about 300, with forty per cent serving in South-East Asia. Parajumpers won more decorations than any other group in the USAF serving in Indo-China; and the most decorated of them all was Airman 1st Class Duane Hackney, who served with the 37th Aerospace Rescue and Recovery Squadron. On 16 February 1967 Hackney was searching for a downed pilot in the jungle undergrowth during a mission in North Vietnam. Having found and strapped him into a Stokes litter, Hackney had just reached the relative safety of the Jolly Green Giant with his patient when the NVA opened fire on the helicopter. The pilot pulled pitch, but the HH-3E caught fire. Hackney put a parachute on the injured man and then climbed into one himself. Suddenly the helicopter exploded, throwing Hackney out, and his parachute opened just above the trees. A second 'high bird' HH-3E swooped down and its own parajumper searched for survivors, but found only Hackney, dazed but uninjured. He was evacuated without further incident.

Less than a month later, on 13 March, Hackney was one of a pair of PJs aboard an HH-3E flying just south of the DMZ. A Marine UH-34 had been shot down and the survivors reported that enemy troops were closing in for the kill. A second Marine helicopter heard the call for help and went to assist their beleaguered comrades. The Jolly Green Giant arrived at the scene just as the CH-46 stalled, rolled over and crashed on top of the first downed helicopter. The Marines gathered their injured and set up a defensive position. While the rescue helicopter circled overhead, A-1 Skyraiders attacked the enemy and laid down a smoke screen. Under its cover the 'Jolly Green' came to a hover over the embattled Marines, and Hackney was lowered to the ground with a Stokes litter. Exposed all the while to enemy sniper fire, he made repeated rides on the hoist, each time loading as many injured Marines on the litter as possible. During one trip up the hoist, just as Hackney and a casualty were at the door, the pilot saw warning lights flash on, indicating that the hydraulics were shot out. With bullets smashing into the fuselage, he fought the controls and headed the damaged helicopter for Da Nang. Meanwhile, Hackney was tending the wounded in the cabin when a bullet grazed his helmet and knocked him out. On regaining consciousness he continued giving first aid until the helicopter landed. For his efforts, Airman Hackney received the Air Force Cross.

Although the HH-3 Jolly Green Giant had proved itself on numerous missions, it had certain limitations and, as the tempo of the war grew, its shortcomings became more apparent—in particular, insufficient protective armour, limited suppressive firepower, and lack of power when operating at a hover in the higher mountains. These deficiencies prompted the acquisition of a new aircrew rescue helicopter. On 19 June 1967 the ARRS took delivery of the first Sikorsky HH-53B specifically designed for aircrew rescue and, on 14 September, two arrived at Vung Tau, from where they were assigned to Detachment 2, 37th Aerospace Rescue and Recovery Squadron at Udorn RTAFB.

At twice the weight and with four times the payload of the HH-3E, the HH-53 was overly large to be an ideal rescue helicopter, but its performance more than met the requirements of the aircrew recovery rôle, and it represented almost as much of an improvement over the HH-3 as that helicopter had been over the HH-43 Huskie. Due to its size, aircrews called it 'BUFF', for 'Big Ugly Fat Fellow'; however, because the crews usually substituted another six-letter word beginning with 'F' for 'Fellow', it was officially designated the Super Jolly Green Giant. More importantly, the HH-53 incorporated an aerial refuelling capability which allowed the helicopter to fly as far as the limit of the crew's endurance.

The ability to refuel in flight revolutionized search and rescue operations. After extensive trials in the United States and the acquisition of a suitable aerial tanker—a converted Hercules designated the HC-130P—the first operational test of in-flight refuelling in Vietnam occurred on 21 June 1967, when a modified HH-3E flew around the Gulf of Tonkin for eight hours with the help of two fuel replenishments from an HC-130P. By September this technique had become routine throughout South-East Asia. It offered a new flexibility by enabling the helicopters to stay airborne during airstrikes against North Vietnam instead of having to reach the operational area from distant bases in Thailand or South Vietnam. On a typical sortie the rescue helicopters flew ahead of a bombing mission, topped up their fuel tanks, and then orbited in a safe area over Laos or the Gulf of Tonkin until the last fighter-bomber had dropped its ordnance, or until they were called upon to make a recovery. The HC-130P, acting as an airborne rescue command post codenamed Crown (later King), orbited in the same pattern and refuelled the helicopters as necessary. All HH-3E Jolly Green Giants in South-East Asia were subsequently fitted with an extendable probe in the nose for in-flight refuelling, while the HH-53s had them installed during manufacture.

Search and Rescue Mission

Although all rescue operations differed in detail, a typical mission was based around the Search and Rescue Task Force comprising seven aircraft: an HC-130P Crown for airborne command and refuelling, two rescue helicopters (a pair of HH-3Es or HH-53B/Cs), and four A-1 Skyraiders in two flights of two for escort. The Douglas A-1 Skyraider—callsign 'Sandy'—with its 7,000 pound bomb load, four 20mm cannons, armour plating, long loiter time, and a speed to match the helicopters, was better suited than any other aircraft to rescue escort. The A-1 was an immensely robust aircraft—which, indeed, it had to be, since its mission of attacking anti-aircraft sites at low level was one of the most dangerous in South-East Asia, and many fell prey to eager communist gunners. On a par with the parajumpers, Sandy pilots were among the most respected aviators of the war and, for a pilot downed in enemy territory, there was nothing more reassuring than the fearsome sight and sound of an approaching, fully-laden Skyraider—except, perhaps, that of the lumbering Jolly Green Giant.

As the task force approached the rescue area the formation divided into two flights, 'Sandy High' and 'Sandy Low', with two Skyraiders

ABOVE LEFT: *Landing in a remote spot of SE Asia, a CH-3E of the 20th Special Operations Squadron lands a SOG team (Special Operations Group) on 30 June 1968 during a 'cross-border' mission. The 20th SOS was the only USAF combat helicopter squadron in Vietnam and it conducted numerous clandestine operations throughout SE Asia, many of which remain classified: but Operation 'Pony Express', the insertion of unconventional warfare forces into Cambodia, Laos and Thailand, was typical of its activities. (USAF)*

ABOVE RIGHT: *A downed pilot clutches the jungle penetrator as he is hoisted aboard a hovering HH-3E on 17 November 1968. Helicopters were at their most vulnerable during this stage of a rescue mission; one problem of the helicopter was the lack of defensive fire on the starboard side when winching. (USAF)*

and a Jolly Green Giant in each, while the HC-130P Crown flew its own flight pattern as overall command post. Once near the scene, Sandy High remained in high orbit to act as an airborne reserve in the event that the other flight failed in the mission. Simultaneously, 'Jolly 1' and 'Sandy 2' were directed to a safe orbit at a given altitude and location close to the crash site, while 'Sandy Low Lead' ('Sandy 1') reconnoitred at low level to discover the exact position of the downed aircrew and the extent of enemy defences. Sandy 1 acted as the on-scene commander and determined when the actual pick-up attempt was to be made. Using direction-finding equipment, Sandy 1 homed in on the URC-11 survival radio of the downed aircrew and, once it was pin-pointed, the Skyraider pilot was careful not to circle around the position so as not to disclose it to any enemy troops in the area.

Forward Air Controllers (FAC), in their Cessna 0-1, 0-2 or Rockwell OV-10 Broncos, were often part of the search and rescue task force. FACs usually worked in the same specific area and, in consequence, knew the terrain intimately and had some knowledge of enemy dispositions. They were also of assistance during the next task for Sandy 1: that of finding the enemy guns, known as 'trolling for fire'. The Skyraider flew low and slow over the area, both to observe and to tempt the guns to open fire so as to reveal their positions, which the FAC was quickly able to identify. Sandy 1 would fly back and forth, often for an hour or more, in a deadly game of hide-and-seek, occasionally firing into the jungle or likely positions, to stir up the enemy gunners who, if experienced, bided their time until the

ABOVE: *The 20th SOS also employed the Huey UH-1F, a model incorporating a General Electric T58-GE-3 engine (the same as that in the HH-3), a forty-eight-foot rotor and an extended tailboom, shown here bearing the 'Green Hornets' emblem of the squadron. When armed with miniguns and rocket launchers as a gunship, this variant was designated the UH-1P. (Robert Steinbrunn)*

valuable and vulnerable helicopters came within their sights. It was a matter of fine judgement for Sandy 1 to determine whether there were any guns waiting in silence, knowing that by delaying the rescue attempt he might be giving the enemy time to position anti-aircraft weapons—or enemy ground troops, attracted to the area by the aerial activity, time to capture the downed aircrew.

Often the decision became academic as enemy guns reacted with an intense barrage of fire. While the FAC spotted their positions, Sandy Low attacked them with 20mm cannons, rockets and bombs, calling Crown to send in further aircraft if necessary. Two Skyraiders remained on the ground at base during rescue missions, fuelled and fully armed for just such a contingency. Often equipped with special ordnance, such as smoke, riot control agents and cluster bombs, they were on immediate stand-by, waiting for the call from Sandy Low Lead. Further suppressive fire was provided by any attack aircraft in the vicinity, such as F-4 Phantoms or F-105 Thunderchiefs, which could be diverted from their primary mission to the rescue area where their strikes were directed by the FAC. Indeed, nothing was spared in support of a search and rescue mission, as was noted by Colonel William Harris IV, commander of the 37th Aerospace Rescue and Recovery Squadron in 1971 and 1972: 'During my tour rescue efforts have called upon every conceivable military resource as well as . . . Air America, special ground teams, clandestine operations, frogmen, aircraft carriers, tanks, and so on. There is no limitation on tactics or concepts to be employed to effect a rescue.'

When Sandy Low Lead determined that the situation was safe for the recovery attempt, Sandy 2 and Sandy High joined the Jolly Green Giant, designated as 'low bird', and escorted it in for the pick-up. The other helicopter, 'high bird', remained in orbit, ready to move in if the need arose. In heavily defended areas it was common practice to employ additional Skyraiders (often seven or eight) as smoke-laying aircraft. Flying in an echelon trail, the 'smokes' screened the 'low bird's' approach to the downed aircrew. Often in zero visibility, the 'low bird' was guided by Sandy 1 flying above the smoke screen until the helicopter pilot saw the red flare released by the downed aircrew. Once they had been picked up, Sandy 1 guided the helicopter back through the smoke.

Rescue attempts generally took precedence over all other missions and often lasted several days. On one operation in December 1969,

336 sorties were flown over a three-day period in the support of rescue forces during the recovery of the 'back seater' of an F-4 Phantom, 'Boxer 22', shot down near Tchepone in Laos. Air Force sorties included fifty by F-105, forty-three by F-4, and four by F-100 aircraft, and the Navy contributed several A-6 Intruder and A-7 Corsair sorties. Eventually the weapons-systems operator, Lieutenant Woodrow Bergeron Jr., was rescued—but in the process five Sandys were badly damaged, five of the ten Jolly Greens damaged during the rescue were so severely shot up that they had to be cannibalized for spare parts, one parajumper was killed and several others injured. The firepower employed during the operation was equal to that used in a small war. A-1 'Dump Trucks' dropped so many white phosphorous bombs, along with other ordnance, that the resulting cloud was clearly visible in television transmissions from weather satellites.

'That Others May Live'

The enemy was well aware of the extraordinary efforts that would be made by the rescue forces, and sometimes lured them into 'flak traps'. Using captured survival radios and laying parachutes on the ground as bait, the enemy ringed the area with anti-aircraft weapons to meet any rescue helicopter with an intense barrage. The flyers who took part in rescue missions were only too familiar with the hazards, which forged strong bonds between them; if one was shot down the others would, as a matter of course, make every possible effort to save him. This knowledge did much to bolster a pilot's morale, but he also realized the risks to his comrades. On one unsuccessful rescue mission in early 1966, a low-flying A-1 Sandy was hit in the wing and set on fire. The pilot might have climbed to sufficient height to bail out; but had he done so, he knew he would have landed among enemy guns that would be trained on his friends when they came for him.

BELOW: *Escorted by four A-1E Skyraiders, an HH-3E is refuelled from an HC-130P over north-east Thailand as a Search and Rescue Task Force conducts a mission on 9 December 1967. (USAF)*

Instead, he chose to stay at low altitude to evade the guns, hoping to reach a safe area before bailing out. Unfortunately, before this could happen, the flames burnt through the aileron cables and the A-1 crashed into a hillside. The pilot was killed, sacrificing himself to spare the helicopter crews who would surely follow.

In the summer of 1969 the ARRS reached its peak strength in South-East Asia with seventy-one aircraft operating in four squadrons—the 37th and 40th at Da Nang and Udorn respectively, the 38th at Tan Son Nhut with detachments at fourteen airbases around South Vietnam and Thailand, and the 39th operating eleven HC-130Ps from Tuy Hoa. Between 1966 and 1970 ARRS units had saved 980 aircrew from captivity or death in Laos and both Vietnams. In other rescue efforts an additional 1,059 lives had been saved. The development of search and rescue operations in South-East Asia was a phenomenon peculiar to America's involvement in a complex and frustrating war. Few other nations would have created such an extensive rescue capability based on the concept of saving so few individuals; even fewer nations could have afforded it. On some occasions, humanitarian considerations jeopardized the tactical situation, as was the case of 'Bat 21' during the Easter Offensive of 1972.

On 2 April, three days after the NVA invaded across the DMZ, Bat 21 and Bat 22, two Douglas EB-66 electronic warfare aircraft, were escorting three B-52s on a strike mission against the enemy when a SAM-2 hit Bat 21, killing all the crew except Lieutenant Colonel Iceal Hambleton, an electronics warfare officer with extensive knowledge of US strategic missile systems. A patrolling OV-10 Bronco, alerted by his 'beeper', soon spotted Hambleton and contacted a nearby airborne search and rescue task force returning from a cancelled mission. Two of its A-1s, Sandy 07 and 08, immediately headed for his position and, amid intense ground fire, bombed and strafed enemy positions while Hambleton, using his survival radio with cool precision, directed their airstrikes against

ABOVE: *The telescopic probe of an HH-53C engages the drogue of an HC-130P for in-flight refuelling during a rescue mission in January 1973. There is a GAU-2B/A 7.62 mm minigun at the starboard doorway. (USAF)*

enemy troops who at times came as close as 100 yards from his position.

The Sandys had determined that the area was too dangerous for the Jolly Greens, but four Army helicopters of F Troop, 8th Cavalry—two Cobra gunships and two UH-1H slicks—decided to make their own unauthorized pick-up attempt. One UH-1H was shot out of the sky, killing all on board; and a Cobra, Blue Ghost 28, limped away and crashed, though its two crewmen were rescued. At this point Air Force operations staff, realizing that Hambleton was located in the middle of a major enemy troop concentration, established a seventeen-mile radius 'no-fire zone' around the downed officer. This restriction encompassed most of the area of operations of the inexperienced ARVN 3rd Division, struggling to stem the communist invaders. During the night, by means of Loran navigation co-ordinating equipment, Hambleton's position was plotted exactly. Because the weather was so foul on the following day, all recent aerial photography of the area was analysed, together with the Loran co-ordinates, and computers printed out targets for the bombers to strike through the clouds.

For the next three days the Seventh Air Force continually bombarded the area around the beleaguered flyer until, on 6 April, the first attempt was made to pick him up, together with a crewman of an OV-10 shot down by another SAM-2. Escorted by a flight of A-1 Sandys, an HH-53, 'Jolly 62', headed towards Hambleton but, on taking fire, it turned to the right over a village where the Sandys knew the enemy to be in force. Over the radio the Sandy pilots screamed 'Turn left, don't turn right, turn left!'—but someone in Jolly 62 had depressed the radio transmission button, and the crew could not hear. The turn brought the HH-53 under intense heavy machine gun fire. The Sandy pilots watched in horror as the helicopter burst into flames and crashed into the ground, killing the entire crew. For the next week, during which another OV-10 was shot down with the loss of its two crewmen, Air Force attention remained focused on the

BELOW LEFT: *With a pair of Colt CAR-15 assault rifles slung across his back, a parajumper renders first aid to a wounded flier during a rescue mission on 16 June 1970. During the conflict in SE Asia, the ARRS saved 3,883 lives at a cost of seventy-one rescuemen and forty-five aircraft. (USAF)*

BELOW RIGHT: *The defensive armament of the HH-53 comprises three General Electric GAU-2B/A miniguns with one in each forward doorway and one on the rear ramp. Capable of firing at 4,000 rounds per minute, the miniguns and titanium armour of the 'Super Jolly Green Giant' made it a formidable rescue helicopter. (USAF)*

plight of two aviators, with up to ninety sorties a day being expended on their behalf. Eventually Hambleton, having spent three nights floating down a river on a log, was extricated by a Marine ground team, together with the other aviator.

The twelve-day operation raised serious questions about the aircrew recovery rôle. Against radar-guided anti-aircraft guns and surface-to-air missiles even the superb HH-53 had been impotent. The only Super Jolly Green Giant to attempt a recovery was shot down. The lives of two OV-10 crew members, five crewmen in the HH-53 and four in the Army Huey had been lost to save a single man. Given the unquestioned value of airpower in ground operations, the decision to establish a 'no-fire zone' cost the ARVN 3rd Division untold casualties. For twelve days the enemy was allowed to advance virtually unchecked through the area of the rescue operation. Many South Vietnamese troops died because air and artillery support was denied to them. More died in the following months during operations to regain the lost ground. The difficult question of how much one man's life was worth when set against the sacrifice of others was not adequately addressed during the war, and was never answered. Yet, to the crews of the Jolly Greens and the Sandys, the question needed no answer because, to them, no effort was too great to fulfil the motto of their service—'That others may live'.

8 US MARINE CORPS HELICOPTERS IN VIETNAM

Operation 'Shufly'

To augment the three Shawnee helicopter companies operating in South Vietnam, Marine helicopter squadron HMM-362 arrived from Okinawa in April 1962 under the codename Operation 'Shufly' in order to increase the airlift capability of ARVN forces. The original intention had been to deploy four US Army CH-21 companies with one in each of the four military regions of RVN. From the outset, it was realized that the more powerful Sikorsky HUS-1 helicopter (later UH-34D) employed by the Marines was better suited than the Vertol CH-21 to the high elevations of the northernmost region of the country, which was subsequently designated I Corps Tactical Zone. In the event, the 93rd Transportation Company (Light Helicopter) moved to Da Nang in I CTZ before the Marines' arrival; HMM-362, with its twenty-four HUS-1 helicopters, was deployed to the Soc Trang airstrip in the Mekong Delta, where it landed on 15 April.

The squadron began combat operations exactly one week after its arrival when, on 22 April, it flew twenty-nine sorties and lifted 400 ARVN troops during Operation 'Lockjaw', in conjunction with the 57th Transportation Company (Light Helicopter). Two days later, during Operation 'Nightingale', a 'Shufly' helicopter suffered the first combat damage when ground fire punctured an oil line and forced it to land. Within two hours it had been recovered after four other helicopters had landed a Marine repair team and an ARVN security force. On 23 May an HMM-362 helicopter flew the first night medical evacuation mission of the war.

In several of the early operations the enemy often eluded the larger ARVN units by fleeing the area of operations in small groups. The Marines of HMM-362 devised a technique to prevent such escapes whereby four HUS-1s carrying fifty ARVN troops circled above the contested area and, once the enemy was located, landed them to block any avenue of escape. Known as 'Chickenhawk', the technique was first used on 8 June when an insurgent carrying a suitcase filled with money and documents was apprehended and identified as a VC leader. This mission, in which the rapid response and mobility of the helicopter provided a means to exploit any sighting of the enemy, was developed into the concept of an airborne reserve for fast reaction known as 'Eagle Flights', which were subsequently employed with success by many helicopter units in Vietnam.

On 20 July 1962 the first helicopter night troop landing in Vietnam was made when troops of the ARVN 7th Division were landed just before dawn by 'Shufly' helicopters in the Plain of Reeds to increase the element of surprise. The landing was completed without incident and, although the ground operation proved inconclusive, it added a

RIGHT: *A flight of 'Shufly' HUS-1 helicopters of HMM-362 lands in a paddy field to pick up ARVN troops prior to an operation in the Mekong Delta in 1962. With a strength of twenty-four helicopters, the Marine medium helicopter transport squadrons of Operation 'Shufly' provided troop lift and logistical support to ARVN forces from April 1962 until the Marine landings at Da Nang in March 1965. (USMC)*

RIGHT: *Troops of the ARVN 21st Infantry Division embark on 'Shufly' HUS-1 helicopters of HMM-362 at Ca Mau for an assault on Cai Ngai, a VC-controlled village twenty-one miles to the south, on 9 May 1962. During the operation eight 'Huss' aircraft were hit by small arms fire, one of which was forced down but later recovered. The increasing number of hits from enemy ground fire led to the installation of armour plate to protect vital components, the addition of M-60 machine guns for suppressive fire, and the introduction of personal body armour for the crews. (USMC)*

RIGHT: *Flying over the typically mountainous terrain of I Corps Tactical Zone, UH-34 'Huss' helicopters of HMM-161 airlift Marines during a 'Tiger Flight' mission for a surprise attack against the Viet Cong on 30 August 1965. 'Tiger Flights' differed from 'Eagle Flights' in that the ready reaction force remained at a designated pick-up zone rather than being airborne. (USMC)*

new dimension to counter-guerrilla warfare. HMM-362 was relieved by HMM-163 on 1 August; since its arrival in April the squadron had executed fifty combat assault landings and flown 4,439 sorties in 5,262 hours of combat flight time. Seventeen of its twenty-four HUS-1s had incurred battle damage, but none were lost and the squadron suffered no casualties.

The 'Ridge Runners' of HMM-163 participated in their first combat mission on the same day. In a subsequent operation in conjunction with a VNAF detachment, the squadron suffered the first Marine helicopter loss in Vietnam on 25 August when a VNAF fighter careered off the runway at Soc Trang into a parked HUS-1, which was damaged beyond repair but stripped of undamaged parts for use as spares. Throughout Operation 'Shufly' helicopter losses were replaced on a one-to-one basis by new machines flown in by USAF C-124 Globemasters from Okinawa, so that the squadrons were able to maintain a constant level of twenty-four helicopters except for brief periods. HMM-163 continued to perform intensive support operations in III and IV Corps Tactical Zones during August, when it logged a total of 2,543 hours of flight time. During that month the helicopters were modified by the addition of an M-60 machine gun in the starboard cabin doorway to protect the aircraft during assault landings and take-offs.

At the beginning of September HMM-163 began redeployment to the coastal city of Da Nang. It was completed on 20 September, with the helicopters arriving in two waves on the 16th and 17th in a seven-hour flight, with three refuelling stops *en route*. The squadron flew its first combat operation in I CTZ on 18 September in support of the ARVN 2nd Division, after VNAF fighter-bombers had prepared the landing zones with airstrikes to neutralize enemy positions. This tactic of 'prep strikes' became standard practice, and was refined in the following weeks, with artillery fire support being employed in conjunction with the airstrikes. Marine helicopter aviators in Vietnam suffered their first fatalities on 6 October when a HUS-1 on a search and rescue mission crashed into a hillside fifteen miles southeast of Tam Ky, killing the five Marines on board. In November all Marine aircraft were redesignated, and the HUS-1 became the UH-34D Sea Horse—but to the Marines it was always known affectionately as 'Huss', a word that survives in Marine Corps jargon to describe something that is both effective and reliable.

On 11 January 1963 the 'Ridge Runners' were replaced by HMM-162.[1] The squadron had flown a total of 10,869 hours, executed 15,200 sorties, and lifted 25,216 combat troops and 59,024 other passengers. During the course of these operations its helicopters had been hit on thirty-two occasions by enemy fire, and two of them were lost due to operational causes. HMM-162 continued the 'Shufly' missions and flew increasing numbers of combat support sorties into the mountainous areas of the region. On 13 April the squadron participated in a major heliborne combat assault in support of the ARVN 2nd Division. For the first time, Marine helicopters were escorted by UH-1B gunships of an UTTHCO detachment stationed at Da Nang. Within a short period Army gunships were

---

[1] Over the next two years, other HMMs followed: 261, 361, 364, 162 for a second tour, 365, and finally, 163 for the second time.

ABOVE LEFT: *A CH-46D of Marine Medium Helicopter Squadron-161 brings in replacements to the 1st Battalion, 3rd Marines during an operation near the DMZ in 1968. On the forward rotor pylon is the 'Pineapple' insignia of HMM-161, a reminder of the squadron's previous posting in Hawaii. Note the air filters fitted over the engine intakes, and the .50 cal. machine gun mounted in the emergency exit door: both modifications proved necessary under Vietnam conditions, although they reduced the Sea Knight's performance and payload. (USMC)*

accompanying all Marine helicopter assault and medical evacuation missions and, when available, resupply sorties to isolated ARVN positions. The effectiveness of their support led directly to the procurement by the Marine Corps of its own gunship in the form of the UH-1E, albeit not without a vigorous and protracted debate within the Corps concerning the value of armed helicopters.

Until such time as the UH-1E entered service, the Huss was further modified for self-protection. As indicated previously, the helicopters of HMM-163 mounted a single M-60 machine gun in the cabin doorway as early as August 1962, while the co-pilot was armed with a sub-machine gun or automatic rifle for firing from the forward cockpit window; however, this failed to give adequate protection to the port side during assault landings, and also distracted the co-pilot from his primary duties. On 10 August 1964 Headquarters Marine Corps initiated the design of a simple, interim fire suppression kit for the UH-34D. Within two weeks the aviation metalsmiths of HMX-1 at Quantico had completed a prototype kit and, following a month of trials, twenty-four armament kits were produced. Meanwhile, the 'Shufly' squadron in Vietnam, HMM-364, had fabricated a flexible mounting for an additional M-60 to be fitted at a port side cabin window, which required another crew member to act as gunner. This, together with the armour protection fitted, reduced the UH-34's troop-lifting capacity from its original specification of twelve to just seven men.

From the time of the first combat damage on 23 April 1962, attempts were made to protect vital components of the helicopters, particularly the oil cooler system. As an interim measure until a purpose-designed armour protection kit was manufactured, a large slab of half-inch aluminium plate weighing 160 pounds was bolted over the bottom of the oil cooler. Effective against .30 calibre gunfire, such plates were fitted to 'Shufly' helicopters soon after their arrival in Da Nang. In late 1964 the armour protection kit was introduced, consisting of armoured seats for the pilot and co-pilot, additional cockpit armour in the form of 0.38 in. steel side panels, and engine

LEFT: *Marine riflemen of the 3rd Battalion, 4th Marines scramble from a CH-46A of HMM-265 which crashed into Landing Zone 'Crow' in the Ngau Valley after colliding with another helicopter at the outset of Operation 'Hastings' on 15 July 1966. Two Marines were killed by the thrashing rotor blades and seven others were injured following the collision. In all, four Sea Knights were lost during the landings in the Ngau Valley; thereafter, the Marines referred to the area as 'Helicopter Valley'. (USMC)*

ABOVE RIGHT: *In the bitter fighting for Hill 362 during Operation 'Hastings', Company I, 3rd Battalion, 5th Marines suffered eighteen dead and twenty-two wounded during repeated night assaults by the 6th Battalion, 812th NVA Regiment; here, a UH-1E evacuates Item Company wounded on 25 July 1966 while enemy fire lashes the pick-up zone. Note the domed housing of the personnel rescue hoist on the cabin roof, a characteristic feature of the 'Echo' model Huey. (USMC)*

armour. The vulnerable oil tank and oil cooler were further protected by half-inch aluminium armour plate. The crew members were protected by personal body armour—originally standard issue M-1951 flak jackets, effective against fragments only, and subsequently ceramic armour which gave protection from small arms fire. The penalty paid for such protection was a considerably reduced payload of either cargo or personnel, especially in the hot and humid conditions of Vietnam.

Even so, helicopters were still being brought down. During 1963 eight Marine UH-34Ds were shot down, all but one being recovered and repaired; during 1964 four were shot down, of which two were recovered and repaired. Operational losses due to non-hostile causes remained higher, with eight in 1963 and four in 1964. Since Army gunships were not always available, three UH-34Ds of HMM-365 were converted to the gunship rôle early in November 1964 with the addition of the TK-1 (Temporary Kit 1) fire suppression kit developed by HMX-1 at Quantico. First used on 19 November, the TK-1 did not prove effective in combat. The inherent limitations of the UH-34D as a gun platform, because of its low speed and lack of manoeuvrability, reduced the value of the system. By the end of April 1965 it had been discontinued after the arrival of fixed-wing Marine aircraft. During the trial period the UH-34 gunships accounted for only fifteen per cent of the total flight time but had taken eighty-five per cent of all hits from ground fire. Early in December 1964 the 'Shufly' squadron received a new title, and was now called Marine Unit Vietnam.

The Expanding War

On 8 March 1965 the 9th Marine Expeditionary Brigade landed at Da Nang as the first American ground combat forces to be committed to the war. There followed a steady build-up of helicopter squadrons, which came under the operational command of 1st Marine Air Wing, and Operation 'Shufly' was terminated. In three years of continuous operations, half of the Marine Corps' medium helicopter transport squadrons had participated in 'Shufly'. During that period they had gained valuable combat experience and introduced new operating procedures that were to influence the employment of helicopters for the next decade. Throughout 1965 and 1966 the UH-34D remained the workhorse of the Marine Corps in Vietnam; to the individual rifleman, the 'Huss' was the vehicle which transported him into battle, provided him with rations and ammunition, and carried him out of combat alive, wounded or dead.

Among the aviation units deployed to Vietnam in support of the 9th MEB were Marine Observation Squadrons (VMO) 2 and 6, equipped with the UH-1E. The Huey was employed by the Marine Corps for myriad tasks including command and control, medical evacuation, visual reconnaissance and observation, as a platform for aerial searchlights and sensors, in the gunship rôle, and as a courier, liaison, administrative support and VIP transport craft. The 'Echo' model differed only slightly in configuration from the Army versions; but it did incorporate a rotor brake so that the engine could be shut down rapidly on the crowded flight decks of assault ships, and it used aluminium rather than magnesium in its construction to reduce the problem of corrosion when exposed to salt air or water.

As a gunship, the UH-1E was fitted with the TK-2 Armament Subsystem comprising four side-mounted M-60C machine guns with a bomb rack below each pair from which 2.75 in. rocket pods were normally suspended, although other weapons could be carried. From April 1967, the TK-2 was augmented by the Emerson Electric TAT-101 chin turret containing a further two M-60 machine guns with 500 rounds. Although the UH-1E was not as heavily armed as the UH-1B/C Army gunships, it suffered less payload degradation—a significant factor in the higher elevations of I Corps Tactical Zone.

BELOW: *A pair of UH-1E gunships of VMO-6 land at a ProvMAG-39 helicopter pad to rearm the 2.75in. rocket pods of their TK-2 (Temporary Kit-2) armament subsystem during Operation 'Nanking/Scotland II' on 5 October 1968. These Hueys are also fitted with TAT-101 chin turrets mounting twin M-60 machine guns. (USMC)*

It also allowed the aircraft fitted with the armament system to perform other rôles than that of gunship, such as reconnaissance, evacuation and supply missions. This was in keeping with Marine Corps doctrine which dictated that fixed-wing, high-performance attack aircraft such as the A-4 Skyhawk were the principal means for tactical air support.

The UH-1E assumed the mission of transport helicopter escort which involved the reconnaissance of a landing zone for enemy activity prior to troop insertion. Often this was combined with landing zone preparation by attack aircraft, followed by the marking of the zone itself with smoke grenades or rockets from the UH-1E to guide the troop transports. As the latter approached and landed, the UH-1E gunships provided suppressive fire to adjacent areas or remained on call in an orbiting pattern overhead. The ratio of armed helicopters to troop transports was commonly one to five with, whenever possible, a minimum of four UH-1E Hueys operating in pairs.

As the intensity of helicopter operations mounted in 1965 a number of maintenance problems arose, which by the summer had assumed acute proportions. Not only were helicopters flying almost twice the programmed hours, but the sand- and dust-laden air on landing and take-off caused severe erosion of rotor blades. In August there was such a shortage of rotor blades for the UH-34 that otherwise flyable aircraft were grounded for want of spares. By the end of the month the situation was similar for the UH-1E: its rotor blades were expected to last 1,000 hours of flight, but in Vietnam they were being worn out after only 200 hours. In addition, tail rotor blades were being expended at a far higher rate than predicted because of the damage caused by ejected ammunition links and cases from the side-mounted machine guns. There was abundant evidence of this problem around the airbases, where virtually every signpost and door marker was painted on a discarded rotor blade. The

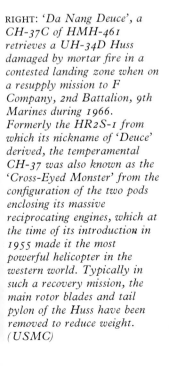

RIGHT: *'Da Nang Deuce', a CH-37C of HMH-461 retrieves a UH-34D Huss damaged by mortar fire in a contested landing zone when on a resupply mission to F Company, 2nd Battalion, 9th Marines during 1966. Formerly the HR2S-1 from which its nickname of 'Deuce' derived, the temperamental CH-37 was also known as the 'Cross-Eyed Monster' from the configuration of the two pods enclosing its massive reciprocating engines, which at the time of its introduction in 1955 made it the most powerful helicopter in the western world. Typically in such a recovery mission, the main rotor blades and tail pylon of the Huss have been removed to reduce weight. (USMC)*

production of rotor blades for both types of helicopter was immediately increased, and by October the supply of replacements was ample.

No sooner had this problem been resolved when disaster struck with the destruction on the 27th of the month of thirteen UH-1E Hueys and damage to four others during a Viet Cong sapper attack against the Marine airbase at Marble Mountain, Da Nang. Six UH-34s were also destroyed and another twenty-six damaged. VMO-2 was reduced to four flyable Hueys; VMO-6 at Ky Ha provided its fellow squadron with seven Hueys, leaving itself with only eleven. In total, there remained only twenty-two UH-1Es in Vietnam; the Marine Corps possessed only eighteen others, most of which were immediately despatched to Vietnam as replacements.

Among the aircraft at Marble Mountain at the time of the attack was a detachment of CH-37 heavy-lift helicopters (formerly the HR2S-1) drawn from HMH-461 and attached to H&MS-16. The six giant 'Deuces' had escaped with only minor damage when concussion grenades blew out their windows. Their principal mission in Vietnam was the recovery of other helicopters which had been shot down or crashed, but they were also used for cargo and troop carrying. Although obsolescent and being phased out of Marine Corps service elsewhere, the idiosyncratic Deuce soldiered on in Vietnam until 1967 when it was superseded by the CH-53 Sea Stallion, having flown over 5,300 hours, carried almost 32,000 passengers, transported 12.5 million pounds of cargo, and even executed over 600 medical evacuation missions.

From Pistons to Turbines

For the US Marine Corps, 1966 saw the transition from the piston-engined UH-34 and CH-37 to the turbine-powered CH-46 Sea Knight and CH-53 Sea Stallion. The latter helicopters represented a major increase in performance but, at the same time, the introduction of far more sophisticated turbine engines than that of the simple Huey presented considerable maintenance and supply problems, especially under the adverse conditions encountered in Vietnam. Although the twelve-year-old UH-34 Huss had given yeoman service, the tempo of the war and the expanding nature of Marine operations demanded greater lift capability. This was significantly increased by the arrival of the twenty-seven CH-46s of HMM-164 on 8 March 1966. In the first three months of operations the squadron flew 7,328 sorties, carried 18,926 passengers and 1,388 tons of cargo, and flew 253 medical evacuation missions. On 22 May a second CH-46 squadron, HMM-265, arrived at Marble Mountain. By the end of the year there were four Sea Knight squadrons in Vietnam, with the two at Da Nang and HMMs-165 and -262 assigned to MAG-36 at Ky Ha, near Chu Lai.

Once in Vietnam, unforeseen technical problems began to plague the CH-46. When operating close to the ground, its rotor blades whipped up large clouds of sand and grit, as well as other debris, which were indiscriminately ingested into the GE 758-8 engines. FOD (Foreign Object Damage) was common to all helicopters operating away from prepared runways, but it caused excessive

BELOW RIGHT: 'Yankee Tango', a CH-46A of HMM-164, the first Marine helicopter squadron equipped with Sea Knights in Vietnam, lifts a damaged UH-34D from a landing zone where it was shot down on 8 August 1966 during Operation 'Colorado'. This CH-46 is armed with M-60 machine guns rather than .50 cal. Brownings in order to save weight. The installation of armour plating and defensive weapons reduced the troop-carrying capability from twenty-five to about fifteen, or the cargo payload from 4,850 pounds to approximately 3,000. (USMC)

RIGHT: *A Marine guides in a UH-34D loaded with ammunition and rations to an outpost landing site during a supply mission on 24 November 1966. Note the personnel hoist above the cabin doorway. (USMC)*

ABOVE: *A maintenance team from HMM-165 rig a hoist sling to a CH-46A stranded in a mountain stream north-west of Chu Lai on 12 May 1967. Enemy ground fire had set the aircraft on fire and the pilot, Captain James Pleva, set his Sea Knight down in the water, dousing the flames. The helicopter was later retrieved and returned to service. (USMC)*

erosion of the compressor blades of the CH-46. The resulting condition, called compressor stall, reduced power, and the engine temperature rose to a dangerous degree because insufficient air was being pumped into the burning chambers. The abrasive dust also damaged its rotor blades and entered the fuel system, causing erratic operation of the engines. Engine life of the Sea Knight was as low as eighty-five hours as compared to 250 on the UH-34, even though the latter's engines had been rebuilt many times. On 21 July all CH-46s in Vietnam were grounded, except for emergency missions. By September the problems had been resolved by fitting more efficient filters, but the venerable UH-34 continued to act as the principal troop lift helicopter throughout 1966.

The performance of the CH-46 also suffered from the addition of a considerable weight of armour plating around the pilots and vital components, such as fuel computers and gearboxes, and by the provision of defensive armament. These factors, together with the climatic conditions, resulted in a lower lift capability than the obsolescent CH-37 Deuce. While the UH-34 could only carry two M-60 machine guns, the CH-46 was able to mount either the 7.62mm or .50 calibre machine guns, with one on each side. The .50 calibre Browning was the more common armament fitted, but it could not be removed and used as a ground defence weapon if the helicopter was forced down. Both had their advocates, but there was also a considerable body of opinion which maintained that the weight penalty of these measures did not justify the reduction in payload. The issue remained contentious throughout the war, but in the event most helicopters were armed and armoured to a degree.

A replacement for the Deuce had been under development since

ABOVE LEFT: *A CH-53A Sea Stallion of HMH-463 drops an external load of C-rations to troops of 1st Battalion, 3rd Marines at FSB 'Spear' on 20 December 1968 during Operation 'Taylor Common'. The 'Super Bird' was capable of lifting sufficient C-rations in a single sortie to feed a whole battalion for three days. (USMC)*

ABOVE RIGHT: *A CH-46D Sea Knight of HMH-262 dumps fuel over typical I Corps terrain west of Da Nang to lighten its gross weight prior to an emergency extraction of a reconnaissance team in trouble on 23 February 1970. (USMC)*

1962 when a Sikorsky design was chosen for the proposed heavy vertical assault helicopter. By 1966 the requirement had become urgent because of the need in Vietnam for a helicopter capable of retrieving aircraft forced down by enemy action or malfunction in disputed territory where they would otherwise have to be destroyed *in situ*. Throughout the year final testing of the Sikorsky CH-53 continued, and modifications made for Vietnam service included protective armour and filters on the air intake of the engines. On 8 January 1967 'Detachment Alpha' from HMH-463 joined MAG-16 at Marble Mountain with four CH-53A Sea Stallions. Although the need in Vietnam was for a helicopter retriever, the Sea Stallion was primarily an assault transport helicopter for the carrying of cargo and troops. Internally the CH-53A had a seating capacity for thirty-eight combat-equipped troops, or it could be rigged with litters for twenty-four patients and seats for four medical attendants. With its external cargo hook, the Sea Stallion was capable of lifting 20,000 pounds, including such loads as the M-50A1 Ontos anti-tank vehicle, the M-114A1 155mm towed howitzer, or other helicopters. On one mission a 'Super Bird'—as the CH-53 soon became known—combined most of these functions by simultaneously carrying a disabled UH-34 externally, a transmission for it and its crew internally, together with a wounded medical evacuation patient, several passengers and hundreds of pounds of assorted cargo.

By the end of 1967 HMH-463 was operating thirty-six CH-53s (including ten from HMH-462) in Vietnam. In that time the Sea Stallions had retrieved more than 370 downed aircraft, although not all of them were from enemy areas. Since the arrival of the full squadron in May the CH-53s of HMH-463 had carried almost seventy-five per cent of MAG-16's total tonnage and passengers, while flying only about sixteen per cent of the flight hours. The deployment of the Sea Stallion was providential because, in September, the CH-46 was once again grounded after a series of catastrophic accidents both in Vietnam and in the United States. In the majority of cases the crashes were caused by the structural failure of the rear pylon which incorporated the engines, main transmission and the aft rotors. An extensive modification programme was necessary to rectify the problem. In the meantime twenty-three UH-34s were despatched from the United States by cargo plane in October, and ten CH-53s in November. In addition, thirty-one US Army UH-1Ds of the 190th Aviation Company were acquired on loan until the Sea Knights could return to full-flight status, which occurred in February 1968. Thereafter the CH-46 performed in an outstanding manner, and was the principal Marine Corps troop-lift assault helicopter for the remainder of the war.

'Bullets, Bodies and Beans'

US Marine Corps helicopters in Vietnam came under the control of Marine Air Groups (MAG) 16 at Da Nang and 36 at Chu Lai, later Quang Tri. They in turn were under the command of 1st Marine Air Wing (MAW). Further helicopter squadrons were under the operational control of 9th Marine Amphibious Brigade, which was not based in Vietnam but did undertake Special Landing Force operations in the coastal regions. A MAG was an administrative and tactical element designed for independent operations, and each MAG was assigned a specific task. Since there was no formal table of

RIGHT: *A sling-load of C-rations and stores is connected to the external cargo hook of a CH-46D of HMM-364 at Dong Ha Logistical Support Area at the outset of a 'Super Gaggle' mission in February 1968, during the seventy-seven day siege of Khe Sanh Combat Base. Once at the point of destination the helicopters simply unhooked the nets with their cargo in order to speed delivery. When a position had accumulated sufficient nets, the defenders bundled them together for a helicopter to retrieve as a sling load. On one occasion a Marine rigger doing this task became entangled in the nets and had a precarious ride at several thousand feet back to Dong Ha. (USMC)*

organization, the MAGs in Vietnam differed but, typically, were structured around four Marine Medium Helicopter Squadrons (HMM), two Marine Heavy Helicopter Squadrons (HMH)—although usually a single reinforced one—and two Marine Observation Squadrons (VMO). From 1968 some VMOs were redesignated as Marine Light Helicopter Squadrons (HML), equipped with twenty-four UH-1E Hueys or, from early 1970, twenty-four AH-1G Cobras[1]. Each HMM was equipped with twenty-one CH-46 Sea Knights, giving a MAG total of eighty-four. Each HMH was equipped with eighteen CH-53 Sea Stallions, giving a MAG total of thirty-six. Due to operational factors, not all squadrons were equipped with normal complements; this was particularly prevalent in HMH, VMO and HMLs.

In all, a MAG possessed approximately 180 helicopters—less than half the 428 machines of an Army airmobile division. Even the combined helicopter assets of 1st MAW, which supported all Marine operations in Vietnam, were fewer than those of 1st Cavalry Division (Airmobile). Of particular note is the difference between the two services' doctrines whereby sixty-two per cent of Marine helicopters were medium or heavy lift types, whereas an airmobile division had eleven per cent, its main transport element being the UH-1 which represented forty-three per cent of its complement. As for attack helicopters and observation aircraft, the Marines had nineteen per

BELOW: *A CH-46 burns fiercely after crashing in the LZ while attempting to evacuate the wounded of Delta Company, 1/3 Marines on 5 May 1968. Another Sea Knight lands to pick up the crew and casualties. (USMC)*

[1] In 1968, VMO-3 became HML-367 while VMO-5 became HML-276. These units operated both armed and unarmed UH-1Es, and gradually absorbed the Hueys from other VMO squadrons. During early 1970, as more AH-1G Cobras entered service, the attack helicopters were concentrated into HML-367 and all UH-1Es reverted to the unarmed configuration within HML-167. The VMO squadrons continued to operate O-1 Bird Dog and OV-10 Bronco observation aircraft.

cent as against forty-six per cent, which emphasized the cavalry concept of Army airmobile operations.

Although each type of helicopter, light, medium or heavy, was designed for a specific task, such a strict division was unrealistic in Vietnam and many missions were undertaken by whatever helicopter was to hand. Thus, a wounded Marine could be extricated by any 'bird' from a UH-1E Huey to a CH-53 Sea Stallion, although the CH-46 performed the majority of medical evacuation missions. However, as the above proportion of types indicates, most Marine helicopters were intended for the transport of troops and cargo during 'vertical assault' operations. In the vernacular of the time, this was referred to as 'bullets, bodies and beans'. Bullets represented all ammunition and weapons transported by helicopters, from the 5.56mm M-16 rifle round to the M-114A1 155mm howitzer. Bodies denoted the movement of troops within the battle zone, for both combat and administrative purposes, and the evacuation of casualties. Beans did not just signify the execrable ham and lima beans of C-rations, but embraced all the consumables used in the field, including hot turkey Thanksgiving dinners, water, fuel, jungle boots, radio batteries, and a host of other items.

Marine helicopters were used for five basic missions: the tactical airlift of troops; the insertion and extraction of reconnaissance teams; supply; the recovery of downed aircraft; and search and rescue, which included the medical evacuation rôle. The latter was particularly hazardous, especially at night or in bad weather. Predictably, most casualties occurred when friendly forces were in close contact with the enemy, thus ground fire in the pick-up zone was only to be expected. Even with gunship or attack aircraft escorts, the evacuation helicopter was highly likely to sustain hits. Indeed, almost a quarter of Marine helicopter losses occurred during medical evacuation missions. An incident in southern Quang Ngai Province

in mid-1967 demonstrates the dangers faced by Marine helicopter aviators.

On 19 August Captain Stephen Pless was piloting a UH-1E gunship of VMO-6 as escort during a medical evacuation mission when he heard another emergency call over the radio net: four US Army soldiers were stranded on a beach north of Duc Pho and were about to be overwhelmed by a large Viet Cong force. Breaking off from the original mission, Pless and his crew—Captain Rupert Fairfield Jr., Gunnery Sergeant Leroy Poulson and Lance Corporal John Phelps—flew to the scene, where they found about fifty VC in the open, some of whom were bayoneting and beating the Americans. The crew opened fire with machine guns and rockets and, in repeated firing runs, killed and wounded many of the VC and forced the survivors into a treeline. The attacks were made at such low level that fragments of the expended ordnance struck the gunship. Although still under heavy small arms fire, Pless manoeuvred the helicopter between the wounded men and the enemy, providing a shield which permitted Poulson and Phelps to retrieve the Americans. The enemy repeatedly rushed the aircraft, closing within a few feet before being cut down by the Huey's machine guns and 'Skeets' Fairfield manning an M-60. With the wounded men aboard, Pless headed the dangerously overloaded helicopter out to sea. Four times the Huey settled into the water, but each time Pless bounced it back into the air while the crew threw out all excess gear to lighten the load. By jettisoning the rocket pods Pless was able to coax the helicopter aloft, and delivered the wounded to a medical facility at Chu Lai. Captain Pless was awarded the Medal of Honor and his crew members the Navy Cross for their actions.

'Super-Gaggle' of Khe Sanh

In October 1967, MAG-36 moved from Chu Lai to a new airfield at Quang Tri as III Marine Amphibious Force (III MAF) concentrated its infantry battalions into the northern two provinces of I CTZ, with 3rd Marine Division deployed in a series of

strongpoints and combat bases along the general line of Route 9 in order to stem NVA infiltration from Laos and across the Demilitarized Zone (DMZ). Its relocation proved to be of decisive importance in the opening months of 1968, when attention was focused on one of these isolated Marine positions—Khe Sanh Combat Base. Situated in a mountainous region near both the DMZ and the Laotian border, it was occupied by nearly 6,000 Marines and ARVN Rangers, with several infantry companies of the 26th Marines holding outposts on the surrounding hills. NVA pressure against Khe Sanh Combat Base (KSCB) increased during 1967, and by the end of the year it was under siege, with all supplies having to be airlifted into the main bastion and its outposts.

The Battle of Khe Sanh escalated into a major operation of considerable political significance, with the entire spectrum of American airpower being employed for tactical air support, including Marine, USAF and Navy aircraft, as well as Strategic Air Command B-52s. NVA anti-aircraft defences were extensive, with numerous 12.7mm and 37mm guns covering the approaches to the hill outposts which could only be resupplied effectively by helicopters. Despite valiant efforts Marine gunship escorts, with their limited firepower, were unable to destroy these well-entrenched gun sites, and towards the end of February the rate of helicopter losses was rising alarmingly. A solution was found whereby all helicopter flights to KSCB were escorted by attack aircraft which provided heavy suppressive fire.

In what became known as the 'Super-Gaggle', the resupply operation was initiated by a TA-4, a two-seat trainer version of the Skyhawk acting as a command and control aircraft, assessing if the weather was clear enough for the Skyhawks of MAG-12 to operate with any degree of success. Once the TA-4 had radioed that the conditions were adequate, an 'H'-hour was set and the Super-Gaggle began. Twelve A-4 'Scooters' were launched from Chu Lai while simultaneously, 100 miles to the north, twelve to sixteen CH-46 helicopters of HMM-262 (later reinforced by HMM-364) lifted off from Quang Tri and proceeded to the Dong Ha LSA (Logistical

RIGHT: *Carrying a 3,000 pound sling-load of ammunition, a CH-46D of HMM-364 leads a 'Super Gaggle' of Sea Knights as it heads for Hill 881 South, an outpost position near Khe Sanh, on 7 March 1968. Flying even in the most adverse weather conditions, the helicopter airlift was crucial to the defence of the embattled combat base. During February, helicopters ferried 465 tons of supplies to KSCB. (USMC)*

Support Area) to pick up supplies. The object was for all the aircraft to arrive in the objective area on schedule. At the appointed time, a proportion of the Skyhawks flew ahead of the helicopters and attacked known enemy positions with bombs and napalm. Two A-4s fitted with CS gas dispensers then saturated known and possible sites of enemy anti-aircraft and automatic weapons. At approximately thirty to forty seconds prior to the approach of the helicopters, two Skyhawks laid a smoke screen along their flight path. While the CH-46 Sky Knights made their final run into the drop zone, four Scooters with bombs, rockets and 20mm guns provided close-in fire suppression. Once the helicopters began their descent, the factors of weather, their 3,000 pound externally slung load, and the terrain did not allow a second chance. The enemy gunners knew the helicopter glide slope to all the Marine positions and fired by sound alone; but even if the guns were not suppressed there was no alternative for the CH-46s but to continue. The only consolation for the crews was the knowledge that UH-1E gunships were close at hand to pick them up if they survived being shot down.

Fortunately, these tactics proved so successful that during the entire period of the Super-Gaggle only two CH-46s were downed near the hill positions, and their crews were rescued immediately by Huey gunship escorts; prior to its introduction, as many as three helicopters were shot down in one day around Khe Sanh. The total Marine helicopter losses for the whole battle were seventeen destroyed and approximately thirty-five damaged. On a peak day, such as 26 February, as many as four Super-Gaggle flights were made, but three was more normal, with one around 0900 hours, one in the afternoon and one about 1700 hours in the evening. Internal loads were also carried, notably reinforcements and water for the hill positions. The usual procedure was for the sling-loads to be dropped on the first pass and for passengers to be disembarked and casualties evacuated on the second. The helicopters continued to supply Khe Sanh Combat Base until it was relieved by the 1st Cavalry Division (Airmobile) on 6 April in an exemplary airmobile operation, codenamed 'Pegasus.'

BELOW: *A wounded Marine is rushed to a Sea Knight of HMM-262 during a medical evacuation mission at the height of the Battle of Hue in February 1968. The foul weather limited air support throughout the battle, but emergency medical evacuations were continually undertaken. (USMC)*

ABOVE: *AH-1G Cobras of HML-367 are refuelled at the POL point at Khe Sanh during 'Lam Son 719' in February 1971. This operation saw the first use in action of the AH-1J Sea Cobra when four were attached to HML-367 on 17 February 1971. The Sea Cobras, especially configured for the USMC with heavier firepower and twin-engined reliability, soon proved themselves in combat. (US Army)*

From Tet to Keystone

While the Battle of Khe Sanh raged, the enemy unleashed the Tet Offensive in I Corps on 30 January. Following rocket attacks against Marine airbases to cripple air support, the VC/NVA attacked urban areas in strength. Hue, the ancient imperial capital of Vietnam, became the scene of one of the bitterest battles of the war as Marine and ARVN units engaged in a gruelling month-long house-to-house fight until the enemy was expelled from the historic city. Throughout the battle the weather was atrocious and the use of tactical air support severely limited, although helicopters flew many medical evacuation and resupply missions. The enemy suffered a serious military defeat on the battlefield; but the political effect of the Tet Offensive had profound repercussions in the United States, that were eventually to lead to the withdrawal of American forces from South-East Asia.

Following Tet, III MAF adopted more mobile tactics, but the intensity of ground combat slackened as the enemy retired to the border regions to recuperate. However, Marine air operations reached a new peak, reflecting this shift in tactics, with the helicopter units flying 639,194 sorties during 1968—almost double the 388,000 of the previous year. The prime example of these new-found tactics was Operation 'Dewey Canyon', when, at the height of the monsoon season, the 3rd and 9th Marines were airlifted by helicopters into the fearsome A Shau Valley. From 22 January to 19 March 1969, the Marines sought out and destroyed numerous enemy camps along the Laotian border. Despite the weather, Marine helicopters continually carried essential supplies to the various bases in the operational area and returned with the wounded. Often flying on instruments because of the low clouds and drizzle, the helicopters flew 14,893 sorties carrying 21,841 troops and 3,515 tons of cargo in 5,050 flight hours.

During the two-month operation only one helicopter was lost, in spite of the adverse weather and terrain, and determined enemy resistance—a tribute to the skill and professionalism of Marine aviators.

Of particular note for Marine helicopter aviation was the retirement from combat of the redoubtable UH-34 and the introduction of the AH-1G HueyCobra in 1969. After its last combat sortie with HMM-362, the original 'Shufly' squadron in 1962, the Huss folded its rotor blades for the last time during a ceremony at Phu Bai on 18 August. The first four Cobras arrived in late April and were assigned to VMO-2 at Marble Mountain Air Facility in Da Nang. The squadron subsequently received another eight Cobras, and they served as escorts as well as flying fire support and armed reconnaissance missions. 1969 also saw the first withdrawals of US servicemen from Vietnam. In a series of increments codenamed Keystone, Marine units departed Vietnam. By late 1970 1st MAW was reduced to four medium helicopter squadrons equipped with CH-46Ds, one heavy squadron of CH-53s, a light squadron with UH-1Es and one with AH-1G Cobras. In February 1971 there followed the major ARVN operation into Laos, LAM SON 719, but Marine Corps involvement was limited, and further helicopter squadrons departed in March and April. In the same month, III MAF was deactivated and superseded by the 3rd Marine

BELOW: 'Crazy Horse', a CH-53D of HMH-463 is refuelled at 'Kilo Sierra' (Khe Sanh) during 'Lam Son 719'. Operating out of Marble Mountain, HMH-463 provided a heavy-lift capability during the Cambodian incursion. One Sea Stallion was lost to enemy fire on 23 February when it was struck by a mortar bomb at FSB 'Hotel Two' while trying to recover a 155 mm howitzer. During March, the CH-53s flew 980 sorties in support of the operation, lifting 1,491 tons of cargo and 1,556 troops. (USMC)

ABOVE: *As the last of the security forces protecting the evacuation of Phnom Penh, Marines of F Company, 2/4 Marines prepare to embark on CH-53D Sea Stallions of HMH-463 at LZ 'Hotel', a soccer pitch adjacent to the American Embassy, during Operation 'Eagle Pull' on 12 April 1975 as the Cambodian capital fell to the Khmer Rouge. (USMC)*

ABOVE: *On 13 December 1974 the NVA launched an attack into Phuoc Long Province which subsequently marked the beginning of the end of South Vietnam. Here, troops of the 2nd Battalion, 7th Infantry Regiment of the ARVN 5th Infantry Division board UH-1Hs at Lai Khe as reinforcements for Phuoc Long in one of the last helilift operations of the war. By this time, few VNAF Hueys were armed with miniguns because of their vast consumption of scarce ammunition. (US Army/Aviation News)*

LEFT: *A VNAF UH-1H Command and Control Huey swoops low along Route 1 as refugees stream towards Saigon. After the fall of Xuan Loc resistance crumbled; the capital fell at midday on 30 April 1975. (US Army/Aviation News)*

Amphibious Brigade incorporating a helicopter group. On 26 May 1971 Marine helicopters flew their last sorties, and the remaining CH-53s of HMH-463, UH-1Es of HML-167 and the Cobras of HML-367 stood down.

Operation 'Frequent Wind'—the Night of the Helicopters

At the time of the Paris Agreement of 27 January 1973, which effectively terminated US involvement in South Vietnam, the VNAF possessed one of the most modern helicopter fleets in the world, comprising almost 600 rotary-wing aircraft in nineteen squadrons of UH-1 Hueys and four of CH-47 Chinooks. Peace, however, did not prevail in Vietnam, and there ensued the 'land-grabbing' campaign of 1973 when both sides repeatedly violated the ceasefire in their efforts to wrest control of the countryside. In the aftermath of the Arab-Israeli War of October 1973 US military aid to RVN was reduced dramatically, whereas communist assistance to North Vietnam continued unabated. VNAF appropriations were cut drastically, compounded by a lack of trained technical personnel to service such sophisticated aircraft, so that during 1974 airlift by helicopter diminished by seventy per cent and reconnaissance by fifty-eight per cent.

RIGHT: *Refugees from the fighting disembark from a VNAF CH-47A and troops of the ARVN Airborne Brigade prepare to board as reinforcements for the final major battle of the war at Xuan Loc, which lasted from 9 to 22 April 1975. (US Army/Aviation News)*

BELOW RIGHT: *An AH-1J Sea Cobra of HMA-369 lifts off from the deck of the USS* Hancock *in support of the CH-53 Sea Stallions during Operation 'Frequent Wind'. Four Sea Cobras were used to provide escorts to the transport helicopters. They were also employed as Tactical Air Co-ordinators and as Forward Air Controllers (Airborne) to direct fixed-wing attack aircraft. During the night, they acted as pathfinders by leading the transport helicopters to their appropriate landing zones. One Sea Cobra was lost due to fuel starvation when the deck of the ship it was heading for was blocked by an Air America Huey which had landed without permission; the crew was saved, however. (USMC)*

FAR RIGHT: *South Vietnamese refugees are ushered from a CH-53D aboard the USS* Hancock. *Helicopter operations continued until 0835 on 30 April. During the day forty-eight VNAF Hueys, three CH-47s and an 0-1 Bird Dog flew out to the carrier fleet and were landed safely, many having to be jettisoned overboard immediately to make room for others. At 2114 on 29 April, a CH-46 of HMM-365 crashed into the sea while returning to the USS* Hancock; *two crewmen were saved, but the pilot and co-pilot were lost—the last US casualties of the Vietnam War. (USMC)*

RIGHT: *CH-53D Sea Stallions land at the 'Alamo', the defended area around the DAO compound at Tan Son Nhut, as darkness falls on 29 April 1975. Of the 682 sorties flown during Operation 'Frequent Wind', 360 were flown during hours of darkness. A total of 395 US citizens and 4,475 other nationals were evacuated from the DAO; a further 978 US and 1,120 other persons were lifted out of the US Embassy, to give a grand total of 6,968. (USMC)*

Thus, when the NVA mounted a major offensive in late 1974 and into 1975, the RVNAF were unable to resist the onslaught. Inexorably, cities and provinces fell to the enemy. By April 1975 it was clear that the collapse of South Vietnam was nigh; and a contingency plan codenamed 'Frequent Wind' (formerly 'Talon Vise') was implemented for the evacuation of the remaining US staff in Saigon and selected South Vietnamese personnel. A fleet of four carriers, two with their normal complement of aircraft and two configured for helicopters, and support ships with 9th Marine Amphibious Brigade was hastily assembled and arrived off the coast of South Vietnam on 20 April. The Marine helicopters comprised thirty-four CH-53s of HMH-462 and -463, twenty-seven CH-46s of HMM-165, six UH-1Es of HML-367 and eight AH-1Js of HMA-369, augmented by six CH-53s of the 21st Special Operations Squadron and two ARRS HH-53s of the US Air Force.

After considerable political prevarication, Operation 'Frequent Wind' got underway on the afternoon of 29 April with the insertion of a Marine security force to guard the principal extraction site at the Defence Attaché's Office (DAO) compound, adjacent to Tan Son Nhut airfield. The evacuation proceeded smoothly, although not without incident, as frantic refugees clambered aboard the helicopters. On 'Jolly Green 12-1', one of the ARRS HH-53s, the parajumper tried to maintain some semblance of order while loading, but one frightened woman clawed her way forward until he pushed her back into line with his rifle butt. Undeterred, she rushed forward again, and once more was jabbed with the rifle. Falling back, she grabbed the barrel of the minigun, which swung towards the waiting crowd of refugees. The woman reached forward, only to grasp the trigger. To the horror of the parajumper, he heard the electric motor that drove the firing mechanism of the 2,000-round-per-minute gun engage. The first round chambered—then the gun jammed . . . The HH-53 took off with ninety-seven men, women and children aboard, twice its normal capacity; but as it flew over the city's suburbs the flight mechanic observed an SA-7 Strella streaking upwards. He fired a flare pistol, causing the missile to veer away and explode at a distance of only sixty feet from the helicopter.

By 2100 hours the evacuation was complete at the DAO compound, and after the complex (including millions of dollars in currency) had been destroyed with explosives, the last two CH-53s lifted off at 0012 on 30 April. Meanwhile, amid the fires of downtown Saigon, the evacuation of the US Embassy proceeded more slowly, compromised by having only two landing pads: one on the roof, and only one large enough for a CH-53 in the carpark, which was illuminated by a slide projector. With the weather deteriorating and increasing anti-aircraft fire from both the enemy and disgruntled ARVN troops, each flight became more hazardous; yet still the stream of refugees seemed endless. Eventually, by presidential order, only Americans were to be transported. At 0458 the ambassador and his key staff took off aboard an HMM-165 CH-46, 'Lacey Ace 09'. Only the Marines guarding the perimeter of the embassy remained. After sealing and barring the building, they climbed the stairwell to the rooftop helicopter pad to board several CH-46s, the last being 'Swift 22' which lifted off at 0753. The 'night of the helicopters' was over, and with it, the helicopter war.

ACKNOWLEDGEMENTS

Many sources, individuals and institutions have been consulted in the preparation of this book and I wish to extend my fulsome thanks to the following:–

American Aviation Historical Society; ARMOR Magazine; Army Aviation; Army Aviation Systems Command; William H. Austin; Australian War Memorial; ALAT (Aviation Légère de l'Armée de Terre); Dana Bell; Boeing Vertol Company; Paul Boyer; 1st Cavalry Division Museum; Bob Chenoweth; Robert A. Carlisle; The Cobra Company; Jerome R. Daley; Walt Darran; Defense Technical Information Center; Department of the Air Force; William Dismukes; Lou Drendel; John R. Dunham Jr.; Colonel Paul Gaujac; Dennis Giangreco; John Graber; Bobby D. Harber; Colonel Michel Henry; Hiller Helicopters; Damian Houseman; Hughes Helicopters; John Humphreys; INFANTRY Magazine; Robert S. Kellar; Military Review; MOD Library; Kenneth Munson; Wayne Mutza; Museum of Army Flying; National Air and Space Museum; Naval Aviation History and Archives; Naval Aviation News; Naval Historical Center; Alfred G. Nichols; Office of Air Force History; Office of Information, Navy Department; Tim Page; James H. Pickerell; Pilot Press Ltd; Service Historique de l'Armée; Sikorsky Aircraft; Albert F. Simpson Historical Research Center of the USAF; Robert Sisk; Soldier of Fortune; James D. Sprinkle; Shelby L. Stanton; Robert Steinbrunn; US Army Aviation Center, Fort Rucker; US Army Aviation Digest; US Army Aviation Museum, Fort Rucker; US Army Command and General Staff College; US Army Military History Institute; US Marine Corps, History and Museums Division; Vietnam Helicopter Pilots Association; Vietnam Veterans of America; Westland Helicopters; Gary G. Wetzel; Martin Windrow; Steven Zaloga.

Finally, I am most grateful to Major General George S. Patton Jr. for providing the introduction to *Vietnam Choppers*.

SIMON DUNSTAN
London 1987

Boeing Vertol CH-47D Chinook

1 Pitot tubes
2 Forward lighting
3 Nose compartment access hatch
4 Vibration absorber
5 IFF aerial
6 Windscreen panels
7 Windscreen wipers
8 Instrument panel shroud
9 Rudder pedals
10 Yaw sensing ports
11 Downward vision window
12 Pilot's footboards
13 Collective pitch control column
14 Cyclic pitch control column
15 Co-pilot's seat
16 Centre instrument console
17 Pilot's seat
18 Glidescope aerial
19 Forward transmission housing fairing
20 Cockpit overhead window
21 Doorway from main cabin
22 Cockpit emergency exit doors
23 Sliding side window panel
24 Cockpit bulkhead
25 Vibration absorber
26 Cockpit door release handle
27 Radio and electronics racks
28 Sloping bulkhead
29 Stick boost actuators
30 Stability augmentation system actuators
31 Forward transmission mounting structure
32 Windscreen washer bottle
33 Rotor control hydraulic jack
34 Forward transmission gearbox
35 Rotor head fairing
36 Forward rotor head mechanism
37 Pitch change control levers
38 Blade drag dampers
39 Glassfibre rotor blades
40 Titanium leading-edge capping with de-icing provision
41 Rescue hoist/winch

42 Forward transmission aft fairing
43 Hydraulic system modules
44 Control levers
45 Front fuselage frame and stringer construction
46 Emergency exit window, main entry door on starboard side
47 Forward end of cargo floor
48 Fuel tank fuselage side fairing
49 Battery
50 Electrical system equipment bay
51 Aerial cable
52 Stretcher rack, up to 24 stretchers
53 Cabin window panel
54 Cabin heater duct outlet
55 Troop seats stowed against cabin wall

56 Cabin roof transmission and control run tunnel
57 Formation-keeping lights
58 Rotor blade cross section
59 Static dischargers
60 Blade balance and tracking weights pocket
61 Leading-edge anti-erosion strip
62 Fixed tab
63 Fuselage skin plating
64 Maintenance walkway
65 Transmission tunnel access doors
66 Troop seating, up to 44 troops
67 Cargo hook access hatch
68 VOR aerial
69 Cabin lining panels
70 Control runs
71 Main transmission shaft
72 Shaft couplings
73 Centre fuselage construction
74 Centre aisle seating (optional)
75 Main cargo floor, 1440 cu ft (40.78 m³) cargo volume
76 Ramp-down 'dam' for water-borne operations
77 Ramp hydraulic jack
78 Engine bevel drive gearbox
79 Transmission combining gearbox
80 Rotor brake
81 Transmission oil tank
82 Oil cooler
83 Engine drive shaft fairing
84 Engine intake screen
85 Starboard engine nacelle
86 Cooling air grilles
87 Tail rotor pylon construction
88 Hydraulic equipment
89 Access door

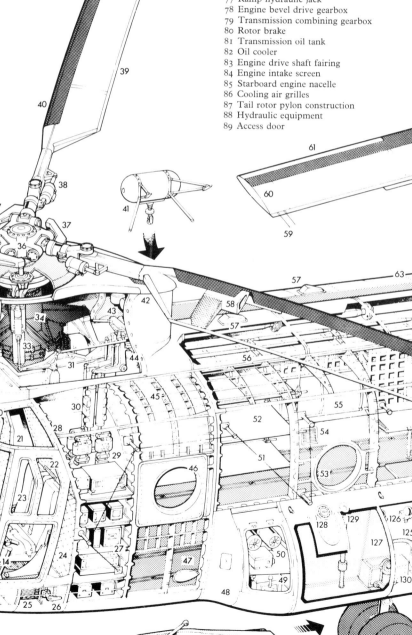

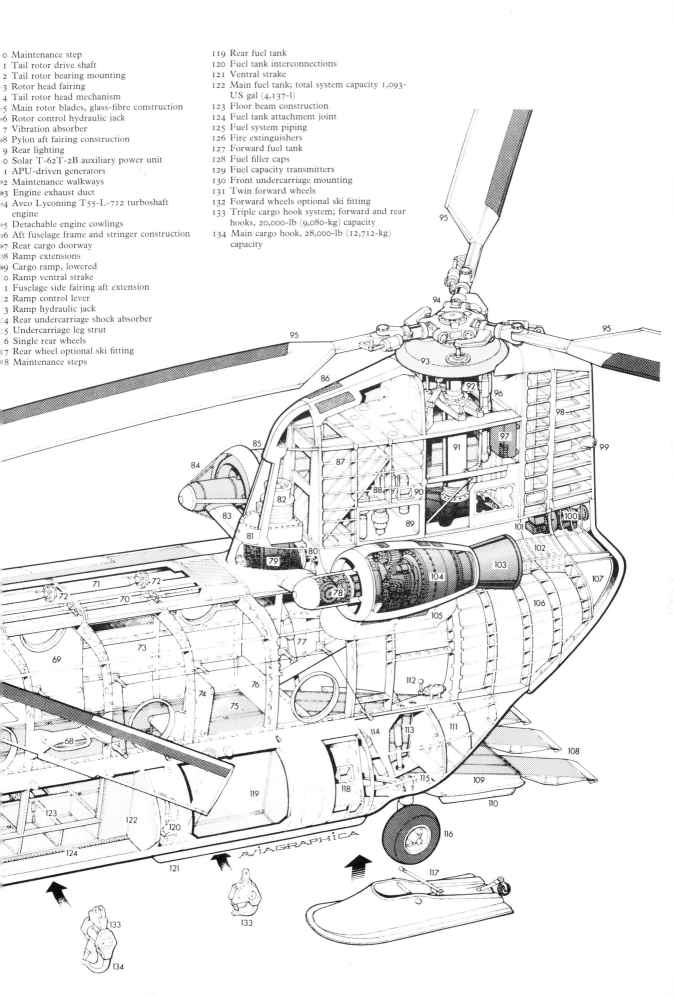

o Maintenance step
1 Tail rotor drive shaft
2 Tail rotor bearing mounting
3 Rotor head fairing
4 Tail rotor head mechanism
5 Main rotor blades, glass-fibre construction
6 Rotor control hydraulic jack
7 Vibration absorber
8 Pylon aft fairing construction
9 Rear lighting
0 Solar T-62T-2B auxiliary power unit
1 APU-driven generators
2 Maintenance walkways
3 Engine exhaust duct
4 Avco Lycoming T55-L-712 turboshaft engine
5 Detachable engine cowlings
6 Aft fuselage frame and stringer construction
7 Rear cargo doorway
8 Ramp extensions
9 Cargo ramp, lowered
0 Ramp ventral strake
1 Fuselage side fairing aft extension
2 Ramp control lever
3 Ramp hydraulic jack
4 Rear undercarriage shock absorber
5 Undercarriage leg strut
6 Single rear wheels
7 Rear wheel optional ski fitting
8 Maintenance steps

119 Rear fuel tank
120 Fuel tank interconnections
121 Ventral strake
122 Main fuel tank; total system capacity 1,093-US gal (4,137-l)
123 Floor beam construction
124 Fuel tank attachment joint
125 Fuel system piping
126 Fire extinguishers
127 Forward fuel tank
128 Fuel filler caps
129 Fuel capacity transmitters
130 Front undercarriage mounting
131 Twin forward wheels
132 Forward wheels optional ski fitting
133 Triple cargo hook system; forward and rear hooks, 20,000-lb (9,080-kg) capacity
134 Main cargo hook, 28,000-lb (12,712-kg) capacity